THE INSIDE STORY

EXODUS

The Inside Story
Volume Two: Exodus

First Edition — 2017

Published by
Meaningful Life Center

ISBN 978-1-886587-63-2

COVER: Batsheva Lubin
ILLUSTRATIONS: Levi Weingarten
LAYOUT: Shimon Gorkin

© Meaningful Life Center 2017
All rights reserved.
Printed in China.
No part of this book may be used or reproduced in
any manner whatsoever without written permission from
the Meaningful Life Center,
except for brief quotations for the purposes of review.

Meaningful Life Center
788 Eastern Parkway, Suite 303
Brooklyn, NY 11213-3409
(718) 774-6448
For more information visit www.meaningfullife.com
or call (800) 3-MEANING

Based on the works of THE LUBAVITCHER REBBE
Adapted by YANKI TAUBER

THE INSIDE STORY

A CHASSIDIC PERSPECTIVE *on* BIBLICAL EVENTS, LAWS, *and* PERSONALITIES

EXODUS

In the merit of
Abigail Ruth bas Sarah Etti

Dedicated by
her loving husband
John Pollitt

Dedicated by
Yosef Leib (Jeff) and Aviva Kashuk

in honor of

the marriage of
our beloved children
Rachel Ora (Kashuk) and Daniel Tzairi

May they be blessed
with a lifetime of happiness

and

our first granddaughter
Maya Leah Morris
daughter of
Drs. Sara Bayla (Kashuk) and Jonathan Morris

May she be blessed with a life of peace, happiness,
and *nachat* for her parents and family

TO THE READER

This book is the second volume of *The Inside Story*, a five-volume series exploring the inner significance of selected events and precepts in the Five Books of Moses. Included in this volume are sixty-two essays covering the eleven *parashiot* (Torah sections) of the book of Exodus.

A hallmark of chassidic teaching is that the Torah, like the human being it comes to instruct, consists of both a body and a soul. The "body" of the Torah is comprised of the events it describes and the laws it legislates; the "soul" of the Torah is the spiritual guidance implicit in these events and laws. The body of Torah is bounded by time and space—the events occurred at a specific point in history, and the laws address specific circumstances and activities. The soul of Torah is timeless; for when we appreciate the inner import of these events and laws, we understand their relevance to our own lives in every place and time.

The essays in this volume are based on the teachings of the Lubavitcher Rebbe, Rabbi Menachem M. Schneerson, of blessed memory. For a discussion of the Rebbe's teachings, and of the approach we have taken with these essays, see our introduction to volume one (Genesis) of *The Inside Story*.

I am deeply indebted to those whose guidance, critique, and assistance have aided me in the writing of these essays, and in the compilation, design, and production of this book: Rabbi Simon Jacobson, Ben-Zion Rader, Chaim Abrahams, Rochel Chana Schilder Riven, Alex Heppenheimer, Gani Goodman, Velvel Farkash, Ya'akovah Weber, Shimon Gorkin, Batsheva Lubin, Levi Weingarten, and Zalman Glick.

Yanki Tauber
Sivan, 5777 (June, 2017)

Note on the spelling of "G-d"

Throughout this book, "G-d" is written with a hyphen instead of an "o." According to Torah law, the divine name is sacred, and great care must be taken to accord it proper care and reverence. For this reason, it is best to avoid writing or printing the word "G-d" in its full spelling in all but the most recognizably sacred books (e.g., a Bible or prayer book), lest it be unwittingly defaced or treated irreverently.

May this also serve to remind us that even as we discuss G-d and His influence upon our lives, He is above and beyond all our words; that even as we are enjoined, by the Almighty Himself, to seek Him with our thought, speech, and deeds, He transcends all human effort to name and describe His reality.

CONTENTS

XIII: SHEMOT 1
Enslavement in Egypt

Essay 1: **Name and Number** 2
To survive the myriad challenges of their first exile, the Children of Israel were fortified with two essential tools: their names and their numbers.

Essay 2: **The Brick Factory** 5
We were forged as a nation at the brick kilns of Egypt, and the manufacture of "bricks" remains the essence of our mission in life.

Essay 3: **The Cult of the River** 8
The spiritual and contemporary significance of Pharaoh's decree to throw Jewish children into the Nile.

Essay 4: **The Infant Shepherd** 10
Moses was eighty years old when he took the Israelites out of Egypt; but his role in charting the spiritual course of his people began on the day he was placed in a basket on the Nile.

Essay 5: **The Runaway Kid** 13
It is not enough for a shepherd to provide water for his flock; he must also understand why they are thirsty.

Essay 6: **A Heart of Flame** 14
What Moses saw: the insatiable fire at the heart of the thorn.

Essay 7: **The Essence of Existence** 16
What is the meaning behind the various names of G-d? And why was this the first question that an enslaved people would pose to Moses?

Essay 8: **The Numerology of Redemption** 21
The difference between singularity and oneness, and the thirteen-point stretch of history joining Moses and Moshiach.

Essay 9: **Moshiach's Donkey** 27
The donkey that makes its appearance as Abraham proceeds toward his greatest test of faith, as Moses embarks on his mission to take the Israelites out of Egypt, and as the world enters the messianic era of divine perfection.

XIV: VA'EIRA 33
The promise of redemption

Essay 1: **Have a Heart** 34
Moses' confrontation with G-d, and the thinking believer's response to evil and suffering.

Essay 2: **On Freedom and Authority** 41
Is the Torah a theocracy?

Essay 3: **Of Snakes and Sticks** 56
The lesson from Aaron's staff: The only good warrior is a lifeless warrior.

Essay 4: **The Red Nile** 58
G-d obviously needed to get the Egyptians' attention. But why the Nile? And why blood?

Essay 5: **The Frog in the Oven** 61
The difference between sacrificing one's life and sacrificing one's self.

Essay 6: **Crime, Punishment, and Suspended Precipitation** 63
What happens when a hailstorm has its past pulled out from under its feet? The Jewish perspective on reward and punishment.

CONTENTS VII

XV: BO 69
Exodus and freedom

Essay 1: The Soul of Evil 70
The secret that terrified Moses and liberated the soul of man.

Essay 2: The Fifth Element 76
Four-dimensional plagues or five? Burn your leaven or throw it in the sea? How deep does change reach?

Essay 3: The Freedom to Passover 85
What do we seek when we strive for freedom? The freedom to be our natural selves, or to liberate ourselves from our own nature?

Essay 4: Great Wealth 94
Apparently, we spent 210 years in Egypt in order to pick up "vessels of silver, and vessels of gold, and garments."

Essay 5: Ambition 100
How do you prepare your daily fare—boiled, baked, stewed, or grilled? Fervid with desire or sodden with contentment? On Passover, there's only one dish on the menu.

Essay 6: Speed in Three Dimensions 107
The significance of the three signs of haste that marked our exodus from Egypt: girdled hips, shod feet, and a staff held firmly in hand.

Essay 7: Dialogue 110
Try describing a Passover *seder* to one who never actually participated in one. Family dinner? Prayer service? Songfest and storytelling marathon? All of the above?

Essay 8: Tomorrow's Child 114
Moses addresses the generation gap.

XVI: BESHALACH 117
A sea splits

Essay 1: **The Mountain and the Sea** 118
No sooner had the Children of Israel departed Egypt, than four types emerged: the insular Jew, the submissive Jew, the fighting Jew, and the praying Jew.

Essay 2: **The Amphibian Soul** 124
The psychological and practical reasons to split the seas in your life.

Essay 3: **On the Essence of Leadership** 129
How do thousands of souls sing the same song? Three kinds of leaders, and the different types of unity they evoke in their people.

Essay 4: **Bringing G-d Home** 135
In many areas of life, it comes down to this: mine or more?

Essay 5: **The Manna Eaters** 137
Food as processed by the stomach and by the mind.

Essay 6: **Reason, Doubt, Faith, and Memory** 140
Who is Amalek and what does he represent? How is he overcome?

XVII: YITRO 147
Revelation and law

Essay 1: **Captains of Thousand** 148
On the significance of Jethro's "addition" to the Torah.

Essay 2: **Shards or Sparks?** 157
When the hammer of divine wisdom strikes the rock of reality, sparks fly.

Essay 3: **Sighting the Sounds** 160
Yes and no, matter and spirit, sight and sound: the different modes of reality that emerged at the revelation at Sinai.

Essay 4: **A Gift and a Test** 169
When the gift of wisdom and purpose is also a challenge.

XVIII: MISHPATIM 171
In the courtroom of the soul

Essay 1: **Oxen and Souls** 172
Crime, conflict, and consensus in the social and spiritual history of Jewish civil law.

Essay 2: **The Four Guardians** 183
Whose life is it, anyway? Do we possess an inherent right to its blessings, or must we earn these rights? Four ways to determine the relationship between responsibility and reward.

Essay 3: **The Resourceful Oath** 190
The legal principles of "partial culpability," "corroborating oath," and "depreciation of property," as applied to the inner life of the soul.

Essay 4: **The Third Crown** 199
Doing, learning, and that which supersedes them both.

XIX: TERUMAH 203
A dwelling for G-d

Essay 1: **Son-in-Law** 204
We are all G-d's children; but we are also married to His daughter.

Essay 2: **Transplanted Cedars** 206
Why carry trees from the Holy Land to plant in Egypt, for use in a building to be constructed centuries later?

Essay 3: **The Altar and the Ark** 209
Which was the primary function of the Holy Temple? A place in which to serve G-d, or a place for G-d to manifest His presence in our world?

Essay 4: **Wood and Stone** 216
A Tabernacle of wood and cloth evolves into a Temple of plaster and stone, mirroring life's progress from achievement to action.

Essay 5: **Model Home** 221
The three spaces of the Holy Temple as the three realms of human life: the mundane, the refined, and the transcendent.

Essay 6: **The Face of a Child** 232
The ark, its cover, and its cherubim in the relationship between G-d and Israel.

Essay 7: **Have Word, Will Travel** 238
The special case of the carrying poles of the ark in the Holy Temple.

Essay 8: **Spiritual Space** 240
The latitude of the mind and the longitude of the heart, as represented in the seven lamps of the *menorah*.

XX: TETZAVEH 251
Garments and coatings

Essay 1: **Noise** 252
What do you call someone who acts contrary to his nature? A hypocrite? A beginner? A beautiful person? Reflections on Aaron's noisy robe, sidewalk hawkers of faith, and the sound bite generation.

Essay 2: **Princesses on Horseback** 260
We might envision Rashi walking to the study hall one day, and coming upon a party of noblewomen on horseback...

Essay 3: **Joined at the Waist** 262
One of the Torah's 613 commandments involves a belt, four gold rings, and two blue ribbons.

Essay 4: **The Superficial Coat** 264
The gold of wealth and extravagance, or the copper of poverty and hardship, are both no more than coatings on the altar of the soul.

CONTENTS   XI

XXI: KI TISA 267
The second tablets

> *Essay 1*: **Partner** 268
> The paradox of partnership: Each contributes its wholeness, while affirming its halfness and partness.

> *Essay 2*: **Foundation** 272
> For fourteen out of the fifteen materials of the Tabernacle, each person donated according to how "their heart impels them to give." The single exception was the silver in the foundation sockets.

> *Essay 3*: **Washstand** 275
> On the spiritual and contemporary significance of the washbasin in the courtyard of the Tabernacle.

> *Essay 4*: **Sin and Sanctuary** 279
> Which came first, the golden Tabernacle or the Golden Calf? There are no less than three different opinions on the matter, all correct.

> *Essay 5*: **The Anonymous Essence** 290
> Moses disappears from the Torah.

> *Essay 6*: **Intellectual Waste** 300
> What happens with the hours we spend pursuing a rejected line of reasoning, or the energy and acumen we expend on a refuted argument? The lesson from the source of Moses' wealth.

> *Essay 7*: **Moses' Mask** 304
> A mask is a barrier; but it is also a filter and attenuator, regulating our balance of distance and involvement vis-à-vis the material in our lives.

XXII: VAYAK'HEL 307
Home and hearth

> *Essay 1*: **Heaven and Earth** 308
> Why does the Torah repeat, almost verbatim, the dozens of verses that describe the construction of the Tabernacle?

Essay 2: **The Vessel** 311
The purpose of a vessel is that it be filled; but it is the making of vessels, rather than filling them, that is life's greatest challenge and its most revolutionary achievement.

Essay 3: **Casual Labor** 317
The difference between "doing" and "having done."

Essay 4: **The Fire** 319
Why do we dedicate buildings and institutions "for the merit" of a departed loved one? A lesson from the Shabbat law of useful ashes.

XXIII: PEKUDEI 325
The edifice

Essay 1: **Weight** 326
Which is heavier—a pound of copper or a pound of gold?

Essay 2: **Assembled Parts** 329
Five lessons on the interplay of community and individuality, as derived from the separate and combined Torah readings of *Vayak'hel* and *Pekudei*.

SOURCES 334

GLOSSARY 337

INDEX 363

PARASHAH
THIRTEEN

SHEMOT

Exodus 1:1–6:1

Enslavement in Egypt

NAME AND NUMBER

These are the names of the Children of Israel who came to Egypt... Reuben, Simeon, Levi, Judah... And all the souls descendant of Jacob were seventy.

Exodus 1:1–5

Although [G-d] had already counted them in their lifetime,[1] He again counted them at the time of their death, to express His love for them. For they are like the stars, which He takes out and brings in by number and name; as it is written (Isaiah 40:26): "He takes out their hosts by number, He calls them each by name."

Rashi, ad loc.

Counting and naming are among love's most powerful expressions. Listen to a child count his candies, or to a beloved's name on the lips of a lover, and you will know what it means to cherish and revere.

The number and the name retain their poignancy where love's more "passionate" signals no longer apply—or never did. A hug or a kiss is meaningless unless its recipient can sense it and respond.

---

[1] See Genesis 46.

But the act of counting will express our affection also for inanimate objects, and the utterance of a name will trigger a rush of feeling long after its bearer has departed from our midst.

As the book of Exodus opens, the twelve sons of Jacob—a fledgling nation's link to the lives of their founding fathers and mothers—have passed on, and the Jewish people are entering their first *galut*, a state of exile and spiritual displacement. At this point, G-d reaffirms his bond with His people by counting them and naming them. G-d is saying: Even if the trials to come will deaden your response to Me, My love for you will not falter.

Two Dimensions

Counting and naming relate to two different—even opposite—aspects of their subject.

Numbers are the ultimate equalizer. The statement, "all the souls descendant of Jacob were seventy," attributes to each soul an equal standing in the total count. Each of these souls is a unique individual, with his or her particular strengths and weaknesses; but in counting them, we underscore their common denominator—the basic fact of their being. On this level, each of the seventy count for no more and no less than "one."

Names, on the other hand, denote the very opposite of commonality. The name identifies, individualizes, distinguishes. This is especially true in the Torah, where names are given to individuals and places to express their unique characteristics and to identify their specific function and role.[2]

Throughout the long and bitter *galut* of Egypt, G-d kept loving watch over both these dimensions of the Children of Israel. G-d

---

2   See Genesis 17:5, 21:31, 25:21, 41:51–52, et al.

counted the quintessence of their being, the indestructible core of the Jewish soul. And G-d named the growing thousands of expressions of this essence, as translated into thousands and then hundreds of thousands of individual lives.

THE BRICK FACTORY

They made their lives bitter with hard labor, with mortar and with bricks...
                                    Exodus 1:14

Before they could become a people, chosen by G-d as His "light unto the nations,"[1] the Children of Israel had to first undergo the "smelting pit of Egypt."[2] For 210 years they were "sojourners in a land that is not theirs,"[3] the last eighty-six of which they were inducted into forced labor by the Egyptians, primarily in the manufacture of bricks.[4]

Why bricks? Nothing is incidental in G-d's world, particularly in the history of His people. If we were forged as a nation at the brick kilns of Egypt, then the brick is significant to our mission in life.

Brick vs. Stone

The human being is a builder. Some build physical edifices: homes, cities, roads, machines, and a host of other structures. Others engage in more metaphysical construction, structuring words, hues, or sounds so that they house ideas or feelings. But we all

---

1 Isaiah 42:6.
2 Deuteronomy 4:20.
3 Genesis 15:13.
4 See Exodus 1:14 and 5:7–19; *Midrash Rabbah, Bamidbar* 15:20.

build our lives, taking materials from our environment, our society, and our own psyche, and forging them into an edifice that serves a certain function and aim. Having been endowed by our Creator with free choice, we might make this a material or a spiritual aim, a selfish or altruistic one, a positive or negative one; or we can make it the ultimate aim of "building a dwelling for G-d"[5] by devoting our lives to the fulfillment of G-d's will as revealed in the Torah.

The materials we use fall under two general categories: G-d-given and man-made. Much of the "matter" out of which we build our lives was already here when we arrived on the scene, ready for use, or with its potential implicit in it, awaiting discovery and realization. But G-d empowered us to do more than simply develop His world. Desiring that we be true "partners in creation,"[6] the Creator imparted to us the ability to create potential where no such potential exists.

Therein lies the deeper significance of the bricks we molded and fired as we matured as a people. In the eleventh chapter of Genesis, the Torah describes the invention of the brick. Originally, the survivors of the Flood inhabited mountainous regions, and quarried stone as a building material. But then they settled in the valley of Shinar (later Babylon), where they desired to build "a city and a tower whose head reached to the heavens."[7] Where would they find a material strong enough for such a massive structure?

> *They said one to the other: "Let us mold bricks, and bake them with fire." And the brick served them as stone, and clay served them as mortar.*[8]

---

5 "G-d desired a dwelling in the physical world" (*Tanchuma, Naso* 16); "This is what man is all about; this is the purpose of his creation, and the creation of all worlds, lofty and lowly" (*Tanya*, chapter 36).
6 Talmud, *Shabbat* 10a and 119b.
7 Genesis 11:4.
8 Ibid., verse 3.

"Stone" represents those materials with which G-d provides us to build our lives. Not that we needn't toil—the stone must be cut from the quarry, transported, hewn into shape, and fitted with many others for a structure to be raised. But the stone is there, solid and fit for the task, awaiting development. In our own lives, these are the elements that are naturally qualified to serve as part of a home for G-d and readily lend themselves to this end: our positive character traits, the sacred times and places in creation (e.g., the twenty-four hours of Shabbat, the Holy Land), objects and forces designated for the performance of a *mitzvah* (e.g., a Torah scroll, a pair of *tefilin*).

Then there are those elements that are as qualified a building material as raw clay: our selfish and animalistic instincts, and a material and materialistic world that obscures the truth of its Creator. These are elements that, by nature, are unconducive, or even contrary, to anything good and G-dly. To include these elements in the "dwelling for G-d" we make of our lives, we must forge "bricks." We must knead and mold them into a shape they have never known, fire them in the kiln of self-sacrifice and love of G-d, until they become as solid and supportive as the sacred "stones" in our edifice.

THE CULT OF THE RIVER

Pharaoh commanded his entire nation: Every boy that is born, you shall throw into the river, and every girl you shall make live.

Exodus 1:22

Very little rain falls in Egypt. Agriculture is completely dependent on the Nile, whose overflow fills a network of irrigation canals. The ancient Egyptians therefore deified the Nile, regarding it as the ultimate source of sustenance and the ultimate endower of life.

This is the deeper significance of Pharaoh's decree to drown the Hebrew children in the Nile. Pharaoh knew that if the next generation of Jews were submerged in the Nile-cult of Egypt—if they were raised to regard the natural purveyors of sustenance as gods—the faith of Abraham would be obliterated. The message of a One G-d who is the creator and source of all, which so threatened his pagan oligarchy, would be silenced forever.

One can say that Nile-worship is as prevalent today as it was in the days of the Pharaohs. Today's "Nile" may be a college degree, a career, social standing—anything that is venerated as a provider of sustenance and life. These are *tools* of sustenance, as the Nile is an instrument of G-d's sustenance of those who dwell along its banks. But when the vehicle is confused with the source—when a person drowns their entire self in the "Nile," investing their choicest energies in the perfection of the instrument rather than the cultivation of their relationship with its divine wielder—this is idolatry.[1]

The people of Israel survived the Egyptian *galut* (exile) because there were Jewish mothers who refused to comply with Pharaoh's decree to submerge their children in his river. If we are to survive the present *galut*, we, too, must resist the dictates of the current "Pharaohs." We must set the spiritual and moral development of our children—rather than their future earning power and careers—as the primary aim of their education.

---

[1] Therein also lies the significance of the second part of Pharaoh's decree, "...and every girl you shall make live." Pharaoh does not say that the girls should be allowed to live, but that they shall be *made to live*—i.e., to be indoctrinated into the life-values and culture of Egypt. The boys were to be physically drowned in the Nile. The girls, too, were to be submerged in the Nile—to be raised in this cult of the river, their souls drowned in a life that deifies the earthly vehicle of material sustenance.

THE INFANT SHEPHERD

[When] she was no longer able to hide him, she took for him a papyrus box, and she smeared it with clay and with pitch; and she placed the child in it. And she placed it in the rushes on the bank of the river. Exodus 2:3

Pharaoh had decreed that all newborn Hebrew males should be drowned in the Nile. In the hope of saving him from that fate, Moses' mother placed the three-month-old infant in a basket and concealed it in the rushes that grew along the riverbank. The baby's older sister, Miriam, was stationed at a distance to stand watch over what would happen to him.

> *The daughter of Pharaoh came down to bathe at the river… and she saw the box amidst the rushes… She opened it, and she saw the child… She had mercy upon him, and she said, "This is of the children of the Hebrews."*[1]

The Torah goes on to relate how the daughter of Pharaoh adopted the child and raised him as his own son. "She called his name Moses *(Moshe)*… because I have drawn him *(meshitihu)* from the water."[2]

---

1 Exodus 2:5–6.
2 Ibid., verse 10.

The Purging of the Nile

There is one detail in this account that is the subject of some confusion. Where, exactly, was Moses' basket placed? In the beginning of the Torah's account we read that "she placed it in the rushes, *on the bank of the river.*" According to this, Moses was not placed in the Nile itself, but on the Nile's shore.[3] A few verses later, however, Pharaoh's daughter declares that "I have drawn him *from the water.*"

The Gaon of Rogachov[4] offers a halachic (Torah-legal) explanation for the basket's change of location. The Nile, upon which Egypt was completely dependent for its sustenance, was worshipped by the Egyptians as a god.[5] Therefore, Moses' mother could not have initially placed him in the Nile, as it is forbidden to make use of an object of idol-worship even to save oneself.[6] However, Torah law also stipulates that if an idol-worshipper renounces their idol, it becomes "nullified" and permissible for use.[7] Our sages tell us that Pharaoh's daughter "came down to the river to bathe"[8] not only in the physical sense, but also "to cleanse herself from her father's idols."[9] Her renunciation of the paganism of Egypt nullified the river's idolatrous status, and its waters could now receive and shelter Moses. It was at this point that Moses' basket entered the Nile.[10]

Why was it important that Moses should be in the Nile, rather than hidden in the rushes on its shore? The Midrash tells us that

---

3   Also see *Targum Onkelos* on the verse.
4   Rabbi Yosef Rozin, 1858–1936.
5   See previous essay, "The Cult of the River," pp. 8–9 above.
6   *Mishneh Torah, Laws of the Fundamentals of Torah* 5:6; see *Likutei Sichot*, vol. 15, p. 13, note 9.
7   *Mishneh Torah, Laws Regarding Idol-Worship* 8:8.
8   Exodus 2:5.
9   Talmud, *Sotah* 12b; *Midrash Rabbah*, ad loc.
10 *Tzafnat Paaneach* on Exodus 2:3.

Pharaoh's astrologers had told him that "the savior of Israel will meet his end by water," which was why Pharaoh decreed that all male Jewish babies should be thrown into the Nile. When Moses was in the river, the astrologers told Pharaoh, "The savior of the Jews has already been cast into the water." Thus Moses' entry into the Nile brought about the end of Pharaoh's decree.[11]

Feeder of Faith

Moses is referred to as the *raaya meheimna*, the "faithful shepherd" of Israel.[12] The words *raaya meheimna* also mean "shepherd of faith"—i.e., one who feeds faith to his flock.[13] Moses' primary role was to nurture the faith of his people, so that they became permeated with a knowledge of G-d and with the understanding that "There is none else besides Him"[14]—that all the "Niles" of the world are not forces or realities in their own right, but merely vehicles of divine sustenance.

Moses was eighty years old when he took the people of Israel out of Egypt, led them to Mount Sinai, and fed them the ultimate infusion of divine knowledge, the Torah. But he was already a "shepherd of faith" at the age of three months, when he was instrumental in dethroning the arch-idol of Egypt and putting an end to the drowning of Israel's children in its waters.

---

11 *Midrash Rabbah, Shemot* 1:24. The true import of what Pharaoh's astrologers saw was that it would be decreed that Moses die in the desert as a result of the "waters of contention," as related in Numbers 20:1–13.
12 *Zohar Chadash* 104a, et al.
13 *Tanya*, chapter 42.
14 Deuteronomy 4:35.

THE RUNAWAY KID

Moses was a shepherd.   Exodus 3:1

"-d tested Moses with sheep," declares the Midrash, and relates:

> When Moses was tending the flock of Jethro in the wilderness, a little kid escaped from him. He ran after it until it reached a shady place … [where there was] a pool of water, and the kid stopped to drink. When Moses approached it, he said: "I did not know that you ran away because of thirst! You must be weary." He placed the kid on his shoulder and walked back. Said G-d: "You are merciful in leading the flock of a mortal—you shall tend My flock, the people of Israel."[1]

In addition to demonstrating Moses' compassion, the incident contains another important lesson: Moses realized that the kid did not run away from the flock out of malice; it was merely thirsty.

When a Jew alienates themselves from their people, G-d forbid, it is only because they are thirsty. Their soul thirsts for meaning in life, but the waters of Torah have eluded them. So they wander about in foreign pastures, seeking to quench their thirst.

When Moses understood this, he was able to become a leader of Israel. Only a shepherd who hastens not to judge the runaway kid, who is sensitive to the causes of its desertion, can mercifully lift it into their arms and bring it back home.

---

1   *Midrash Rabbah, Shemot* 2:2.

A HEART OF FLAME

The angel of G-d appeared to [Moses] in the heart of the fire[1] from within the thornbush. And he saw that, behold, the thornbush burned with fire, but the thornbush was not consumed.

Exodus 3:2–3

aid Rabbi Israel Baal Shem Tov: In his vision of the burning thornbush, Moses beheld the heart of the simple Jew.

"Man is a tree of the field."[2] But the field has many types of trees. The Talmud[3] compares the righteous Torah scholars to fruit trees—stately, beautiful trees who bestow fragrance and nourishment upon the world. Like the thornbush that Moses beheld at Mount Horeb, these trees also burn. They burn with the ecstasy of their Torah learning, with the fervor of their prayer, with the warmth of their good deeds. But theirs is a fire that burns and burns out—a fire that is satiated by the wisdom acquired, by the feelings experienced, and by the sense of achievement they attain in their G-dly endeavors.

---

1. *Be'labat aish*, in the Hebrew. The word *labah*, commonly translated as "flame," literally means "heart" (see Rashi on this verse).
2. Deuteronomy 20:19. See the essays, "Of Trees and Men" and "Fruit for Thought," in *Inside Time* (MLC 2015), Vol. II, pp. 217–227.
3. Talmud, *Taanit* 7a.

The thornbush, however, burns with a fire that is never satiated. The simple Jew, who cannot fathom the depths of Torah, who can barely articulate his or her prayers, who has little understanding of the significance of a *mitzvah*—theirs is a thirst never quenched. Their heart burns with a yearning for G-d they can never hope to still, with a love they can never hope to consummate.

What was Moses' reaction when he beheld this sight?

> *Moses said: "I shall now turn away and I shall see this great sight, why the thornbush does not burn up."*[4]

Rashi, in his commentary on this verse, dwells on the meaning of the word Moses uses—*asurah*, "I shall turn away"—and explains that Moses is saying: "I must turn away from where I am, in order to get closer to there."

Moses is described by Maimonides as "the most perfect human being." But when Moses beheld the heart of flame that smolders within the thornbush, he was humbled by this great sight. I must remove myself from where I am, he said to himself. I must strive to awaken in myself the insatiable fire of the simple Jew.

---

4 Exodus 3:3.

THE ESSENCE OF EXISTENCE

I shall be that which I shall be.
Exodus 3:14

I was with you in your present distress, and I shall be with you in future exiles and persecutions.
Talmud, Berachot 9b

When G-d appeared to Moses in the burning bush and charged him with the mission to take the people of Israel out of Egypt, Moses said to the Almighty:

> Here I will come to the Children of Israel and say to them, "The G-d of your fathers has sent me to you," and they will say: "What is his name?" What shall I say to them?[1]

G-d replied:

> *I shall be that which I shall be... Say to the Children of Israel, "Eh'hehyeh ('I Shall Be') has sent me to you."*[2]

What is the meaning of this enigmatic exchange?

---

[1] Exodus 3:13.
[2] Ibid., verse 14.

An Anonymous G-d

To name something is to describe and define it. It therefore follows that G-d, who is infinite and undefinable, cannot be named. Indeed, G-d has no name, only names—descriptions of the various behavior patterns that can be ascribed to G-d's influence on our lives. In the words of the Midrash,

> G-d said to Moses: "You want to know My name? I am called by My deeds. I might be called El Shadai, or Tzeva'ot, or Elokim, or Havayah. When I judge My creations, I am called Elokim. When I wage war on the wicked, I am called Tzeva'ot. When I tolerate the sins of man, I am called El Shadai. When I have compassion on My world, I am called Havayah."[3]

Therein lies the deeper significance of the question that Moses anticipated from the Children of Israel.

"What is His name?", they were sure to ask. What type of behavior are we seeing on the part of G-d in these times? You say that G-d has seen the suffering of His people in Egypt, that He has heard their cries and knows their pain, and has therefore sent you to redeem us.[4] Where was G-d until now? Where was He for the eighty-six years that we are languishing under the slave driver's whip, that our babies are being torn from their mothers' arms and cast into the Nile, that Pharaoh is bathing in the blood of Hebrew children? What "name" is G-d now assuming, after all these years that He has apparently been nameless and aloof from our lives?"

---

3 *Midrash Rabbah, Shemot* 3:6.
4 Exodus 3:7–10.

G-dly but Not Holy

As explained above, each of the divine "names" describes another of the attributes by which G-d has chosen to relate to His creation: *Elokim* describes G-d's assumption of the attribute of justice, *Havayah* denotes G-d's assumption of the attribute of compassion, and so on. *Eh'hehyeh* ("I shall be"), the name by which G-d here identifies Himself to Moses, denotes G-d's assumption of being and existence.

This is why there is some question as to whether the name *Eh'hehyeh* should be counted among the "seven holy names of G-d." Torah law forbids erasing or defacing G-d's name, as the very ink and paper (or other medium) upon which it is inscribed assumes a holiness by virtue of its representation of something that relates to the Divine.[5] While there are many names and adjectives that describe G-d's many-faceted involvement with His creation, there are seven primary divine names to which the strictest provisions of this law apply. Yet despite the fact that *Eh'hehyeh* is considered the loftiest of divine names,[6] it is not included in certain versions of the seven-name list as it appears in the Talmud and the halachic authorities. Indeed, the final halachic conclusion is that it is *not* one of the "seven holy names."[7]

---

[5] This is why the word "G-d" and other divine names are written with a hyphen breaking up the letters and/or with a letter substituted or some other alteration (e.g. substituting a "k" for an "h" in *Elokim* or transfiguring the four letters Y-H-V-H as *Havayah*). Were a divine name to be spelled precisely, anyone destroying or disposing of the page on which it is printed would be violating a severe halachic prohibition.

[6] See *Zohar* 3:11a; *Sefer Ho'arochim Chabad*, vol. I, pp. 645–649.

[7] See Talmud, *Shevuot* 35, and *Dikdukei Sofrim*, ad loc.; *Mishneh Torah, Laws of the Fundamentals of Torah*, 6:2; ad loc., Venice 1524 and Venice 1540 editions; *Kesef Mishneh* commentary on *Mishneh Torah*, ad loc., *Shulchan Aruch, Yoreh De'ah* 276:9.

The reason for this paradox is best understood by understanding the meaning of the term "holiness." What makes something holy? The term *kadosh* (Hebrew for "holy") means "transcendent" and "apart." G-d is holy, as He transcends our earthly reality; Shabbat is a holy day, because it is a day of withdrawal from the mundane labors of the everyday; a Torah scroll or a pair of *tefilin* are holy because these are objects that have been set apart to serve a G-dly end.

The same applies to the seven holy divine names. Each of these names describes a divine activity that goes beyond the mundane norm, a divine *intervention* in reality—G-d as ruler, G-d as judge, G-d as provider, G-d as savior, etc. *Eh'hehyeh*, on the other hand, is G-d as being—G-d as the essence of reality.[8] So *Eh'heyeh* is beyond "holiness." If holiness is a feature of G-d's transcendence, the being-ness of G-d transcends holiness itself, describing a dimension of divine reality that pervades every existence even as it transcends it, and thus relates equally to them all, "holy" and "mundane" alike.

(Nevertheless, *Eh'hehyeh* is a *name*—that is, an assumed "behavior pattern"—of G-d's. The very phenomenon of "existence" is part and parcel of G-d's creation, and G-d certainly cannot be defined by something He created. Ultimately, G-d can be described as a "being" or "existence" only in the sense that we speak of Him as a "provider" or "ruler." These are mere "names," describing not G-d's essence but a certain perception that G-d allows us to have of Him by affecting our reality in a certain manner.)

---

8   *Guide for the Perplexed*, 1:62; Ralbag and Abarbanel on Exodus 3; *Ikarim* 2:27; et al. See also *Gevurot Hashem*, end of chapter 25.

The Answer

This was G-d's answer to the people's outcry, "What is His name?!"

    Tell the Children of Israel, said G-d to Moses, that My name is *Eh'heh yeh*. Where was I all these years? With you. I am being, I am existence, I am reality. I am the groan of a beaten slave, the wail of a bereaved mother, the spilled blood of a murdered child. Certain things must be, no matter how painful and incomprehensible to your human selves, in order that great things—infinitely great and blissful things—should be. But I do not orchestrate these things from some distant heaven, "holy" and removed from your existential pain. I was there with you, and I shall be there with you, suffering with you, praying for redemption together with you.[9]

    If you cannot see Me, it is not for My ethereality; it is because I am so real.

---

[9] See Rashi, Exodus 3:2: "G-d revealed Himself to Moses in a thornbush, and not some other tree, to emphasize that He is together with [Israel] in their affliction." Also see *Midrash Rabbah, Shemot* 2:9: "Why from a thornbush? To teach us that there is no place devoid of the divine presence."

THE NUMEROLOGY OF REDEMPTION

Moses said to G-d: "Who am I, that I might go to Pharaoh, and that I might take the Children of Israel out of Egypt? ... Please, my Lord, send by the hand of the one whom You will send."   Exodus 3:11, 4:13

"Send by the hand of the one whom You will send"—by the hand of Moshiach, who is destined to be revealed.   Midrash Lekach Tov, ad loc.

Our sages state that "the first redeemer is the final redeemer."[1] This is not to say that Moses, who delivered the Jewish people from their first exile, and Moshiach, who will bring about the final redemption, are the same person. Moses was from the tribe of Levi,[2] while Moshiach is identified as a descendant of King David,[3] from the tribe of Judah. Rather, it means that the redemption achieved by Moses is the source for the redemption by Moshiach.

---

1 See *Midrash Rabbah, Shemot* 2:4; *Zohar* 1:253a; Ari, *Shaar HaPesukim, Vayechi*; *Torah Ohr, Mishpatim* 75b.
2 Exodus 2:1–2.
3 Isaiah 11:1; *Mishneh Torah, Laws of Kings*, 11:5; et al.

The purpose of the Exodus, as G-d said to Moses when He revealed Himself to him in the burning bush, was that "when you take this people out of Egypt, you will serve G-d on this mountain"[4]—that the Jewish people should receive the Torah at Mount Sinai. The final redemption represents the full and ultimate implementation of the Torah, G-d's "blueprint for creation,"[5] in the world. Thus, "the first redeemer is the final redeemer"—Moses' Torah is the essence of Moshiach's perfect world.

Yet when Moses appealed to G-d that G-d send Moshiach and make the Exodus the first *and* final redemption, G-d did not accept his plea. First the Jewish people must be taken out of Egypt and given the Torah—a task that only Moses could achieve. Then they will be able to embark on their mission to "perfect the world as the kingdom of G-d"[6] via the Torah, until its ultimate realization through Moshiach.

Two Degrees of Oneness

The relationship between Moses and Moshiach is reflected in the numerical value of their names.[7] The numerical value of *Mosheh* (Moses) is 345,[8] and that of *Moshiach* is 358.[9] So the difference

---

[4] Exodus 3:12.
[5] *Midrash Rabbah, Bereishit* 1:2.
[6] *Siddur, Aleinu* prayer.
[7] In the Holy Tongue every letter is also a number, so that a word is also a string of numbers; the sum of these numbers is the word's numerical value, or *gematria*. The *gematria* of a word represents a deeper stratum of significance than its linguistic meaning. Thus, the fact that two different words have the same numerical value indicates that they are variant expressions of the same truth.
[8] *Mem*=40, *shin*=300, *hei*=5.
[9] *Mem*=40, *shin*=300, *yud*=10, *chet*=8.

between Moses and Moshiach is represented by the number 13. Otherwise stated, Moses plus 13 makes Moshiach.[10]

Thirteen is the numerical value of *echad*,[11] a word that is the keystone of the Jewish faith. Every morning and evening of our lives we recite the verse, *Shema Yisrael, Ado-nai Elo-hei-nu, Ado-nai echad*—"Hear O Israel, G-d is our G-d, G-d is *echad*."[12] The Jewish people are called "an *echad* nation on earth" because they reveal the *echad* of G-d in the world.[13] The era of Moshiach is described as "the day that G-d will be *echad*, and His name *echad*."[14]

Echad means "one." The *Shema* proclaims the oneness and unity of G-d, which the people of Israel are charged to reveal in the world, and which will be fully manifest in the era of Moshiach. But the Hebrew language has two words for oneness: *yachid* and *echad*. *Yachid* means "singular," and "only one"; *echad* means "one" and "unified." Unlike the word *yachid*, the word *echad* does not preclude the existence of other objects. It can refer to the first item of a sequence (as in "one, two, three..."), or to an entity that is composed of parts (as in "one nation," "one forest," "one person," and "one tree," each of which consists of many units or components). Why, then, do we use the term *echad* to express the divine oneness? It would seem that the term *yachid* more clearly expresses

---

10 The same concept is also expressed in the verse "The scepter shall not depart from Judah ... until Shiloh will come." The *gematria* of "Shiloh," an appellation of Moshiach, is 345, expressing the idea that "the first redeemer, he is the final redeemer." The word *yavo* ("will come") has a numerical value of 13, so that the words *yavo Shiloh* ("Shiloh will come") equal 358, the *gematria* of "Moshiach."

11 *Alef*=1, *chet*=8, *daled*=4.

12 Deuteronomy 6:4.

13 *Siddur, Amidah* for Shabbat afternoon; *Tanya, Igeret HaKodesh*, ch. 9.

14 Zechariah 14:9.

the "perfect simplicity"[15] of G-d and the axiom that "there is none else besides Him."[16]

Chassidic teaching explains that, on the contrary, *echad* represents a deeper unity than *yachid*. *Yachid* is a oneness that cannot tolerate plurality—if another being or element is introduced into the equation, the *yachid* is no longer *yachid*. *Echad*, on the other hand, represents the union of diverse elements into a harmonious whole. The oneness of *echad* is not undermined by plurality; indeed, it employs plurality as the very ingredients of unity.

G-d did not have to create a world to be *yachid*. G-d was singularly and exclusively one before the world was created, and remains so after the fact.[17] It was to express His *echad* that G-d created us, granted us freedom of choice, and commanded us the Torah. G-d created existences that, at least in their own perception, are distinct from Him, and gave them the mandate and the tools to bring their lives in harmony with His will. When a diverse and plural world chooses, by its own initiative, to unite with its Creator, the divine oneness assumes a new, deeper expression—G-d is *echad*.[18]

---

15 I.e., the fact that there are no parts, components, or aspects to His being. See *The Second Principle*, Maimonides' introduction to *Perek Chelek*; *Mishneh Torah, Laws of the Fundamentals of Torah*, 1:7; et al.

16 Deuteronomy 4:35.

17 See *Tanya*, chapter 36: "Prior to the world's creation, He was one alone, singular, and unique, filling all the 'space' in which He created the world. Now, too, this remains the true reality... The change is only from the perspective of those who receive the life and light emanating from Him, which they receive via many 'garments' that conceal and obscure His light."

18 This is expressed in the three letters/numbers that comprise the word *Echad—alef, chet, daled*, or 1, 8, 4: that the oneness of G-d be made to pervade the "seven heavens and the earth" (8) and the four (4) points of the compass.

The Limits of Revelation

Moses plus *echad* equals Moshiach.

Moses revealed the divine wisdom and will to man. But this was a *revelation*, a burst of light from Above. It was not something the world understood or agreed with, but something imposed upon it by the force of a higher truth. It was a display of the divine *yachid*, of the exclusive, all-obliterating reality of G-d.

Moses wanted that G-d should send Moshiach to take the Children of Israel out of Egypt—that the Exodus should lead to the implementation of the divine *echad* in the world. But an *echad*-oneness, by definition, cannot be imposed by a revelation from above. It must come from within, when a diverse world chooses, by its own initiative, to become one with G-d. Moses could provide the key, the formula. But the process had to unfold in the course of the thousands of years in which the world would absorb the divine truth and implement the divine will.

In the words of Rabbi Schneur Zalman of Liadi:

> *The era of Moshiach... is the culmination and fulfillment of the creation of our world—it is to this end that it was created... In the future [world of Moshiach], the light of G-d will be revealed without any obscuring garment, as it is written: "No longer shall your Master be shrouded; your eyes shall behold your Master"*[19]...
>
> *A semblance of this was already experienced on earth at the time that the Torah was given, as it is written: "You have been shown to know that G-d is the G-d, there is none else besides Him"*[20] *... [But] then their existence was lit-*

---

[19] Isaiah 30:20.
[20] Deuteronomy 4:35.

*erally nullified by the revelation, as our sages have said, "With each utterance [the people of Israel heard from G-d at Mount Sinai], their souls flew from their bodies..."*²¹ *In the end of days, however, the body and the world will be refined, and will be able to receive the revelation of the divine light ... via the Torah.*²²

---

21 Talmud, *Shabbat* 88b.
22 *Tanya*, ch. 36.

MOSHIACH'S DONKEY

Moses took his wife and children, and he set them upon the donkey; and returned to the land of Egypt.

Exodus 4:20

The prophet Zechariah describes Moshiach as "a pauper, riding on a donkey."[1] The plain meaning of the verse is that Moshiach, the most important human being in history,[2] is the epitome of self-effacement. Indeed, humility is the hallmark of the righteous, who recognize that their talents and achievements, and the power vested in them as leaders, are not theirs but their Creator's. They live not to realize and fulfill themselves, but to serve the divine purpose of creation.

On a deeper level, Moshiach's donkey represents the very essence of the messianic process—a process that began with the beginning of time and which constitutes the very soul of history. In the beginning, the Torah tells us, when G-d created the heavens and the earth, when the universe was still empty, unformed, and shrouded in darkness, the "spirit of G-d hovered" above the emerging existence.[3] Says the Midrash: "*The spirit of G-d hovered*—this is the spirit of Moshiach."[4] For Moshiach represents the divine

---

1 Zechariah 9:9.
2 "He shall be greater than Abraham, higher than Moses, and loftier than the supernal angels" (*Yalkut Shimoni* on Isaiah 52:13).
3 Genesis 1:1–2.
4 *Midrash Rabbah, Bereishith* 2:5.

spirit of creation—the vision of the perfected world that is G-d's purpose in creating it and populating it with willful, thinking, and achieving beings.

Moshiach's donkey has a long, prestigious history. Time and again it makes its appearance through the generations, surfacing at key junctures of the messianic process. Each time we see this donkey fulfilling the same function, but in a slightly different manner—reflecting the changes our world undergoes as it develops toward its ultimate state of perfection.

Abraham, Moses, and Moshiach

Moshiach's donkey first appears in the twenty-second chapter of Genesis, as Abraham heads for the "binding of Isaac," his tenth and greatest reiteration of his faith in G-d. "Abraham rose early in the morning, and he readied his donkey," the Torah relates, and loaded it with supplies for the "binding" ("the wood, the fire, and the knife") for the three-day trek to Mount Moriah in Jerusalem.[5]

Seven generations later, Moses was sent by G-d to take the Jewish people out of Egypt and bring them to Mount Sinai to receive the Torah.[6] To embark on this mission, "Moses took his wife and his children, and set them upon the donkey."[7] *The* donkey, stresses the Torah—the very same donkey, our sages explain, that served Abraham and that will bear Moshiach.[8]

Thus we find that Abraham, Moses, and Moshiach are three personages who employ this erstwhile donkey in their fulfillment

---

5 Genesis 22:3.
6 Exodus 3:12.
7 Ibid., 4:20.
8 *Pirkei d'Rabbi Eliezer*, ch. 31.

of a divine mission. But the extent to which the donkey is involved in their mission differs. With Abraham, it carries his supplies; with Moses, it carries his wife and children; whereas Moshiach is described as himself riding the donkey.

To understand the varying role "the donkey" plays in these three missions, we need to first understand the significance of what transpired at Mount Sinai—the goal of Moses' mission, which followed Abraham's mission and was the forerunner of the mission of Moshiach.

The Rescinded Decree

Conventional wisdom has it that the spiritual is greater than the physical, the ethereal more lofty than the material. Nevertheless, our sages have taught that the entirety of existence, including the loftiest spiritual "worlds," was created because "G-d desired a dwelling in the lowly realms."[9] Our physical existence is the objective of everything that G-d created, the environment within which the divine purpose in creation is realized.

G-d desired that we refine and elevate the material existence; that the physical reality, whose obtuseness and self-centeredness obscure our inner vision and distort our true priorities, be redirected as a positive force in our lives; that we bring to light the goodness and perfection inherent in all of His creation, including—and especially—the "lowliest" of His works, the material world.[10]

---

9 *Midrash Tanchuma, Nasso* 16; *Tanya*, ch. 36.
10 See the essay, "To Be or to Be Not," in vol. 1 (Genesis) of *The Inside Story*.

The Hebrew word for "donkey" is *chamor*, from the word *chomer*, "material." Moshiach's donkey is the material beast harnessed, the physical directed to higher and loftier ends.

Humanity's mission of elevating the material is a long and involved process, a historic effort in which each generation builds upon the attainments of its predecessors. This is because the physical and the spiritual are worlds apart; indeed, the very nature of G-d's creation is such that a vast gulf divides the two, making them natural antagonists. By nature, almost by definition, a person devoted to spiritual pursuits shuns the material, while material life coarsens a person's soul and dulls their spiritual sensitivity. Only at Mount Sinai was the divide between spirit and matter breached. The divine reality revealed itself within the earthly reality; the Torah was given to mankind, empowering us to sanctify the mundane, to express the all-pervading truth of G-d within, and via, the material world.

The Midrash[11] uses the following parable to explain the significance of the event:

> Once there was a king who decreed, "The people of Rome are forbidden to go down to Syria, and the people of Syria are forbidden to come up to Rome." Likewise, when G-d created the world He decreed, "The heavens are G-d's, and the earth is given to man."[12] But when G-d wished to give the Torah to Israel, He rescinded His original decree, and declared: "The lower realms may ascend to the higher realms, and the higher realms may descend to the lower realms. And I, Myself, will begin"—as it is written, "G-d

---

[11] *Tanchuma, Va'eira* 15.
[12] Psalms 115:16.

descended on Mount Sinai,"[13] and then it says, "And to Moses He said: Go up to G-d."[14]

Precursor, Initiator, and Culminator

This explains the difference in the extent to which Abraham, Moses, and Moshiach involve the material "donkey" in their respective missions.

Abraham, the first Jew, began the process of sublimating the material, of realizing, through his service of G-d, the physical world's potential to express the goodness and perfection of the Creator. But Abraham lived before the revelation at Sinai—before G-d rescinded the decree that had divided the world between "higher" and "lower," between matter and spirit. In Abraham's day, the original order instituted at creation still held sway—the physical and the spiritual were two separate, incompatible worlds. The most Abraham could do was to harness the physical to *serve* the spiritual, to use "the donkey" to carry the accessories of his divine service. The physical remained as coarse as ever, and could not directly be involved in his spiritual life. Nevertheless, Abraham took the first step in wresting the material from its inherent self-absorption by utilizing it, albeit peripherally, to assist in his service of G-d.

Moses, on the other hand, was embarking on the mission that was to culminate in his receiving the Torah—the medium by which G-d empowered us to dissolve the dichotomy between the "higher" and "lower" domains. The Torah instructs and enables us to sanctify even the most mundane aspects of our lives, to

---

13 Exodus 19:20.
14 Ibid., 24:1.

integrate our material selves and environment into our spiritual goals. So Moses used "the donkey" to carry his wife and children. A person's wife and children are an extension of his own self—in the words of our sages, "a person's wife is like his own body"[15] and "a child is a limb of his father."[16] Beginning with Moses, the material began to play a central and intimate role in our life's work.

But Moses marks only the beginning of Torah's effect on the physical world. Ever since Sinai, whenever we use a material resource to perform a *mitzvah*—e.g., giving money to charity, using the energy our body extracts from the food it consumes to fuel our fervor in prayer—we refine these physical objects and forces, divesting them of their mundanity and selfishness. With each such action, the physical world becomes that much holier, that much more in harmony with its innate function. Each such action brings closer the day when our world will fully shed the husk of coarseness that is the source of all ignorance and strife, heralding a new dawn of universal peace and perfection.

So Moshiach, who represents the ultimate fulfillment of Torah, himself rides the donkey of the material. Moshiach represents a world in which the material is no longer the "lower" or secondary element, but an utterly refined resource, no less central and significant a force for good than the most spiritual creation.

---

[15] Talmud, *Berachot* 24a.
[16] Ibid., *Eruvin* 70b.

PARASHAH FOURTEEN

VA'EIRA

Exodus 6:2–9:35

The promise of redemption

HAVE A HEART

G-d spoke to Moses and He said to him: "I am G-d. I have made Myself seen to Abraham, to Isaac, and to Jacob…"
Exodus 6:2–3

It was the darkest hour yet in the history of the fledgling nation. Slaves in a foreign land, subject to the cruelest and most inhuman of decrees. Just as it seemed that things could never be worse, the first glimmer of hope appeared. Then things *did* get worse.

Moses had come with a message of salvation to the Children of Israel: The time for your redemption has come. G-d has sent me to Egypt to free you from slavery, and to open a new phase in your lives. You will become G-d's chosen nation; you will soon inherit the Land of Israel, the rich and bountiful land, in both the spiritual and material sense, promised to your forefathers.

Moses and Aaron went to Pharaoh and delivered G-d's demand to, "Let My people go, and they shall serve Me!" The result? Not only does Pharaoh disregard the divine message, he also increases Israel's toil and suffering.[1] Full of pain,

> *Moses returned to G-d, and he said: "My Lord! Why have You done bad to this people? Why did You send me? For since I came to Pharaoh to speak in Your name, he has made it worse for this people; neither have You saved Your people."*[2]

---

[1] Exodus, chapter 5.
[2] Ibid., verses 22–23.

Moses' cry reverberates through the next hundred generations of our blood- and tear-soaked history: Why, G-d, why? Why have You done bad to Your people? It resounds as a universal cry for all suffering in G-d's world: Why, G-d, must the human story contain so much cruelty and anguish? Surely You, the very essence of good, could have created a world free of evil, strife, and pain?

The Response

G-d says many things in response to Moses' question, but none of them seem to address the burning issue which lies at its heart.

G-d repeats the promise that things will get better ("Now you will see what I will do to Pharaoh. For by [the force of My] strong hand he will let them go."[3]). He explains that Israel's sufferings in Egypt are the birth pangs of their glorious future as G-d's people ("I will take you out from under the burdens of Egypt, and I will deliver you from their servitude... I will acquire you as My people, and I will be your G-d."[4]). But surely Moses did not doubt G-d's promises. The crux of his question was: Why must it be this way? Why can't we achieve all these great things without the terrible preliminaries?

The Talmud explains that G-d's response to Moses' challenge lies in the words, "I have made Myself seen to Abraham, to Isaac, and to Jacob...." Why is G-d evoking the memory of the Patriarchs?

> *G-d said to Moses: I regret the loss of those who have passed away and are no longer found. Many times I revealed Myself to Abraham, Isaac, and Jacob. They did not question My ways.... I said to Abraham, "Arise, walk*

---

3 Ibid., 6:1.
4 Ibid., verses 6–7.

the land in its length and breadth, for I shall give it to you";⁵ yet he searched for a plot to bury Sarah and did not find one until he purchased it for four hundred silver shekels.⁶ Nevertheless, he did not question My ways. I said to Isaac, "Dwell in this land, and I will be with you and bless you [for to you, and to your descendants, I shall give all these lands]";⁷ yet his servants searched for some water to drink and did not get it without a fight⁸... Nevertheless, he did not question My ways. I said to Jacob, "The land upon which you lie, I shall give to you and to your descendants";⁹ yet he searched for a place to pitch his tent and did not find one until he purchased it for one hundred kesitah.¹⁰ Nevertheless, he did not question My ways...¹¹

Why, indeed, this difference between the Patriarchs and Moses? Did they have greater faith in G-d? Did they know something he did not? Did they care less about the suffering in G-d's world?

Teacher and Father

Moses was the one through whom G-d communicated the Torah, the divine wisdom that is the essence of all knowledge. He was the one human being empowered to fathom the mind of G-d and teach it to humanity.

---

5   Genesis 13:17.
6   Ibid., chapter 23.
7   Ibid., 26:3.
8   Ibid., verse 20.
9   Ibid., 28:13.
10 Ibid., 33:19.
11 Talmud, *Sanhedrin* 111a.

On the other hand, the focal point of the Patriarchs' lives was of a more "emotional" nature. "Abraham, who loves Me,"[12] is how G-d refers to the first Jew. Isaac exemplified fear and awe of G-d, while Jacob represents the emotional integrity that is achieved through the integration of the love of Abraham and the awe of Isaac.[13] The Patriarchs also studied and disseminated the wisdom of Torah,[14] and Moses certainly loved and feared G-d; but insofar as their primary roles in the development of the people of Israel are concerned, Moses is the mind of Israel, while Abraham, Isaac, and Jacob are the "heart" of our relationship with G-d.[15]

The mind has explanations for everything. Then it questions those very explanations. The mind can come to appreciate the "reasons" for G-d's creation of evil and suffering. It can understand that suffering refines us, teaching us compassion and sensitivity; that there is no greater satisfaction than the overcoming of adversity and no greater pleasure than the conquest of hardship; that a person's finest and most potent abilities are unleashed only under conditions of challenge and trial; that without a free choice between good and evil, nothing we do could possibly be of any significance.

---

12 Isaiah 41:8.
13 In Jacob's own words, "the G-d of Abraham and the awe of Isaac were to me" (Genesis 31:42). See the essay "Redigging the Wells of Love" in vol. 1 (Genesis) of *The Inside Story*.
14 Talmud, Yoma 28b; *Midrash Rabbah, Bereishith* 61:1; *Mishneh Torah, Laws Concerning Idol Worship*, 1:3.
15 To this day we refer to Moses as *Moshe Rabbeinu* ("Moses our Teacher") and to the Patriarchs as *Avraham Avinu* ("Abraham our Father"), *Yitzchak Avinu*, etc. In the terminology of kabbalah, the soul of Moses stems from the divine attribute of *chochmah* ("wisdom"), and those of the three Patriarchs from *chesed* ("benevolence"), *gevurah* ("rigor"), and *tiferet* ("harmony") respectively.

The mind can understand all this, question it, and find answers for its questions. But then comes the ultimate question: Why must it be this way? These are all rational explanations, based on our understanding of human nature and of the natural order of creation. But G-d, the creator of nature and logic, are certainly not bound by its laws. G-d could have created a logic that imparts significance to what our current logic dictates is of no significance. G-d could have ordered reality so that there *is* gain without pain, so that the best in us could be realized without the threat and challenge of evil, so that the highest peaks of life could be scaled without the momentum of its lowest descents. Thus, the mind of the believer will never accept the "necessity" for evil and pain.

The heart, of course, also perceives the pain—indeed, it senses it more deeply than the objective mind. But while the mind categorizes everything in terms of yes or no, the heart tolerates contradiction. Can you "prove" to a mother that her child is undeserving of her love? It's not that she is blind to his deficiencies and sins, but that they are simply irrelevant to her love. Outrage and devotion, judgment and acceptance, pain and pleasure—a heart that loves accommodates them simultaneously in its embrace.[16]

Moses, said G-d, you are the mind of My people; the mind that is the instrument for grasping My truth and, with it, illuminating

---

16 Therein lies the significance of G-d's words to Moses, "I have made Myself seen to Abraham, to Isaac, and to Jacob..." "Seeing" denotes a degree of certitude and conviction exceeding that of any other sense. When we hear of something, or when something is proven to us logically, subsequent developments can undermine the initial conviction. But seeing is absolute: the thing that was seen may be denied by the entire world, it may be utterly illogical, but the person who has seen it knows it is true. Likewise, the Patriarchs' faith in G-d was on the level of sight: they "saw" G-d's truth in a way that the most blatant logical contradiction could not shake.

the world. As such, you question My creation of evil and suffering, and can find no logically satisfying answer. But you, too, are a child of Abraham, Isaac, and Jacob. You, too, have inherited from them the Jewish heart—the intrinsic bond with your G-d that cannot be shaken by the most terrible of contradictions.[17]

THE PARADOX

Does this mean that it was a lack of faith on the part of Moses to confront G-d over His treatment of His people? Is that what G-d wants from us—a blind acceptance of whatever He sends our way?

Here, we find G-d rebuking Moses to employ the unquestioning faith of the Patriarchs. Yet on another occasion, we find G-d doing the very opposite—encouraging Moses to challenge His decrees.

When the people of Israel sinned with the Golden Calf, G-d said to Moses: "Now, let Me alone; My wrath shall flare against them and I will destroy them."[18] Asks the Midrash: Moses had

---

17   This explains the meaning of an enigmatic commentary by Rashi. On the verse, "I have made Myself seen to Abraham, to Isaac, and to Jacob," Rashi comments, "To the Patriarchs." Every schoolchild knows that Abraham, Isaac, and Jacob are the three fathers of the Jewish nation. What is Rashi telling us?

The fact that Abraham, Isaac, and Jacob are the Patriarchs of the Jewish people, means that the degree of faith in G-d that they achieved—faith on the level of "seeing"—is achievable by each and every one of us. Just as a child inherits the physical and psychological characteristics of his or her parents, in the same way, each and every Jew inherits the qualities of Abraham, Isaac, and Jacob; their every trait, experience, and achievement are stamped in our spiritual genes. Because our forefathers' faith in G-d was absolute and unequivocal, the potential for such faith exists within each and every one of us.

18   Exodus 32:10.

yet to utter a word in defense of Israel; why does G-d say to him, "Now, let Me alone"? The Midrash explains that G-d was saying to Moses: If you let Me alone, I shall proceed with My intended plans. But if you interfere and protest, I will heed your cries and retract My decree.[19]

In recording both these confrontations with Moses in the Torah, G-d is telling us to employ both the challenging mind and the accepting heart in our relationship with Him. G-d is telling us that the mind's most searching questions must never affect the unequivocal bond of love that is the essence of our relationship. But G-d is also telling us that the heart's acceptance must never silence our prayers and protests, "Why, G-d, have You done bad to Your people?!"—and that these challenges can, and do, make a difference.

The heart aches, the mind explains; the mind questions, the heart accepts. Both live the paradox of faith and challenge: On the one hand, King David's affirmation that "G-d is just in all His ways and benevolent in all His deeds";[20] and on the other, Isaiah's vow, "On your walls, O Jerusalem, I have set watchmen, who shall never hold their peace, day or night. You that evoke the mention of G-d, take no rest, and give Him no rest, until He establishes, until He makes Jerusalem a praise in the earth."[21]

---

19 *Midrash Rabbah*, ad loc.
20 Psalms 145:17.
21 Isaiah 62:6–7.

ON FREEDOM AND AUTHORITY

"Let My people go, and they shall serve Me."
Exodus 7:16

No longer will a man instruct his fellow… for all shall know Me, from the least of them to the greatest.
Jeremiah 31:33

Freedom and liberty are axiomatic to Judaism. The Exodus from Egypt, celebrated each year as "the time of our liberation,"[1] is described by the prophet Ezekiel as the birth of the Jewish people,[2] and we are commanded to "remember the day that you went out of Egypt, every day of your life."[3] According to Maharal,[4] the Exodus not only achieved the liberation of the Jewish people from Egyptian slavery, but also the creation of a new type of person—the free human. As a result of the Exodus, the Jew, even if subsequently conquered and oppressed, remains inherently free.[5]

---

1. *Zeman cheiruteinu* in the Hebrew, as the festival of Passover is referred to in the *Siddur* (prayer book).
2. Ezekiel 16. See *Mechilta, Beshalach* 14:30; *Midrash Tehillim* 107:4; *Yalkut Shimoni* on Deuteronomy 4:34; et al.
3. Deuteronomy 16:3. We fulfill this commandment by reciting the third section of the *Shema* (Numbers 15:37–41) every morning and evening (see Passover *Haggadah*, s.v. *Amar Rabbi Elazar*; see also Talmud, *Pesachim* 116b).
4. Rabbi Judah Loewe of Prague, c. 1512–1609.
5. *Gevurot Hashem*, chapter 61; based on Leviticus 25:42.

Indeed, the image of Moses standing before Pharaoh and demanding, "Let my people go!" has inspired numerous liberation movements in the thirty-three centuries since, including the American revolution of 1776[6] and the abolitionist movement in America in the mid-nineteenth century. This defining moment in Jewish history became a paradigm of freedom for peoples as diverse as British colonists objecting to "taxation without representation" and African slaves yearning for the most basic of human freedoms.

The centrality of the Exodus to Judaism is most strongly emphasized by the fact, noted by many of the biblical commentaries, that when G-d appears to the people of Israel at Mount Sinai, He does not say, "I am G-d your G-d, creator of the heavens and the earth"; rather, G-d says, "I am G-d your G-d, who took you out of the land of Egypt, from the house of slavery."[7] That event, the giving of the Torah at Mount Sinai—occurring seven weeks after the Exodus—is regarded as the extension and fulfillment of the Exodus from Egypt, the next step in the path toward the attainment of true freedom.[8] "There is no free person," says the Talmudic sage Rabbi Joshua ben Levi, "save one who is occupied with the Torah."[9]

If the whole of Jewish history is the outgrowth of the liberation from Egypt, it is also the movement toward a higher liberty—

---

[6] Interestingly, Benjamin Franklin proposed that an engraving of the Children of Israel exiting Egypt be incorporated into the Great Seal of the United States.

[7] Exodus 20:2.

[8] Thus Shavuot, the festival celebrating the giving of the Torah at Mount Sinai, is not defined by a particular date on the Jewish calendar (as all other festivals) but rather as the 50th day from the first day of Passover. See also G-d's words to Moses in Exodus 3:12, cited on p. 45 below.

[9] Ethics of the Fathers 6:2.

toward "the true and complete redemption" of Moshiach. The messianic age is the completion of the process, begun at the Exodus and the giving of the Torah at Sinai, of the liberation of the human soul.

The G-dliness of Freedom

The quest for freedom is central to Judaism because it is as a free being that we actualize our synonymy with the Divine.

The human being was formed in the "image and likeness" of G-d.[10] Just as G-d acts in absolute freedom, so too is the human being unique and distinct among all creations[11] in that man alone possesses free choice.[12] In creating the human being and "breathing into his nostrils" a soul that is "literally a part" of Himself,[13] G-d created the single creature with a potential for freedom—a potential that is, in essence, divine.

It is this potential that drives us to constantly challenge the constraints that are imposed on us, including even the limits of our own nature. In the words of G-d's blessing to Jacob, "You shall burst forth to the west and to the east, to the north and to the south."[14] Indeed, it is only as a free being that humanity has realized its highest potentials in the sciences and the arts, and in the

---

10 Genesis 1:26–27.
11 Even the celestial angels are called "holy animals" because, like terrestrial animals, their actions are dictated by the nature imparted to them by their Creator.
12 Sforno on Genesis 1:26; Maharal, *Derech Chaim* 3:15; also see Maimonides, *Guide for the Perplexed* 1:1–2; *Mishneh Torah, Laws of Repentance*, 5:1.
13 Genesis 2:7; *Tanya*, chapter 2.
14 Genesis 28:14. The Talmud (*Shabbat* 118a–b) refers to this blessing as a "boundless heritage."

quest to know and serve G-d. The purpose of the Exodus and the giving of the Torah was to provide us with the tools for the actualization of this potential—a process which attains its ultimate realization in the messianic redemption.

The Yoke of the Sovereignty of Heaven

This conception of Judaism as a liberation movement is contrasted by another, no less axiomatic principle of Judaism: the Jew's utter and unequivocal submission to the authority of G-d.

Twice a day we recite the *Shema*, declaring, "Hear O Israel, G-d is our G-d, G-d is one." The purpose of this declaration, says the Talmud, is to "accept upon oneself the yoke of the sovereignty of Heaven," as one cannot begin one's day as a Jew without this acceptance. The very stuff and substance of Judaism are the six hundred and thirteen *mitzvot* of the Torah, and the very concept of a *mitzvah*—a divine commandment—is predicated on a prior acknowledgement of the *mitzvah*'s Commander and the absolute obedience to His will.[15] This is the idea behind the many references in the words of the sages and in the texts of our prayers to G-d as "King", "King of the Universe", "King of All Kings", "Master of the World", and the like.

We mentioned earlier how the image of Moses, representing a clan of powerless slaves and confronting the ruler of the mightiest nation on earth to boldly demand, "Let my people go," has become a paradigm of the quest for freedom. But a closer examination of that scene shows it to be something quite different than commonly perceived. Simply stated, Moses is being quoted out of context. What Moses actually says to Pharaoh is: "So said G-d...

---

15 Talmud, *Berachot* 13a.

'Let My people go, and they shall serve Me.'"[16] G-d, for His part, is clear about His purpose in taking the Jews out of Egypt from the very start. When He first appears to Moses in the burning bush, G-d says: "This is the sign that I have sent you: When you take this people out of Egypt, you will serve G-d on this mountain."[17] G-d also says: "The children of Israel are My servants; they are My servants, who I have taken out of the land of Egypt; they cannot be sold into slavery."[18] (This last statement, incidentally, is the basis for the Maharal's above-quoted assertion that following the Exodus, the Jewish people will never again be slaves to any mortal power.)

In Human Nature

We have seen that Judaism paradoxically—often in the same breath—defines itself both as liberator of the human soul and as a covenant of submission to a Higher Authority. Let us also acknowledge that these two impulses reside side by side in the human psyche.

Man's striving for freedom requires no proof or documentation. But the human impulse for submission to authority is no less apparent. We see it in the simple fact that billions of people accept as a matter of course the authority of parents, teachers, government officials, and religious leaders to dictate matters pertaining to every area of their lives. We see it in the phenomena of patriotism, hero-worship, and cultism. We see it in the survival, and even blossoming, of religious observance long after its political braces

---

16 Exodus 4:23, 7:16, 7:26, 8:16, 9:1, 9:13, et al.
17 Ibid., 3:12.
18 Leviticus 25:42.

have been dismantled. The human being, it seems, has a deep-seated need to be part of something greater than him or herself, to negate their own will and ego in the face of a will and ego greater than their own. Chassidism has a name for this ideal, which it regards as a great virtue: *bittul* ("self-abnegation").

The human soul is both rebellious and submissive. It is left to education, conditioning, and environment to emphasize and cultivate—or alternately, to deemphasize and suppress—either of these tendencies.

Because both these impulses are fundamental to Judaism's vision of human potential, and because the cultivation of one presumably will mean the suppression of the other, the question arises: Which should be given priority over the other? Or, to otherwise state the question: In what sort of environment would the Torah prefer to see the Jew—as a member of a free society, or as the subject of an authoritarian regime?

The Holy Side of Tyranny

This dilemma is illustrated by an anecdote told of the *mashpiah* (chassidic teacher and mentor) Rabbi Dovid Kievman, also known as "Reb Dovid Horodoker." It is said that Reb Dovid wept when Czar Nicholas II was overthrown in the Russian Revolution of 1917. When asked why he would shed tears over the fall of a tyrant, Reb Dovid replied: "I weep because a *mashal* (analogy) in chassidic teaching is gone."

The analogy, or *mashal*, is an elementary tool of chassidic teaching. The premise is that to truly understand something, one must experience it, or something like it, oneself. This is even more so when we seek to understand spiritual realities: to make the ethereal palpable to the human mind, we must first find the corresponding model in the human experience. Chassidic teaching therefore makes extensive use of analogies from everyday experience to explain abstract and spiritual concepts such as the nature of G-d's relationship with the created reality, the essence and purpose of creation, and the like.

We have already mentioned the extensive use of the analogy of "kingship" in the teachings of the sages; this is further expanded on in chassidic teaching. The chassidic masters note that the Torah employs a variety of analogies in speaking of our relationship with G-d, comparing it to the relationship between a child and its parent, of a beloved and her lover, a disciple and his teacher, a flock and its shepherd, among others. While each of these models expresses another facet of the bond between us and G-d, there is a dimension to the relationship that can be expressed only by the model of a subject's relationship to their king.

So when the czar was overthrown, a teacher of chassidism wept. To live as a subject of the czar was, in many ways, a great hindrance to living as a Jew. But Reb Dovid was thinking of the deeper, more fundamental effect of authoritarianism: not of the blatant ways that a tyrant's authority intruded upon one's life, but of the particular mindset and psychological makeup it cultivated in a person. How, agonized this *mashpiah*, will a kingless generation possibly understand the utter surrender of self that the king-subject relationship exemplified? How will they comprehend the awe accorded one whose rule is absolute and incontestable? What model would they have for a figure who transcends the personal to embody the soul of a nation? Never mind that most kings of history were unworthy analogies of divine sovereignty; central to our relationship with G-d is something that only one who has been subject to a king can truly appreciate.

The Pitfalls of Freedom

But what about the capacity for freedom? While monarchical rule certainly made submission to authority a tangible reality in the lives of its subjects, it also suppressed their quest for freedom—a quest which, as we have seen, is part and parcel of the soul's formation in "the image of G-d," and which impels us toward the state of freedom that is the end goal of creation.

And yet, there is another side to freedom as well. All too often, personal freedom translates into selfishness, anarchy, and violence; into the exploitation of the weak by the strong; into the abandonment of giving and altruistic relationships (marriage, family, community) for an egomaniacal lust for power, wealth, and corporeal pleasure. Instead of freeing himself, the human being enslaves himself to the most base and animalistic elements of his nature. Set free from the bonds of authority, the worst in man is often the first to assert itself.

Chassidic teaching sees this, too, as a factor of how deeply rooted the quest for freedom is in the soul. There is a kabbalistic rule: the higher a thing is, the lower it falls.[19] Precisely because it is an expression of the soul's synonymy with the Divine, the drive for freedom is susceptible to the most destructive of corruptions.

Hence the dilemma: Presuming that we can in some way influence world events and the nature of the society in which we live, which should we prefer? Should we prefer an authoritarian society which breeds the type of mind and personality that more readily submits to "the yoke of Heaven" and minimizes the dangers of freedom gone amok, but which suppresses the most divine of human potentials? Or should we prefer a free society, in which a state of *bittul* is far more difficult to achieve, and in which one is far more vulnerable to the pitfalls of freedom, yet which nurtures

---

19   Rabbi Schneur Zalman of Liadi, *Likutei Torah*, Emor 34c.

that aspect of ourselves with the potential for deeper identification with our Creator?

Napoleon and the Czar

In the first two decades of the nineteenth century, this question was embodied by two massive armies slaughtering each other on the battlefields of Europe. On one side stood Napoleon, heir of the French Revolution, espousing the ideals of "liberty, equality, and fraternity," and promising emancipation to the oppressed peoples of the continent. Opposing him were the monarchs of Europe, claiming a divine right to rule, casting themselves as defenders of the family, institutionalized religion, law and order—indeed, of civilization itself—and warning of the havoc the apostasy of freedom had wreaked in France.[20]

---

20 At the time that the French Revolution was plunging that country into G-dlessness, anarchy, and bloodshed, another revolution, the American, was espousing and institutionalizing the tenets of freedom on the other side of the Atlantic. But the freedom of the American Founding Fathers was not the freedom from divine authority and moral constraints of Marat and Danton. They envisioned a society beholden to G-d, with the values that later found expression in the mottos, "One nation under G-d," and "In G-d we trust." When they incorporated freedom of religion into the Bill of Rights, their intent was to safeguard the freedom of every person to worship G-d according to his conscience, not to advocate G-dlessness; to them, man's subordination to G-d was a fact of reality, not some "religious" principle (the current trend to interpret the First Amendment as a mandate for the banishment of G-d from the classroom and the prohibition of public support for anything of a nonmaterialistic nature is an unfortunate distortion of its authors' intent). The American Revolution was thus a far closer approximation of Torah's ideal of freedom. G-d has indeed blessed their effort: the republic they founded has endured, and is today the most powerful of nations and in a position to positively influence all inhabitants of earth.

The leaders of European Jewry were likewise divided. There were rabbis and chassidic rebbes who eagerly awaited liberation by Napoleon's armies. No longer would the Jewish people be confined in ghettos and deprived of their means of earning a livelihood; no longer would the state be allied with a religion hostile to the Jewish faith. Liberated from the persecution and poverty that had characterized Jewish life on European soil for a dozen centuries, the Jewish people would be free to deepen and intensify their bond with G-d in ways previously unimaginable. Indeed, there were those who believed that a French victory would ready the world for the coming of Moshiach and the final redemption.[21]

But there were other voices in the Jewish community as well, voices that prophesied the exchange of material poverty for spiritual woe. Yes, the ghetto walls would fall; yes, professional alliances and universities of Europe would open their doors to the Jew. But at what price! The winds of freedom would portend the destruction of traditional Jewish life, the breakdown of the Jewish family and community, and the compromising of the Jews' commitment to Torah. Yes, Napoleon would liberate the Jewish body, but he would all but destroy the Jewish soul.

A major force in the Jewish opposition to Napoleon was Rabbi Schneur Zalman of Liadi, founder of Chabad chassidism. In a letter to one of his loyal followers, Rabbi Moshe Maizlish of Vilna, he wrote:

> *If Bonaparte will be victorious, Jewish wealth will increase, and the prestige of the Jewish people will be raised; but their hearts will disintegrate and be distanced from their*

---

[21] These included the chassidic masters Rabbi Shlomo of Karlin; Rabbi Israel, the Maggid of Kozhnitz; Rabbi Levi Yitzchak of Berditchev; and Rabbi Mendel of Riminow.

> *Father in Heaven. But if Alexander will be victorious, although Israel's poverty will increase and their prestige will be lowered, their hearts will be joined, bound, and unified with their Father in Heaven.*[22]

Rabbi Schneur Zalman did more than warn against the dangers of freedom; he rallied all his forces, both material and spiritual, to halt Napoleon's "emancipation" of Europe. There was even a chassidic spy—the same Moshe Maizlish to whom the above letter is addressed—who, at Rabbi Schneur Zalman's behest, worked as an interpreter for the French high command and relayed their battle plans to the czar's generals. On the spiritual plane, Rabbi Schneur Zalman interceded on high to effect Napoleon's downfall.[23]

Rabbi Schneur Zalman gave his very life to the effort. As Napoleon's armies neared his hometown of Liadi in the late summer of 1812, he fled his home. Though confident of Napoleon's eventual defeat, he refused to live under his rule for even a single moment. He died many miles from home in December of that

---

22 *Igrot Kodesh, Admur HaZaken*, letter #64.
23 Chassidim tell of a contest that took place on the morning of Rosh Hashanah between Rabbi Schneur Zalman and the Maggid of Kozhnitz, to decide the outcome of Napoleon's war against Russia. According to kabbalistic tradition, the sounding of the *shofar* on Rosh Hashanah effects G-d's coronation as king of the universe and the divine involvement in human affairs for the coming year; each of these two rebbes therefore endeavored to be the first to sound the *shofar* in the fateful year of 5573 (1812–1813), and thereby influence the outcome of the war. The Maggid of Kozhnitz arose well before dawn, immersed in the *mikvah*, began his prayers at the earliest permissible hour, prayed speedily, and sounded the *shofar*. But Rabbi Schneur Zalman departed from common practice and sounded the *shofar* at the crack of dawn, before the morning prayers. "The *Litvak* (Lithuanian, as Rabbi Schneur Zalman was affectionately called by his colleagues) has bested us," said Rabbi Israel of Kozhnitz to his disciples.

year, weakened by the tribulations of his flight and the harsh Russian winter. His role in the defeat of Napoleon was recognized by Alexander I, who awarded him the title and privileges of an "Honored Citizen."

Rabbi Schneur Zalman's fears were borne out by the events of the next two centuries. When emancipation did come to European Jewry, it came as a gradual process, and traditional Judaism had by then developed an array of intellectual and moral responses (most notably, the chassidic and *mussar* movements). Still, the spiritual toll of freedom was high, with many abandoning traditional Jewish life after being influenced by the spread of antireligious "enlightenment." We can only imagine what the toll might have been had Napoleon conquered the continent in the early years of the nineteenth century.

The Custom of the City

Napoleon did fall and monarchial authority was restored in Europe. But not for long. History was set on a course that could be slowed and tempered but not stopped—a course in which freedom was replacing authority; in which personal will was becoming less and less subject to rulers, laws, and societal norms.

History is not blind. Divine providence provides each generation with the challenges it is equipped to meet and the potentials it is empowered to realize.[24] If we today live in a free world, it is

---

24 Indeed, many of life's greatest questions—including questions of right and wrong, and even good and evil—are, in truth, questions of context and timing rather than of intrinsic positivity or negativity. A case in point is the first sin of history—Adam and Eve's eating from the Tree of Knowledge—which the Torah describes as being responsible for everything wrong in our world. Yet, if Adam and Eve had waited three hours,

because we have been deemed capable of dealing with this volatile force and harnessing it toward positive and G-dly ends.

"When you come to a city," says the Midrash, "do as their custom."[25] This is more than a bit of traveling advice designed to avoid awkward moments for dinner guests in a foreign country; it is a rule to be applied to our journey through history. We are not here to fight the world, the Midrash is saying, but to mold it, develop it, and sublimate it. Each era and society has its "customs," its unique *zeitgeist* and cultural milieu that is to be exploited to serve your creator and your mission in life. If you live under the

---

until nightfall of that fateful Friday and the onset of Shabbat, the fruit of the Tree of Knowledge would have been permitted to them. Eating from the Tree of Knowledge was not, in and of itself, an undesirable action, but a premature action, a phase in the unfolding of the divine plan for creation whose time had not yet come.

Another example is Korach's rebellion against Moses, recounted in the 16th chapter of Numbers. Korach is treated in the harshest way in the biblical narrative, and described in the harshest terms in the Talmudic and midrashic literature. But all he seems to be seeking is spiritual empowerment for the ordinary man—the right to relate to G-d directly, independently of a spiritual hierarchy. "The entire community is holy," Korach challenges Moses, "and G-d is amongst them; why do you raise yourself above the community of G-d?" (Numbers 16:3). What was undesirable in Korach's campaign? Does not the prophet Jeremiah describe the messianic age as a time when "no longer shall a man instruct his fellow... for all shall know Me, from the least of them to the greatest"? But precisely that was Korach's sin: he was preempting history. His vision was a positive and holy vision, but the timing was wrong, destructive, and thus evil.

This concept is best understood in light of the kabbalistic doctrine of evil as concealment. G-d is the essence of good, and all that flows from Him (i.e., everything in existence) is therefore good in essence. This means that there is nothing that is intrinsically evil. There are only negative forms of essentially positive forces, like a healing medicine that is administered in the wrong dosage or in the wrong manner.

25 *Midrash Rabbah, Shemot* 47:5. See also Talmud, *Bava Metzia* 86b.

hegemony of a czar, channel the submission to authority to which this indoctrinates you to feed your commitment to the supernal King of all kings. If you live in a world profaned by an "everything goes" freedom, recast it as a G-dly freedom—as the facilitator of the uninhibited expression of the "image of G-d" that is your truest self.

Indeed, our generation has proven itself equal to the challenge of freedom. In the 1960s and '70s the youth of the Western World rebelled against the conformity, materialism, and sterile religions of their parents and teachers. They redefined freedom as the freedom to seek a higher purpose to life, the freedom to transcend an ego-encumbered self to discover a truer, more altruistic self within. Much of it was misguided and destructive, as rootless and unfocused revolutions are wont to be. But it also brought about a great liberation of the soul in the form of the *teshuvah* ("return") movement. Many thousands of Jews shed the shackles of habit and ignorance to embrace a Torah-true life, a life that answers the soul's deepest yearnings and realizes its quintessential purpose.

Significantly, France—the very France that two hundred years ago epitomized the corruptibility of freedom—has been the scene of one of the greatest successes of the *teshuvah* movement, with thousands of French Jews rediscovering and recommitting themselves to Torah. Today, the land of Voltaire is undergoing a spiritual renaissance and libertine Paris is dotted with *yeshivahs* and reborn communities. Even the anthem of the French revolution, the *Marseillaise*, has been "appropriated" as a chassidic melody. Freedom is being reclaimed and directed toward its true, G-dly end.[26]

---

26 It is noteworthy that the numerical value (*gematria*) of *Tzarfat*, the biblical name for "France" (Obadiah 1:20), is 770, the same as *(u)faratzta* ("you shall burst forth"), G-d's blessing of a "boundless heritage" to

Freedom Redefined

The last frontier is before us—the frontier of self. Who are we, really? What happens when we are freed of all external constraints and authority structures? Is our commitment to G-d something to be enforced upon a resisting self, or is it the ultimate fulfillment of the self's incessant quest for freedom?

Our sages tell us that there will come a day when, "A fig tree shall cry out: Do not pick my fruit! Today is Shabbat!"[27] A day when G-d's blueprint for creation will be the natural state of every created thing. A day when reality will be a flawless mirror of its divine source.

We are now on the threshold of that day. Living in a world that grows perceptibly freer by the day, we face our final challenge: to bring to light a freedom that is not a challenge to the sovereignty of G-d but its ultimate complement. A freedom in which the ego of man is but a reflection of the divine "I".

Jacob. *Tzarfat* is also Hebrew for "to refine," alluding to our mission in life to refine and perfect all elements of creation, including the most challenging element of them all—the phenomenon of freedom.

27 *Midrash Tehillim*, 73.

OF SNAKES AND STICKS

Moses and Aaron came before Pharaoh, and they did as G-d had commanded: Aaron threw his staff before Pharaoh and before his servants, and it turned into a serpent. Pharaoh summoned also [his] wise men and sorcerers... each cast his staff, and they turned into serpents; but Aaron's staff swallowed up their staffs.   Exodus 7:10–12

The Torah emphasizes that it was Aaron's *staff* that consumed the serpent-staffs of the Egyptian sorcerers. In other words, first Aaron's staff miraculously turned into a snake; then, when the Egyptians replicated the feat with their sorcery, Aaron's staff-turned-snake turned back into a staff, and swallowed the staff-snakes of the Egyptians.

The Midrash explains that since it is natural that a snake should swallow another snake, G-d made it that Aaron's staff should swallow the others *after* it had reverted to its original, inanimate form, thereby demonstrating the impotence of Egypt's idols in a manifestly miraculous way.[1]

---

1   *Midrash Rabbah, Shemot* 9:5.

The Dispassionate Battle

There is also a lesson here, to each and every one of us, on how to confront the various "Pharaohs" we must deal with in the course of our lives.

The Torah declares that "its ways are ways of pleasantness, and all its paths are peace."[2] Our mission is to create light, not to battle darkness. Nevertheless, there are times when we are forced to resort to battle, when we must vanquish those who seek to vanquish us. Thus Moses, the gentle shepherd of Israel,[3] and Aaron, the epitomic man of peace,[4] found themselves in the role of "judge and chastiser of Pharaoh,"[5] crushing the might of Egypt and obliterating, one after another, its icons and myths.

But even when we must wage war, we should not become warriors. Even when we need to consume the serpents of our enemies, we should not be serpents ourselves, spewing poison and hate. Our instrument of vengeance should be as devoid of vengeful feeling as the stoic staff, as cold to the rage of war as a lifeless stick.

---

2   Proverbs 3:17.
3   See "The Runaway Kid," p. 13 above.
4   "Be of the disciples of Aaron: One who loves peace, pursues peace, loves G-d's creatures and brings them close to the Torah" (*Ethics of the Fathers*, 1:12).
5   Exodus 7:1 (see Rashi, ad loc.).

THE RED NILE

Moses and Aaron did so, as G-d had commanded. [Aaron] raised the staff and struck the water that was in the Nile, before the eyes of Pharaoh and before the eyes of his servants; and all the water that was in the Nile turned into blood.

Exodus 7:20

On the most basic level, the Ten Plagues were brought upon the Egyptians to punish them for their cruelty and to force Pharaoh to free the Children of Israel. But they also had a far more significant function.

The purpose of the Exodus was not only to get the Children of Israel out of Egypt but also, and more importantly, to get the Egypt out of the Israelites. Four generations of servitude to the pagan culture of Egypt had enslaved the Jews in soul as well as in body. For Israel to become a free people in the true sense of the word, they had to divest themselves of their spiritual subjugation to the idols and debased mores of their Egyptian taskmasters.

The plagues were thus directed to the Children of Israel as much as they were to the Egyptians. They came not only to punish and threaten Pharaoh and his henchmen, but also to crush the icons of Egyptian culture, to expose the fallacy of the very soul of Egypt in the eyes and minds of its Hebrew slaves.

Thus, the very first plague was directed against the Nile, turning its waters to blood. The Nile was the very backbone of Egypt, the mainstay of its economy, its arch idol, its most dependable god. During the flood season the Nile would overflow its banks, filling a network of canals and irrigating the fields and orchards of Egypt. It was the source of all sustenance in this rainless land.

The farmer who depends on rainfall to water his seedlings is forever aware of his dependence on forces beyond his control, forever lifting his eyes heavenward in hopeful prayer. But the Nile-sustained society of Egypt, which trusted in a river-god whose waters rise with seasonal clockwork, was a society in which the self reigned supreme—a society which arrogantly rejected the very notion of a Supreme Authority, a binding morality, or a higher purpose to life.

Freedom as Servitude, Servitude as Freedom

Such a society, supposedly free of all constraint and responsibility, is a society enslaved to the most base and animal elements of human nature. The Exodus came to liberate the people of Israel from this pagan mentality, to free them from this servitude to the temporal and the mundane.

The purpose of the Exodus was to bring the Children of Israel to Mount Sinai, where the slavery in the guise of freedom of Egypt was replaced by a commitment to be servants of G-d—a servitude which, in truth, is the ultimate spiritual emancipation. A life that is faithful to the divine purpose in creation releases the soul from the strictures of the material and enables it to realize its higher, more worthy potentials. The fulfillment of G-d's will, as expressed in the edicts of the Torah, is the means, and only means, by which the human being can reach beyond the inherent limitations of his or her own existence and connect to their infinite and all-pervading Source and Creator.

So when the time came for Israel to be redeemed, the first thing the Almighty did was to destroy the Nile before their eyes.

Its unfaltering waters turned to blood, shattering the illusion of Egypt's faith in its self-sufficiency and exposing the lie in the "freedom" of its corporeal life.

The Warmth of Life

The fact that the Nile was discredited by its waters turning to *blood* is also significant. This represents another aspect of the transformation that the people of Israel had to undergo in their spiritual exodus from Egypt to Sinai.

Rabbi Shalom DovBer of Lubavitch once said:

> *Between coldness and heresy stands an extremely thin wall. The Torah states that, "G-d your G-d is a consuming fire."*[1] *G-dliness is a blazing flame. Anything G-dly and holy is warm, vibrant, fervently alive.*

Water is the antithesis of the vibrancy of spirituality: cold, damp, and still. The waters of the Nile characterized the coldness and apathy of Egypt's self-worship and apostasy. Blood represents the warmth and throb of life. So with the first plague, the waters of the Nile were transformed into blood. This was the first step in Israel's redemption, the first step in the process to extricate them from the spiritual frigidity of Egypt and ignite in them the fervor of life—life as ultimately defined by the verse, "You who cleave to G-d are alive."[2]

---

[1] Deuteronomy 9:3.
[2] Ibid., 4:4.

THE FROG IN THE OVEN

The river will swarm with frogs. They will come up and enter into your home, and into your bedroom, and onto your bed ... and into your ovens, and into your kneading bowls.

Exodus 7:28

The biblical book of Daniel tells the story of Hananiah, Mishael, and Azariah, three Jewish officers in the court of Babylonian emperor Nebuchadnezzar, who faced the choice to either bow before an idolatrous image or be thrown into a fiery furnace. The three elected to face the fire rather than renounce their faith.[1] The Talmud relates that their decision was inspired by the frogs that plagued Egypt in Moses' time. If the frogs entered the ovens of Egypt to carry out the will of G-d, they reasoned, we, certainly, should be willing to sacrifice ourselves for our Creator.[2]

"Self-sacrifice" is more than the willingness to die for one's beliefs—it is the way in which one lives for them. It is the willingness to give up one's very self—one's most basic wants, desires, and aspirations—for the sake of G-d. Indeed, the Hebrew term for self-sacrifice, *mesirat nefesh*, means both "the giving of life" as well as "the giving of will."

---

[1] Daniel, chapter 3.
[2] Talmud, *Pesachim* 53b.

It is therefore significant that the lesson of self-sacrifice is learned from a frog—a cold-blooded creature—who entered a burning oven. The ultimate test of faith goes beyond the issue of physical life and death; it is the willingness to go against the grain of one's nature for the sake of a higher truth.

VA'EIRA (6)

CRIME, PUNISHMENT, AND SUSPENDED PRECIPITATION

Moses went out from Pharaoh, out of the city, and spread out his hands to G-d; and the thunder ceased, and the hail and the rain did not reach the ground.

Exodus 9:33

Also those that were in the air did not reach the ground.

Rashi, ad loc.

The seventh of the Ten Plagues to be visited on Egypt was *barad*—a devastating storm of rain, fire, and ice. Pharaoh was persisting in his refusal to let the Children of Israel go; the divine response was to unleash "thunder and hail, and fire which ran down upon the earth... the likes of which there was not in Egypt from when it had become a nation" and which wreaked havoc on the Egyptians, their cattle, and their crops.[1]

Pharaoh seemed to have gotten the message this time. As the Torah relates,

> *Pharaoh sent and called for Moses and Aaron, and he said to them: "I have sinned this time; G-d is righteous, and*

---

[1] Exodus 9:22–25.

I and my people are in the wrong. Entreat G-d that there be no more divine thundering and hail; and I will let you go..."

Moses went out from Pharaoh, out of the city, and spread out his hands to G-d; and the thunder ceased, and the hail and the rain did not reach the ground.[2]

Suspended or Vaporized?

Almost everything about the plague of *barad* was supernatural. Two sworn enemies, fire and ice, collaborated to create the "hail with fire flaring within it"[3] that rained down on Egypt. And when the time came for the plague to end, Moses lifted his arms and the storm ceased instantaneously: even the hail and rain which had already begun its descent from the heavens "did not reach the ground."

What happened to these orphaned raindrops and hailstones? There are, in fact, two versions of their fate: (a) they remained suspended in mid-air; (b) they ceased to exist altogether.[4]

The reason why the plagues that struck Egypt were supernatural occurrences is spelled out in the Torah's account. As G-d says to Moses, "I will multiply My signs and My wonders... and Egypt will know that I am G-d."[5] The purpose of the plagues was not just to punish the Egyptians, but also to undermine their faith in nature

---

2   Ibid., verses 27–33.
3   Ibid., verse 24.
4   These two versions are derived from the two different interpretations of the Hebrew word *nitach* ("reached" or "poured") cited in Rashi's commentary on Exodus 9:33. See *Likutei Sichot*, vol. 6, pp. 46–48.
5   Exodus 7:3–5.

and nature's processes, and force them—and the Israelites who were also held captive in the nature cult of Egypt—to acknowledge that there is a Higher Force that created nature and can supersede it at will.[6]

But why the need for the supernatural ending for the plague of *barad*, in which "the hail and the rain did not reach the ground"? Our sages teach "G-d desires to uphold the workings of the world as much as possible; nature is precious to Him, and He does not interfere with it unless it is critically necessary."[7] Why not allow the already falling raindrops to conclude their natural descent to the ground?

Crime Repays

The principle that good deeds are rewarded and evil deeds are punished is a fundamental dictum of the Jewish faith.[8] But there is much discussion in works of Jewish philosophy and mysticism regarding the dynamics of this principle—on when, how, and why it operates.

The famed mystic and sage Shaloh posits that punishment for wrongdoing is not a divine "revenge" any more than frostbite is G-d's "revenge" for a barefoot trek in the snow. Rather, it is the natural consequence of one's deeds. Just as the Creator chose to run His world in accordance with the laws of physics, so, too, He has instituted a spiritual "natural order" that governs the moral universe. The fact that a good deed is beneficial to its doer, and an

---

[6] See the essay, "The Red Nile," pp. 58–60 above.
[7] *Derashot HaRan, derush* 8. See also Genesis 8:22; Talmud, *Shabbat* 53b.
[8] See Maimonides' *Thirteen Principles* (commentary on Mishnah, introduction to Chapter *Chelek*), principle 11.

evil deed is detrimental, is an outgrowth of the essential natures of these actions.⁹

Every good deed that a person does is a realization of his or her divine purpose, and thus an intensification of their bond with their Creator. Because the ultimate source of life and bliss is G-d, the obvious result is a more enhanced flow of sustenance and well-being. On the other hand, a person who transgresses the divine will is disavowing the very purpose for which G-d grants them existence and life. The suffering and afflictions that consequently befall them are a direct result of their having sabotaged their lifeline to their divine Source.

Pharaoh's Punishment

The fire and ice which rained down on Pharaoh's Egypt was in punishment for his enslavement of the Jewish people and his repeated defiance of the divine command, "Let My people go." But when Pharaoh repented his crime, acknowledging his guilt ("I have sinned this time; G-d is righteous, and I and my people are in the wrong") and committing himself to its rectification ("I will let you go"),¹⁰ the root cause for the plague of *barad* no longer was. The dynamics of reward and punishment now dictated that Pharaoh's evil, now repented, was no longer to afflict him.

The laws of physics may have dictated the continued descent of the hail and rain already en route. But the laws of physics are only the implementors of a higher moral-spiritual "nature." For even a

---

9 In the words of the prophet (Jeremiah 2:19), "Your evil does afflict you." See Shaloh, *Bayit Acharon* 12a.

10 Thereby meeting the three requirement of *teshuvah* (repentance): regret, verbal confession, and the resolve to never repeat the offence in the future.

single hailstone or raindrop to now strike Egypt would have been a violation of the spiritual natural order which the Creator has established to govern our reality.

Two Versions

This also explains the two versions as to what happened to those hailstones and raindrops which Pharaoh's repentance disarmed in mid-flight: Did they halt in midair, or did they cease to exist entirely?

There are two levels of *teshuvah* (repentance). One level is a *teshuvah* that affects only the future. A person who has acted contrary to their ordained mission in life has turned their back on their Creator; as long as they do not repent their deed, they remain in a state of "estrangement" from G-d. When they express regret for their crime and commit henceforth to be faithful to G-d, they repair the damaged relationship; all is forgiven as they turn a new leaf in their life. All this, however, does not change the fact that, prior to their repentance, they had been in a state of disconnection from their divine source and from their own intrinsic goodness. The evil deed remains a past reality; all that the person has done is discontinue its negative effects on his or her life.

But there is also a higher level of *teshuvah*—a *teshuvah* that reaches back in time to change the past.[11] This is the *teshuvah* of a penitent who succeeds in exploiting their past wrongs as an impetus for good; who exploits the momentum of their spiritual descents to achieve otherwise unattainable heights. The estrangement from G-d caused by the sin becomes a source of yearning for

---

11 This is the deeper significance of the Hebrew word *teshuvah*, which means "return."

G-d—a yearning whose depth and intensity surpasses anything the spiritually pristine soul can feel. A negative past is thereby transformed into positive force.

This is the difference between the two scenarios for the suspended *barad*. If Pharaoh's repentance was of the first, "from here on" sort, then his past evil, and what it has caused, remained in existence. Only its future *effects* on him were neutralized. The hail and rain remained—only they did not continue their punishment of the now repentant sinner.

But if Pharaoh was capable of achieving the deeper dimension of *teshuvah* which rectifies the past, then the negative cause of the *barad* would have been retroactively undone. Because it is "your evil that does afflict you," the erasure of Pharaoh's evil would have spelled the immediate un-being of all that ever resulted from it,[12] including the physical water, fire, and ice that came to afflict its perpetrator.

---

12 An even more physically "supernatural" occurrence than the first possibility. If a hailstone's midair halt violates the law of gravity, its dis-existence defies a far more fundamental tenet of physics: the law that nothing can never produce something, and something can never become nothing.

PARASHAH FIFTEEN

BO

Exodus 10:1–13:16

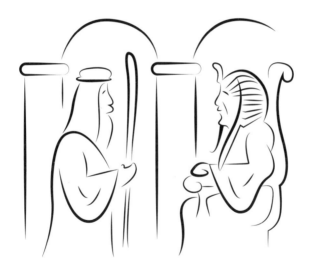

Exodus and freedom

THE SOUL OF EVIL

G-d said to Moses: "Come to Pharaoh; for I have hardened his heart and the hearts of his servants, in order that I might show My signs in their midst..."

Exodus 10:1

Why does it say, "Come to Pharaoh"? It should have said, "Go to Pharaoh".... But G-d brought Moses into a chamber within a chamber, to the ... supernal and mighty serpent from which many levels evolve ... which Moses feared to approach himself...

Zohar 3:34a

*A*mong the fifty-four *parashiot* (sections) of the Torah, several stand out as milestones in its narrative of the history of humanity and of the people of Israel. The *parashah* of *Bereishith* (Genesis 1:1–6:8) recounts G-d's creation of the world in six days; *Lech Lecha* (Genesis 12:1–17:27) describes Abraham's journeys to bring the truth of the One G-d to a pagan world; *Yitro* (Exodus 18:1–20:23) includes the revelation at Sinai and the giving of the Torah to Israel; and so on.

A list of pivotal Torah sections would certainly include the *parashah* of *Bo* (Exodus 10:1–13:16), which tells of the Exodus of the Children of Israel from the land of Egypt. The Exodus marked our birth as a people,[1] and we are enjoined to "Remember the day that you went out of Egypt, all the days of your life."[2] Indeed, when G-d revealed Himself to us at Sinai, He introduced Himself not as the Creator of heaven and earth, but as "...your G-d, who has taken you out of the land of Egypt"[3]! For the defining element of our relationship with G-d is not that we are beings created by Him (of which there are many others in G-d's world), but that we are *free beings*: beings in whom G-d has invested of His own infinity and eternity; beings empowered by G-d to transcend the constraints of the material world and the limits of their own natures.

The Name of the Parashah

Bo means "come." The name derives from the *parashah*'s opening verse, in which G-d instructs Moses to "come to Pharaoh" to warn him of the eighth plague (the plague of locusts) and once again deliver the divine demand that the ruler of Egypt set free the Children of Israel.

The Torah considers the name of a thing to be the articulation of its essence;[4] certainly, such is the case with the Torah's own names for itself and its components. The name of a Torah section always conveys its primary message and the common theme of all its subsections and narratives.[5]

---

1 See Ezekiel 16, and sources cited in footnote 2 on p. 41 above.
2 Deuteronomy 16:3.
3 The first of the Ten Commandments, Exodus 20:2.
4 See Genesis 2:19, and *Midrashim* and commentaries on that verse; *Tanya, Shaar HaYichud Ve'haEmunah*, chapter 1; et al.
5 Often, the name of a Torah section seems to merely derive from its opening verses, with little visible connection to its overall contents. But an in-depth examination and analysis of a section's contents always reveals that its common theme and axial principle are expressed by its name.

One would therefore expect the *parashah* of the Exodus to be called "Exodus," "Freedom," or some other name that expresses the significance of this defining event in the history of Israel. Instead, it derives its name from Moses' coming to Pharaoh—an event that seems but a preliminary to the Exodus. Indeed, the idea that the leader of the people of Israel has to come to Pharaoh's palace to petition him to let the Jewish people go, implying that the Jews are still subservient to Egypt and its ruler, seems the very antithesis of the Exodus!

Come or Go?

The phrase "Come to Pharaoh" also evokes much discussion in the commentaries. Why does G-d tell Moses to *come* to Pharaoh? Would it not have been more appropriate to say, "Go to Pharaoh"?

Zohar explains that Moses feared confronting Pharaoh inside his palace, at the hub of his power. (On earlier occasions, Moses had been directed to meet Pharaoh in other places, such as on the king's morning excursions to the Nile.[6]) So G-d promised Moses that He Himself would accompany him to Pharaoh. The word "come" is thus to be understood in the sense of "come with me"; G-d is saying to Moses, "Come with Me to Pharaoh."

Zohar goes on to say that Moses is being invited by G-d to meet with the innermost essence of Egypt's ruler and idol. Thus we have another meaning of the phrase "Come to Pharaoh"—"come" in the sense of "enter within." To liberate the people of Israel from the "great and mighty serpent," it was not enough to merely go to Pharaoh; Moses had to enter into the innermost essence of Pharaoh, into the very core of his power.

---

6   See Exodus 7:15, 8:17, et al.

My River

Who is Pharaoh and what does he represent? What is his "innermost essence"? Why did Moses dread confronting Pharaoh in his palace if G-d Himself had sent him there? And how does "coming into Pharaoh" hold the key for the Exodus from Egypt and the liberation of the soul of man?

The prophet Ezekiel describes Pharaoh in the following manner:

> *The great serpent who couches in the midst of his streams; who says, "My river is my own, and I have made myself."*[7]

In other words, the evil of Pharaoh is defined not by the promiscuity that characterized the pagan cults of Egypt; not by Pharaoh's enslavement and torture of millions; not by his bathing in the blood of slaughtered children; but by his egocentrism, by his regarding his own self as the source and standard for everything.

For this is the root of all evil. Self-centeredness might seem a benign sin compared to the acts of cruelty and depravity to which man can sink, but it is the source and essence of them all. When a person considers the self and its needs to be the ultimate arbiter of right and wrong, his or her morality—and they might initially be what is regarded as a moral person—is devoid of significance. Such a person is ultimately capable of committing any act, should they regard it as crucial to themselves or to their self-defined vision of reality.

Ultimately, every good deed is an act of self-abnegation, and every evil deed is an act of self-deification. When a person does a good deed—whether it involves contributing a single coin to charity or devoting an entire lifetime to a G-dly cause—he or she

---

7   Ezekiel 29:3.

is saying: There is something greater than myself to which I am committed. When a person violates the divine will—whether with a minor transgression or with the most heinous of crimes—they are saying: "My river is my own, and I have made myself." Good is what is good for me, evil is what is contrary to my will. I am the master of my reality; I am a god.

The Secret

So is the ego evil? Is this fundamental component of our soul an alien implant that must be uprooted and discarded in our quest for goodness and truth?

In the final analysis, it is not. The cardinal law of reality is that "There is none else besides Him"[8]—that nothing is contrary to, or even separate from, the Creator and Source of all. The ego, the sense of self with which we are born, also derives from G-d; indeed, it is a reflection of the divine "ego." Because G-d knows Himself as the only true existence, we, who were created in the divine image, possess an intimation of G-d's "sense of self" in the form of our own concept of the self as the core of all existence.

It is not the ego that is evil, but the divorcing of the ego from its source. When we recognize our own ego as a reflection of G-d's "ego" and make it subservient to His, it becomes the driving force in our efforts to make the world a better, more G-dly place. But the same ego, severed from its divine roots, begets the most monstrous of evils.

When G-d commanded Moses to "Come to Pharaoh," Moses had already been going to Pharaoh for many months. But he had been dealing with Pharaoh in his various manifestations: Pharaoh

---

8   Deuteronomy 4:35.

the pagan, Pharaoh the oppressor of Israel, Pharaoh the self-styled god. Now he was being told to enter into the essence of Pharaoh, into the soul of evil. Now he was being told to penetrate beyond the evil of Pharaoh, beyond the mega-ego that insists, "I have created Myself," to confront Pharaoh's quintessence: the naked "I" that stems from the very "self" of G-d.

Moses did not fear the evil of Pharaoh. If G-d had sent him, G-d would protect him. But when G-d told him to enter into the essence of Pharaoh, he was terrified. How can a human being behold such a pure manifestation of the divine truth? A manifestation so sublime that it transcends good and evil and is equally the source of both?

Said G-d to Moses: "Come to Pharaoh." Come with Me, and together we will enter the great serpent's palace. Together we will penetrate the self-worship that is the heart of evil. Together we will discover that there is neither substance nor reality to evil—that all it is, is the misappropriation of the divine in man.

If this truth is too terrifying for a human being to confront on his own, come with Me, and I will guide you. I will take you into the innermost chamber of Pharaoh's soul, until you come face to face with evil's most zealously guarded secret: that it does not, in truth, exist.

When you learn this secret, no evil will ever defeat you. When you learn this secret, you and your people will be free.

THE FIFTH ELEMENT

On the first day,[1] you shall exterminate all leaven from your homes... For seven days, no leaven shall be found in your homes... Do not eat anything that is leavened...

Exodus 12:15–20

Rabbi Judah says: Leaven can be exterminated only by burning. The [other] sages say: One can also crumble it and cast it to the wind, or throw it into the sea.

Talmud, Pesachim 21a.

More than a people's redemption from slavery to freedom, the Exodus was a transition "from darkness to a great light."[2] The Children of Israel were wrested from pagan Egypt's "forty-nine gates of impurity"[3] and elevated to become G-d's chosen "kingdom of priests" and "holy nation."[4]

A primary feature of the festival of Passover is the purging of all leavened foods from our diet and possession. Leaven is dough that has fermented, causing it to swell and rise. Within the human being, "leaven" is the propensity for pride and self-aggrandizement,

---

1 I.e., the day before Passover.
2 Passover *Haggadah*.
3 See *Zohar* 3 93a.
4 Exodus 19:6.

which was the primal sin of Egypt and is the ultimate source of all evil.⁵ On Passover, we relive the experience of the Exodus by cleansing our soul of its spiritual "leaven." The physical and spiritual being two faces of the same reality, this is complemented by the removal and destruction of all physical leaven in our possession.

This explains the uniqueness of the prohibition of leaven among the other prohibitions of the Torah. The Torah forbids the consumption of various foods, but nowhere is the prohibition as extreme and as all-embracing as the prohibition of leaven on Passover. In most cases, only the actual eating of a substance is forbidden. For example, the Torah forbids eating the meat of a nonkosher animal, but permits deriving benefit from it in other ways—selling it to a non-Jew, feeding it to one's animals, using it in the preparation of non-dietary products, etc. In certain instances (such as meat cooked in milk), the Torah also forbids all benefit from the substance. But in regard to leaven, it carries the prohibition even further: not only is it forbidden to eat leaven on Passover or to derive benefit from it in any way, it is also forbidden to possess leaven or to keep it in one's domain for the duration of the festival. Another stringency of the prohibition of leaven is that even the most minute amount of it is forbidden, as opposed to other prohibited substances which are "nullified" by a certain quantity.⁶

Furthermore, in addition to the "negative commandments" that forbid the consumption, use, and possession of leaven, there is a "positive commandment" to destroy all leaven that is found in one's possession before the onset of the festival. One need only observe the activity in a Jewish home in the weeks preceding

---

5 See the previous essay, "The Soul of Evil," on pp. 70–75 above.
6 For example, if a drop of milk falls into a pot of meat, it is nullified if it is less than one-sixtieth of the contents of the pot.

Passover to appreciate the exactitude and vehemence with which the Jew fulfills the injunction to "exterminate all leaven from your homes."

Degrees of Negativity

When the Torah forbids the consumption of something but permits its other uses, it is saying that the thing itself is not negative to the core—only a certain form thereof (i.e., its function as a food). A prohibition of benefit implies a deeper negativity—one that extends to all forms of beneficial use. However, the fact that the Torah does not forbid an object's possession implies that the object *per se* is not wholly evil.

Evil, as a rule, is a "superficial" phenomenon. Only rarely is there any depth of commitment behind an evil deed, or any profundity of thought and feeling behind an evil desire. Evil might inflict terrible harm, but is usually only skin deep, relating only to the most external surface of the evil person or object, and having but a shallow and temporary effect on its surroundings.

But the evil of Egypt, the most potent and malignant of evils, penetrates deeper than all others, extending beyond the external form to permeate its very substance. Hence the extreme severity of the prohibition of leaven, which embodies the evil of Egypt: a prohibition that relates not to a particular form or forms of the forbidden object, but to the object itself.

Function, Object, and Essence

The above statement, however, requires further clarification. What is "the object itself," as opposed to its form? A physical object, by definition, is of a certain form—there are no formless objects. Yet the very fact that an object can change form (to the extent that the second form might be completely different from, or even antithetical to, the first) leads us to distinguish between the substance of a thing and the forms it assumes, and to speak of "substance" and "form" as two distinct components of a thing's existence.

Thus, a physical object can be viewed on three different levels. The first, most external level, is the object's definition in terms of its particular function: a piano is a musical instrument, a loaf of bread is a food. This might be broadened to include a more generalized definition—the loaf of bread might be regarded as "an object of value to the sustenance of human life," a description that would include its utility as animal feed, fuel, saleable merchandise, etc.[7]

On a second, more basic level, a thing is defined in terms of its physical form, rather than its particular use (or uses). A piano is an object of a certain size and shape, and a loaf of bread is an object of a certain size and shape. We are regarding them as objects in time and space, rather than as instruments of a certain utility.

The third, most elementary, level is the thing's "essence"—that unquantifiable "it" that lies behind the manifold forms it might assume. A loaf of bread is not an "object" but an intrinsically formless essence, whose particular form—and the fact that it possesses a form at all—is completely incidental to its being.

In most of the substances forbidden by the Torah, the prohibition relates only to the first, most external, level of existence. When a substance is forbidden only as a food, this means that

---

7   Indeed, the prohibition against deriving benefit from leaven is derived from the Torah's use of the term "shall not be eaten" (as the Torah writes in regard to the prohibition of leaven on Passover in Exodus 13:3) instead of "do not eat," implying the prohibition of anything that might lead to eating—i.e., any use that yields a profit which can then be utilized to purchase food.

only a certain function of the substance has been deemed negative by the Torah. Even when the Torah forbids deriving any benefit from the substance, the prohibition relates only to a more broadly defined function of the thing, not to its form or "objectness," and certainly not to its essence.

The prohibition of leaven, however, extends beyond function and utility: its very existence in our possession is forbidden, and its destruction constitutes a *mitzvah*, the fulfillment of a divine commandment. But how far does the prohibition extend? Does it relate to leaven as an "object"—a physical substance of a certain form—or does it penetrate even deeper, to its very essence?

This question is the issue behind the Talmudic debate cited in the beginning of this essay, which concerns the obligation to destroy all leaven in one's possession on the morning of the day before Passover:

> *Rabbi Judah says: Leaven can be exterminated only by burning.*
>
> *The [other] sages say: One can also crumble it and cast it to the wind, or throw it into the sea.*

According to the second opinion (that of "the sages"), destroying the *form* of the leaven constitutes the fulfillment of the commandment to "exterminate leaven from your homes." The loaf of bread has been stripped of its objectness. Since the prohibition against leaven extends only to this stratum of its existence, the *mitzvah* of exterminating leaven has been fulfilled.

Rabbi Judah, however, maintains that the prohibition against leaven relates not only to its form, but also to its very essence. So it is not sufficient to destroy the form of the leaven. One must eliminate its very being, something that can be achieved (to the extent that it is humanly possible) only by burning.

Four Aspects of Form

The elimination of leaven from our domain is the physical analogue of the imperative to eradicate the evil of Egypt from our souls. So the question of the extent of the prohibition of leaven on Passover derives from a more basic question: How deeply does the evil of Egypt penetrate its subject?

This, too, is the underlying issue in a debate between our sages, which we read each Passover as part of the *Haggadah*, the discussion of the story of the Exodus that accompanies the Passover *seder*:

> *Rabbi Eliezer says: Every plague that G-d brought upon the Egyptians in Egypt was comprised of four plagues...*
>
> *Rabbi Akiva says: Every plague that G-d brought upon the Egyptians in Egypt was comprised of five plagues...*[8]

The classical philosophers taught that every object is comprised of four elements: fire, water, air, and earth.[9] As understood by the sages of Israel, the "four elements" relate to the various qualities a thing possesses—heat, moisture, etc. In other words, they are not of the substance of the thing, but rather aspects of its form.[10] Beyond them is the thing itself, the essence that is the subject of these qualities.

Thus, commentaries on the *Haggadah*[11] explain the significance of this dispute between Rabbi Eliezer and Rabbi Akiva. The number of aspects to each plague expresses the degree to which the

---

8 *Mechilta*, Exodus 14:31; *Haggadah*.
9 See *Mishneh Torah, Laws of the Fundamentals of Torah*, 4:1; *Tanya*, chapter 1; et al.
10 See *Igrot Kodesh*, vol. 19, p. 239.
11 *Kolbo*, Ritva, and Rashbatz on *Haggadah*.

plagues affected the people and resources of Egypt. A four-fold plague means that the plague involved every aspect of its subject's form, infiltrating each of its four "elements." A five-dimensional plague means that the devastation of Egypt extended not only to the four elements of form, but also to the essence behind them.

Rabbi Eliezer is of the opinion that the evil of Egypt extended to its "four elements"; hence the four-fold plagues that came to crush the pagan "form" of Egypt and liberate Israel from its grasp. This opinion is reflected in the ruling of the sages who maintain that the destruction of the *form* of leaven (by "crumbling it and casting it to the wind, or throwing it into the sea") eliminates the negative qualities it embodies.

Rabbi Akiva, on the other hand, is of the opinion that the evil of Egypt permeated its very essence, necessitating plagues with a fifth dimension—plagues that vanquished also the formless essence of Egypt. The same must be done each Passover, when we endeavor to achieve a personal Exodus by overcoming the "Egypt" within ourselves. Rabbi Akiva's understanding of the evil of Egypt is thus reflected in Rabbi Judah's ruling that, "Leaven can be exterminated only by burning," as also its essence must be annihilated.

The Personal Exodus

What is the significance of all this to our everyday lives?

The human soul also possesses "four elements" that give form to its transcendent essence. The four elements are: (a) behavior—our actual deeds, words, and conscious thoughts; (b) our character and emotions; (c) our intellect; and (d) the suprarational self, which includes qualities such as will, faith, and self-sacrifice.

These, however, are only the elements that comprise the "form" of the soul, not the soul itself. Then there are those things that relate to a person's essence—things relating to our core identity, to the quintessential self that cannot be categorized or quantified by any of the above states of the soul.

"In every generation, a person should regard himself as one who has himself come out of Egypt."[12] On the most basic level, "coming out of Egypt" entails liberating ourselves from our negative actions and habits; this is self-liberation on the behavioral level, the first and most basic of the soul's "four elements." A deeper liberation is when we rise above our emotional limitations—those feelings that hamper and hinder the soul's quest for the divine. Yet a higher achievement is the personal Exodus from the limitations of the intellect—to free ourselves from the various preconceptions and mindsets that confine our soul. Finally, the truly liberated person eradicates the "leaven" that might taint even their suprarational self—the hint of self-consideration that might be found even in the purest faith and the most altruistic sacrifice.

According to Rabbi Eliezer (and the sages who disagree with Rabbi Judah), this is the extent to which a person should strive to "come out of Egypt." This is the extent to which "leaven" can infiltrate the soul of man; these are the elements of self that can be liberated and transformed. As for the essence of the soul, there is no leaven to be eradicated, no Exodus to be achieved. The essence of the soul is beyond being affected by the ferment of ego, and consequently, beyond being liberated or elevated.

Rabbi Akiva disagrees. As lofty as the soul is, its potential for perfection is infinite; it can surmount even itself, liberating itself from the confines of its very essence. Rabbi Akiva was a living example of this: the descendant of converts to Judaism, his was a soul that knew the meaning of utter transformation, of

---

12 Talmud, *Pesachim* 116b; *Haggadah*.

transcending one's very identity. In his own life, Rabbi Akiva overcame forty years of ignorance of and hostility to everything holy, to become one of the greatest sages in Jewish history.[13] Self-liberation, according to Rabbi Akiva, involves not only the "form" of a life, but can be achieved also on the deepest, most quintessential level of one's being.

---

13   See *Avot d'Rabbi Natan*, 6:2.

THE FREEDOM TO PASSOVER

Moses said to the people: "Remember this day, on which you went out of Egypt..."
                                                    Exodus 13:3

On the night of the fifteenth of Nissan, it is a positive commandment to relate the miracles and wonders that were performed for our ancestors in Egypt, as it is written, "Remember this day, on which you went out of Egypt"—just as it is written (Exodus 20:8), "Remember the day of Shabbat."
                    Mishneh Torah, Laws of Leaven and Matzah, 7:1

What is freedom? When pressed to define this most basic human need and aspiration, we usually find ourselves explaining what freedom is not. Freedom is not slavery, it is not confinement, it is not inhibition. But is that all there is to freedom—the absence of subjugation? Is there a positive/dynamic aspect to the state of freedom?

THE CREATION OF REST

The same question could be asked about another much desired and little understood state: the state of rest. Rest is not movement, not toil, not innovation. But what *is* it? Is it merely the negation of activity, or is rest itself an active pursuit?

The Torah implies that it is the latter. In the second chapter of Genesis we read,

> G-d finished, on the seventh day, the work that He had made; and He rested on the seventh day from all the work that He had made. And G-d blessed the seventh day, and He sanctified it, for on it He rested from all His work, which G-d created to make.[1]

At first glance, these verses seem to contradict themselves. First it says that G-d finished His work *on* the seventh day, implying that the seventh day, too, was a day of creative endeavor. But then it says that G-d rested on the seventh day and sanctified it as a day of rest, implying that the entire seventh day was free of labor. One explanation offered by the sages is that on the seventh day, G-d created the final and culminating element of His creation—the element of rest:

> What was the world lacking? Rest. With the onset of Shabbat came rest.[2]

In other words, rest is not merely the absence of work, but an existent phenomenon, a creation.

"Work" is the movement from the self outward, the projection of one's creative powers to effect change on one's environment. "Rest" is the opposite movement—the endeavor to strive inward, to the quintessential core of one's being. For six days, G-d projected outward, creating a universe that is "outside" and distinct of

---

1 Genesis 2:2–3.
2 Rashi, ad loc. *Midrash Rabbah, Bereishith* 10:10.

Himself. On the seventh day of creation, G-d rested—He shifted the movement of creation inward, drawing the created reality back into His all-inclusive being.³ Shabbat is therefore a "holy" day, a day of heightened spiritual sensitivity, a day on which the created reality more deeply identifies with its supernal source.

---

3   Rabbi Schneur Zalman of Liadi (*Likutei Torah, Shabbat Shuvah* 66c) offers the following analogy from human creativity: As an artisan works, his or her ideas and emotions are concentrated in the task. There is an almost palpable outward streaming of thought and emotion from the soul of the artisan into the work. Then, when the work is completed, this stream reverses direction, flowing back from the created work to be reabsorbed within its source in the artisan's mind. The difference is that with a human artisan, it is only the thoughts and feelings that are retracted, while the work itself remains outside of him or her. But with G-d's creation, the created reality is the stream itself (projected as divine speech). When the projection ceases, the world itself is reabsorbed within its source.

(This explains how the world continues to exist on Shabbat, even though G-d ceases to create it. What ceases is the *speaking* of the ten utterances—"speech" being a communication to an "other" outside oneself; but these utterances continue to be projected in the realm of divine thought. So the world still exists, albeit on a more elevated level, for it is now subsumed within the mind of its creator.)

In truth, "there is no place that is void of Him" (*Zohar, Tikunim* 57)—G-d pervades every corner of reality; in the words of the Midrash, "The world is not his place; He is the place of the world" (*Midrash Tehillim*, 90:10). But the act of creation involved a *tzimtzum* ("constriction")—the creation of a vacuum of awareness in the consciousness of creation; in its own mind, the created reality is something distinct of its Creator. On Shabbat, however, G-d's "drawing in" of creation into Himself results in an alleviation of the *tzimtzum*. The guise of apartness that shrouds our existence becomes that much more transparent, making the truth that "there is none else besides Him" (Deuteronomy 4:35) that much more accessible to our perception.

(See the essay, "A Spoken Word," in vol. I of *The Inside Story*, pp. 19–21. Also see the essays, "The Seventh Element," "A World of Thought," and "A Private World," in vol. I of *Inside Time* [MLC 2015].)

The same applies to our weekly implementation of the divine cycle of creation in our own lives. Six days a week we project our talents and prowess outward, developing and perfecting G-d's world. On Shabbat, we actualize our "partnership with G-d in creation"[4] by resting—by delving into the inner essence of our own souls and of the soul of creation.

Shabbat is not a day of inactivity, but a day devoted to the activity of rest. It is a day of prayer, Torah learning, and communion with family and community. It is a day in which we endeavor to seek our own spiritual center, to better attune ourselves to the self that is one with the divine essence of all.

Remember and Keep

The laws of Shabbat are replete with forbidden activities; in order to rest, one must cease to outwardly project. But the prohibition against work is only one aspect of the phenomenon of rest. Indeed, the Torah contains two versions of the Sixth Commandment. In Exodus 20, it reads, "Remember the day of Shabbat, to sanctify it"; whereas in the fifth chapter of Deuteronomy, it reads, "Keep the day of Shabbat." The Talmud explains that,

> *"Remember" and "Keep" were expressed by G-d in a single utterance.*[5]

The dynamic inward focus of Shabbat ("Remember"), and the avoidance of materially creative deeds ("Keep"), are the active and passive dimensions of a single endeavor: the endeavor of rest.

---

4 Talmud, *Shabbat* 119b.
5 Ibid., *Rosh Hashanah* 27a.

Thus Maimonides begins his codification of the laws of Shabbat with the statement:

> Resting from work on the seventh day is a positive commandment, as it is written, "On the seventh day you shall rest."[6] Whoever works on this day negates [this] positive commandment, and also transgresses a negative commandment—"Do not do any work."[7]

Maimonides is emphasizing that although the bulk of Shabbat's laws (twenty-eight out of the thirty chapters in Maimonides' own section on Shabbat) address what is *not* to done on the seventh day, the imperative to rest on Shabbat is, first and foremost, a *positive* commandment. In the words of the Gaon of Rogatchov, commenting on the above passage in Maimonides: "The positive commandment of Shabbat is to rest, not merely to cease work."[8]

A Dynamic Equation

This explains the enigmatic passage in Maimonides' *Mishneh Torah*, quoted at the beginning of this essay, in which Maimonides compares the commandment to "Remember this day, on which you went out of Egypt" to the imperative to "Remember the day of Shabbat." Indeed, this comparison also has a biblical precedent: Passover is the only festival that is referred to by the Torah as "the Shabbat."[9] The commentaries on *Mishneh Torah* puzzle

---

6   Exodus 23:12.
7   Ibid., 20:10. *Mishneh Torah, Laws of Shabbat*, 1:1.
8   *Tzafnat Paaneach*, ad loc.
9   Leviticus 23:15; see Talmud, *Menachot* 65b. See also *Midrash Rabbah*,

over the significance of this comparison, and offer various halachic explanations for it.¹⁰

Legal constructs aside, Maimonides is alluding to a conceptual correlation between the defining characteristic of Shabbat and that of Passover. On Passover, as on Shabbat, we are empowered to experience a state that, on the surface, seems to have no intrinsic content of its own, being only the negation of something else. But just as Shabbat rest is more than the absence of toil, so too the freedom of Passover is a dynamic freedom, not merely the absence of enslavement.

Exodus to Sinai

Freedom is commonly perceived as the removal of all external constraints on a person's development and self-expression. Freedom—this line of reasoning implies—is the natural state of the human being; free him or her of all external forces that limit and inhibit them, and you have a free person.

Passover represents a more ambitious freedom: not just the freedom to be our natural selves, but freedom from the constraints of our own nature. Attaining this freedom entails more than the removal of external impediments. It means accessing and actualizing the power to transcend the finitenesses of our own being and nature.

The Exodus from Egypt, which marked the end of Israel's subjugation to their Egyptian enslavers, was but the first step of a

---

Shemot 19:8.

10 See *Migdal Oz* on *Mishneh Torah, Laws of Leaven and Matzah*, 7:1; *Minchat Chinuch, Mitzvah* 21; *Gevurot Hashem*, chapter 2; et al. Also see Maimonides' *Sefer HaMitzvot, Mitzvat Assei* 157.

seven-week journey, a forty-nine-step climb in the conquest and transcendence of self that culminated in our receiving the Torah at Mount Sinai on the festival of Shavuot. As G-d tells Moses at the onset of his mission to liberate the Jewish people, "This is your sign that I have sent you: when you take this nation out of Egypt, you shall serve G-d at this mountain."[11] Standing before Pharaoh, Moses did not merely demand, in the name of G-d, that he "Let My people go," but that he "Let My people go, that they may serve Me."[12]

What is the significance of this liberating "service"? It means that as human beings, no matter how free we might be of external constraints, we are still finite creatures, ever subject to the limits of our own nature and character. In order to attain true freedom we must transcend our humanity—our emotional, intellectual, even spiritual self—and access the "spark of G-dliness" that is our infinite, suprahuman self. The Torah, G-d's blueprint for life on earth, outlines the observances and practices that enable us to realize our divine essence in our daily lives.

Perpetual Exodus

On the day that we left the borders of Egypt, we were "free" in the conventional sense. No longer could a foreign taskmaster dictate what we must or may not do. We then proceeded to also

---

[11] Exodus 3:12. Accordingly, Shavuot is the only festival that has no calendar date. The Torah designates it not as a certain day of a certain month (as it does all other festivals), but as the day following the seven-week count that begins on the second day of Passover. This emphasizes that Shavuot is an outgrowth of Passover—that the significance of the Exodus was realized on the day we stood at Sinai.

[12] Exodus 7:16, et al.

free ourselves of the negative influences that constrained us from within—the pagan habits and sensibilities that centuries of subjection to the depraved culture of Egypt had imposed on us, and our own inborn negative inclinations.[13] This was accomplished during the forty-nine-day self-refinement "count" that connects the festivals of Passover and Shavuot.

Then, at Sinai, we were empowered to strive for yet a deeper dimension of freedom: a freedom that is not the negation of adversarial forces and influences, whether external or internal, but is the surmounting of our *positive* psychic and behavioral patterns. There is nothing negative about our human potential; but we are capable of more, of raising our achievements to a level in relation to which yesterday's "liberated" self is limited and subjective.

Our sages have said: "In every generation a person must see himself as if he has himself come out from Egypt."[14] The Hebrew word for "Egypt," *mitzrayim*, means "boundaries," and the endeavor to free ourselves from yesterday's boundaries is a perpetual one. For no matter how much we liberate ourselves from negative inhibitors, we remain defined by the boundaries of self and self-definition. Freedom is the incessant drive to "pass over" these boundaries, to draw on our divine, infinite potential to constantly overreach what we are.

Beyond Creation

When we stood at Sinai to receive the Torah, the very first words we heard from G-d were, "I am G-d your G-d, who has taken you out of the land of Egypt, from the house of slavery."[15] Many have

---

13   See Genesis 8:21.
14   Talmud, *Pesachim* 116b; Passover *Haggadah*.
15   Exodus 20:2.

puzzled over this declaration.[16] Would it not have been more appropriate for G-d to introduce Himself as "I am G-d your G-d who has created the heavens and the earth"?

But if our commitment to G-d were based on G-d's creation of the natural reality, this would only demand of us the utmost of our natural capacities and potentials. At Sinai, however, we forged a relationship with G-d that is predicated upon the nature-trouncing miracles of the Exodus.

To live as a Jew is to never accept the *mitzrayim*s of contemporary norms. True, we live and work within the constraints of nature and society; but we do not see them as invincible. We refine and develop them from within, but we also surmount them by actualizing the bond with G-d that was gifted to us at Sinai.

---

[16] See commentaries on Exodus 20:2 by Ibn Ezra, Nachmanides, Chizkuni, et al.

GREAT WEALTH

The Children of Israel did as Moses said: They requested of the Egyptians vessels of silver and vessels of gold and garments... and they salvaged Egypt.

Exodus 12:35–36

For much of our history, we have been in a state of exile. There was the Egyptian Exile that preceded our birth as a nation; the Babylonian Exile that followed the destruction of the first Holy Temple; the Persian Exile that followed the Babylonian; the Greek Exile during the Second Temple Era; and our present exile, which began with the Roman destruction of the second Holy Temple in 69 CE.

Exile—*galut*, in Hebrew—is much more than a person or a people's removal from their homeland. A person in exile is a person severed from the environment that nourishes their way of life, their principles and values, their spiritual identity. In exile all these are in jeopardy, for the onus is now on the exiles themselves; they must call upon their own resources of resolve and perseverance to survive. In the words of our sages, "All journeys are dangerous."[1]

Why are we in exile? *Galut* is commonly regarded as a punishment for our national and individual failings. Indeed, the prophets repeatedly describe it as such, and in our prayers we lament the fact that, "Because of our sins, we were exiled from our land."[2]

---

1 Jerusalem Talmud, *Berachot* 4:4.
2 *Siddur, Musaf* prayer for the festivals.

But long before the sins for which *galut* atones were committed, G-d made a covenant with Abraham—the "covenant between the parts"[3]—in which G-d established His special bond with Abraham's descendants. On that occasion, G-d informed Abraham that his children will experience *galut*:

> *As the sun began to set, a deep slumber fell upon Abram; behold, a dread, a great darkness, descended upon him. And [G-d] said to Abram: "Know that your children will be strangers in a land not theirs, and they will enslave them and afflict them... and afterwards they will go out with great wealth."*[4]

Obviously, then, there is also a deeper purpose to *galut* than atonement for our sins—a purpose that goes to the heart of the Jewish mission in history.

The Salvaging of Egypt

A clue to a deeper significance of *galut* can be found in the "great wealth" that G-d promised to Abraham as the result of his children's sojourn in the land of Egypt. Indeed, this promise is a recurrent theme in the Torah's account of the Egyptian exile and the Exodus—to the extent that one gets the impression that this was the very purpose of our enslavement in Egypt.

In G-d's very first communication to Moses, when He revealed Himself to him in the burning bush and charged him with the mission of taking the Jewish people out of Egypt, G-d includes the promise:

---

3 Described in detail in the fifteenth chapter of Genesis.
4 Genesis 15:12–14.

> *When you go, you will not go empty-handed. Every woman shall request from her neighbor... vessels of gold and vessels of silver and garments... and you will salvage Egypt.*[5]

Just prior to the Exodus, G-d again says to Moses:

> *Please, speak into the ears of the people, that each man ask his [Egyptian] fellow, and each woman her fellow, for vessels of silver and gold.*[6]

G-d is virtually *begging* the Children of Israel to take the wealth of Egypt! The Talmud explains that the Jewish people were disinclined to hold up their departure from Egypt in order to gather its wealth:

> *To what is this comparable? To a man who is locked up in prison and is told, "Tomorrow you shall be freed from prison and be given a lot of money." Says he: "I beg of you, free me today, and I ask for nothing more" ... [So G-d had to beseech them:] "Please! Ask the Egyptians for gold and silver vessels, so that the righteous one [Abraham] should not say: He fulfilled 'they will enslave them and afflict them,' but He did not fulfill 'and afterwards they will go out with great wealth.'"*[7]

But surely Abraham, too, would have been prepared to forgo the promise of "great wealth" if this were to hasten his children's

---

[5] Exodus 3:21–22.

[6] Ibid., 11:2. According to the Midrash (*Shemot Rabbah* 14:3), one of the purposes of the plague of darkness brought upon the Egyptians was that the Israelites—whom the plague did not affect—were able to move about freely inside the Egyptians' homes and take an "inventory" of the wealth of Egypt, so that the Egyptians could not deny the existence of any valuable objects the Israelites asked for when they left Egypt.

[7] Talmud, *Berachot* 9b.

liberation. Obviously, the gold and silver we carried out of Egypt was not some side benefit or compensation for our enslavement in Egypt, but an indispensable component of our redemption.

Sparks of Holiness

The Talmud offers the following explanation for the phenomenon of *galut*:

> The people of Israel were exiled amongst the nations only so that converts might be added to them.[8]

On the most basic level, this is a reference to the many non-Jews who, in the course of the centuries of our dispersion to all corners of the globe, have come in contact with the Jewish people and have been inspired to convert to Judaism. But chassidic teaching explains that the Talmud is also referring to souls of a different sort that are transformed and elevated in the course of our exiles: the "sparks of holiness" contained within the physical creation.[9]

The great kabbalist Rabbi Isaac Luria taught that every object, force, and phenomenon in existence has a "spark of holiness" within it, a pinpoint of divinity that constitutes its soul—i.e., its spiritual essence and design. This "spark" embodies the divine desire that the thing should exist, and its function within G-d's overall purpose for creation. Every time we utilize something to serve the Creator, we penetrate its shell of mundanity, revealing and realizing its divine essence. It is to this end that we have been dispersed across the face of earth: so that we may come in contact

---

[8] Talmud, *Pesachim* 87b.
[9] *Torah Ohr, Bereishith* 6a.

with the sparks of holiness that await redemption in every corner of the globe.

Every soul has "sparks" scattered about in the world which actually form an integral part of itself: no soul is complete until it has redeemed those sparks related to its being. Thus a person moves through life, impelled from place to place and from occupation to occupation by seemingly random forces; but everything is by divine providence, which guides us to those possessions and opportunities whose soul is intimately connected with ours.

Thus the Torah relates how Jacob risked his life to retrieve some "small jugs" he had left behind after crossing the Yabbok River.[10] "The righteous," remarks the Talmud, "value their possessions more than their bodies."[11] The righteous recognize the divine potential in every bit of matter, and see in each of their possessions a component of their own spiritual integrity.

The Lesson

At times, we might be inclined to escape *galut* by enclosing ourselves in a cocoon of spirituality, devoting our days and nights to Torah study and prayer. But instead of escaping *galut*, we are only deepening our entrenchment in it. For we are abandoning pieces of our own soul—the sparks of holiness belonging to it—in the wasteland of unrefined materiality.

It is only by meeting the challenges that divine providence sends our way—by utilizing every bit of material "gold" and "silver" toward a G-dly end—that we extricate these sparks from their exile. And by achieving a personal redemption of our own

---

10 Genesis 32:25; Rashi, ad loc.; Talmud, *Chulin* 91a.
11 Talmud, ibid.

soul and the sparks of holiness related to it, we hasten the universal redemption when "The great *shofar* shall be sounded, and the lost shall come from the lands of plenty, and the forsaken from the lands of stricture, and they shall bow to G-d on the Holy Mountain in Jerusalem."[12]

---

[12] Isaiah 27:13. The Hebrew word *Ashur* (Assyria) in this verse literally means "fortune," and *Mitzrayim* (Egypt) means "stricture."

AMBITION

They shall eat the flesh [of the Passover offering] on that night, roasted on the fire, with matzot and bitter herbs. Do not eat of it half-done, or cooked or boiled in water; only roasted on the fire.   Exodus 12:8–9

We experience life as an endless chain of urges and strivings. We desire something, agonize over our lack of it, and expend our energies and resources in its pursuit. And when our goal is actually attained, our pleasure and satisfaction are short-lived; already the next striving is forming in our hearts, already the fire of desire is consuming our lives.

We might, at times, envy the tranquility of those who are free of ambition, but it is the relentless seekers whom we admire and emulate. In our own experience, we look upon our periods of agitated quest as the high points of our lives. For we sense that while the tranquil person is at peace with themselves, the striving person is relating to something greater than the self, something more than the here and now.

THREE OFFERINGS

In the twelfth chapter of Exodus, G-d communicates to Moses the laws of the *korban pesach*, the Passover offering. When the Holy Temple stood in Jerusalem, every Jewish household (or group of smaller households) would bring a lamb or kid to the Temple on the fourteenth of *Nissan*, the day preceding the festival of Passover. The lamb would be slaughtered in the Temple courtyard, its blood would be sprinkled on the altar, and certain portions of it would be burned atop the altar. It would then be roasted on a spit over an open fire. That night—the first night of Passover—the meat of the *korban pesach* would be eaten with matzah and *maror* (bitter herbs), together constituting the three staples of the *seder*.[1]

Various types of *korbanot* (animal and meal offerings) were offered in the Holy Temple, but the Passover offering was unique in many ways, as it was governed by a set of laws that applied to no other offering. Some of these differences are specified in the fifth chapter of the Talmudic tractate of *Zevachim*, where the Talmud compares the Passover offering with two other *korbanot*—the "firstborn offering" (*korban bechor*) and the "tithe offering" (*korban maaser*).

> *The firstborn, tithe, and Passover offerings are* kodashim kallim; *they can be slaughtered anywhere in the Temple courtyard, and their blood requires only one sprinkling, as long as it is directed toward the foundation of the altar. They differ, however, in how they are to be eaten. The firstborn offering is eaten by the priests, the tithe offering by anyone; both can be eaten throughout the city [of Jerusalem], in any form of food preparation, for two days and one night. The Passover offering can be eaten only at night, and only up to midnight, and only by those registered for it, and only roasted by fire.*[2]

---

1 Today, the meat of the Passover offering is represented at the *seder* by the *afikoman*, a piece of matzah eaten at the end of the meal.
2 Talmud, *Zevachim* 56b.

The Torah commands to bring the firstborn of cattle or sheep as an offering to G-d.[3] Also to be offered is a tithe of the animals born in the herd or flock: once a year, the year's yield was herded into a pen and let out one at a time, and every tenth animal to emerge was marked, pronounced "holy to G-d," and brought as an offering.[4] The firstborn, tithe, and Passover offerings all belong to a class of *korbanot* called *kodashim kallim*,[5] and they resemble each other in the procedure of their offering upon the altar. But the rules pertaining to the eating of the Passover offering differ from those relating to the first two.

The firstborn and the tithe offerings can be eaten for "two days and a night" (on the day it was offered, on the following night, and on the following day until sunset), whereas the Passover offering can be eaten only on the night following its offering, and only until midnight. Another difference is that the firstborn and the tithe offerings can be prepared in any way the eater desires—boiled, stewed, baked, roasted, etc.—while the Passover offering has to be roasted on a spit over the fire, and cannot be prepared in any other way, not even as a "pot roast" cooked in its own juices with no other liquid added.[6]

For the most part, the Torah speaks of physical objects and actions; but its every word also refers to the spiritual dynamics of our lives. Each law of the Torah—each organ and limb of its "body"—has its corresponding element in the "soul" of Torah. The same is true of the abovementioned laws: the firstborn, tithe, and Passover offerings, and the differences between them, all have their counterpart in the inner life of the soul.

---

3   Exodus 13:2, 12; Deuteronomy 15:19.
4   Leviticus 27:32.
5   "Lightly sacred," as opposed to the *kodashei kodashim*, "sacred of sacred," to which a stricter set of rules apply.
6   *Tosafot* on Talmud, *Pesachim* 41a, s.v. *ikka*; Rashi, ibid., s.v. *tzli kadar*.

First, Last, and Over

The teachings of kabbalah describe our world as founded upon ten divine attributes (*sefirot*) from which derive the spiritual form and substance of reality. Thus, the number "ten" represents the *seder hishtalshelut* (literally, the "order of evolution")—the spiritual order of things that G-d instituted in creation. "Firstborn" represents *chochmah*, the first and loftiest phase of the *seder hishtalshelut*; "tithe" refers to *malchut*, the last and lowest of the order.[7] Together, the first and the tenth embrace the totality of the created reality.

"Passover," as its name indicates, relates to that which transcends *seder hishtalshelut*, that which overleaps the standard processes of creation. The Passover offering is so named in attestation to the fact that G-d "leaped over" the homes of the Israelite firstborn when He killed all Egyptian firstborn on the night of the Exodus,[8] despite the fact that, by all standard criteria, the Jews were no more deserving of life than the Egyptians.[9] Passover is G-d's disregarding of the very rules by which He ordered His world, and our reciprocation of G-d's action by rising above the dictates of nature and normalcy in our devotion to Him.

---

7 Thus the firstborn offering was eaten by the *kohanim*, who represent the higher, more spiritual callings of life (see *Mishneh Torah, Laws of Shemittah and Yovel*, 13:13), while the tithe offering was eaten by the farmer who brought it, representing the "lowest," or most material, stratum of creation.

8 Exodus 12:27; Passover *Haggadah*, s.v. *pesach zu*.

9 After more than two centuries of exile and slavery in Egypt, the Children of Israel had assumed the pagan practices of the Egyptians; in many ways, their spiritual state was no better than their enslavers. Indeed, the Midrash relates that when the sea parted for the Israelites and then drowned the Egyptians, the divine "attribute of justice" argued: "How are these any different from these? These are idol-worshippers, and these are idol-worshippers!" See *Zohar Chadash*, beginning of Yitro; *Yalkut Reuveni, Shemot* 14:27; *Zohar* 2:36 and 2:170b.

Fire and Water

This explains the difference in how the Passover offering is eaten, as opposed to the "firstborn" and "tithe" offerings.

As we have remarked in the opening lines of this essay, our lives can be seen as a cycle of striving and realization, yearning and gratification. The common metaphors for these two states are "fire" and "water." Fire denotes thirst and upward striving; water suggests "settling down" and satiation.

A "normal" life—life as defined by the "order of evolution" from *chochmah* to *malchut*—is nourished by both fire and water. Some meals are cooked steeped in the water of contentment; others have lesser degrees of liquid to temper the fire of life; occasionally, one even partakes of a "roast"—a spurt of utter striving, of desire unsated by a single drop of gratification.

The Passover offering, however, can be experienced only one way—roasted on the fire. When a soul reaches for G-d—not for the glimmers of divinity to be found within creation and experienced by conventional spiritual endeavor, but for G-d Himself, as He transcends existence and reality—it is utterly consumed by an unceasing desire. For the human being can never capture anything of the divine essence. We can only strive for it, our soul a pure fire, with nary a drop of water to slake our thirst, without even a "pot"—a vessel to contain our fervor.[10]

Nighttime Meal

The firstborn and tithe offerings were eaten for "two days and a night." The Passover offering was eaten only at night.

---

10 See the essay, "A Heart of Flame," pp. 14–15 above.

In the course of our history, we have experienced days of divine light, as well as nights of spiritual darkness. Generally speaking, there were two "daytime" eras—the periods during which the first Holy Temple, and then the second, manifested the divine presence in our world.[11] Between these two days was a brief night—the seventy-year Babylonian *galut*, when the Holy Temple lay in ruins and the people of Israel were exiled from the Holy Land. Following the sunset of the second day, we were plunged into the blackest of nights—into our current centuries-long *galut*, rife with suffering and persecution, confounded by doubt and spiritual dissonance, and marked by the near-total concealment of the face of G-d.

A "normal" relationship with G-d could be had only on the "two days and a night" that preceded our present *galut*. These were times in which G-d showed Himself to man—even in Babylon we had prophets and other expressions of divine immanence. But when the sun set on the second day, the "firstborn" and "tithe" offerings could no longer be consumed. No longer could the divine truth be experienced within the workings of nature or accessed by the conventional processes of spiritual endeavor. No longer could we experience gratification in our spiritual lives, for a glimpse of the divine had become an elusive dream.

In this night of nights,[12] our striving for the divine is an unquenchable fire, an unrealizable yearning, an unconsummatable love. But for that very reason, it is deeper and truer than the fire-and-water concoctions of the past. In this night of nights, our

---

[11] The first Holy Temple stood for 410 years, from the year 2928 from creation (833 BCE) to 3338 (423 BCE). The second Holy Temple stood for 420 years, from 3408 (353 BCE) dates to 3829 (69 CE).

[12] The Passover offering can be eaten "only until midnight." In kabbalistic teaching, the first half of the night is its harsher part, in which the attribute of *gevurah* ("severity") dominates.

yearning for G-d is not focused on "first" or "tenth" attributes, or filtered through "orders of evolution." In this night of nights, our yearning for G-d is not mitigated by plateaus of gratification. It passes over all systems and processes to strive for the very essence of G-d—an endless striving for the most endless of objectives.

SPEED IN THREE DIMENSIONS

And so you shall eat it: your hips girdled, your shoes on your feet, and your staffs in your hands. Eat it in haste; it is a Passover offering to G-d.

Exodus 12:11

Our life endeavors can be divided into three general categories. First there is the quest for self-improvement and for the development of our own talents and potentials. Then there is our involvement with our personal "portion in the world"—our family, profession, social circle, and the natural resources we consume or develop. Finally, there is our effect upon the macro-universe—world events, the progress of history, creation as a whole.

While many of us might consider this last realm to be beyond our sphere of influence, the truth is that our every deed impacts the world in which we live, whether we are aware of it or not. "A sneeze in New Jersey can cause a hurricane in China," is how one scientist illustrated the integrity of the physical universe. In the words of Maimonides, "Man should always view himself as equally balanced: half good and half evil. Likewise, he should see the entire world as half good and half evil... so that with a single good deed he will tip the scales for himself, and for the entire world, to the side of good."[1]

---

[1] *Mishneh Torah, Laws of Repentance,* 3:4.

From Passivity to Activity

The Exodus marks our birth as a nation—the time when G-d extracted "a people out of the bowels of a people,"[2] granted them the gift of freedom, and empowered them to realize the divine goodness and perfection in their own lives and in the world He created.

A key theme in the story of the Exodus is "haste." The Children of Israel are described as having "fled" Egypt.[3] Matzah is the bread that didn't leaven because we were "driven from Egypt and could not tarry."[4] And the Passover offering, the key to the redemption and the axis around which the entire festival of Passover revolves, was eaten "in haste."[5]

The alacrity of the Exodus emphasizes that life, for the Jew, is never again to be the passive and static experience it was for the clan of Hebrew slaves under Egyptian bondage. Life is to be a vigorous, vibrant movement forward, an unceasing quest to advance and achieve.

Extension Rod

The state of haste in which the first *seder* was held was expressed in three ways: "Your hips girdled, your shoes on your feet, and your staffs in your hands." These correspond to the three dimensions of the forward movement of our lives outlined above—our self-development, our effect upon our immediate surroundings, and our universal impact.

---

2 Deuteronomy 4:34.
3 Exodus 14:5.
4 Ibid., 12:39.
5 Ibid., verse 11. See also Deuteronomy 16:3.

The hips, which are "the base that holds up the entire body,"[6] represent the human being as an individual. "Your hips girdled" thus refers to the endeavor to develop our personal potentials.

The feet are the person's means of locomotion. Equip the feet with shoes, and you enable them to traverse hostile terrain that would otherwise impede their movement from place to place. Shod feet thus represent our ability to journey from the enclave of self to points beyond the range of a "barefoot," home-bound personality.

But we are more than foot travelers in life. The human race is unique among its fellow creatures in that we make extensive use of "tools"—implements that we fashion that enable us to manipulate our environment in ways we could not with our own body and its faculties. If we can scarcely lift the equivalent of our own weight with our own two hands, we have learned to literally move mountains with the machines we devise. If our own two feet, bare or shod, can carry us only so far so fast, we have explored the depths of the sea and the astronomical heights with vehicles of our invention.

Therein lies the significance of the third marker of the alacrity of the Exodus—"your staffs in your hands." The "staff" represents the uniquely human conviction that nothing is impossible, that we can always find a way to extend our reach beyond the distance dictated by our natural arm-span. The conviction that we each possess the capacity to positively influence all people, all elements, and all events of our world, no matter how distant and unrelated to our lives they may seem.

---

6   *Tanya, Igeret HaKodesh*, 1.

DIALOGUE

Your child will ask you...
you shall say to him...   Exodus 13:14

Try describing a Passover *seder* to someone who never actually participated in one, and you'll find yourself groping for models that only partially fit the bill. The *seder* is part family dinner, part prayer service, part ritualistic consumption of symbolic foods, part songfest and storytelling marathon, part child-parent quizzing session... among other things.

The *seder* straddles a number of otherwise distinct areas of our lives because the event it commemorates—the exodus and liberation of the Children of Israel from slavery in Egypt—likewise combines realities and categorizations that we normally see as distinct and apart from each other.

The Emancipation of G-d

The divine promise of redemption was conveyed to Moses in a formula that came to be known as "the four expressions of redemption":

> *I will take you out from under the burdens of Egypt; I will deliver you from their servitude; I will redeem you with an outstretched arm and great judgments; I will acquire you for Myself as a people ..."*[1]

---

[1] Exodus 6:6–7.

In the Torah scroll, the biblical text is written without vowel points (*nikud*). This means that in addition to the traditional pronunciation, which conveys the basic meaning of the text, the text also allows for alternate readings, revealing additional layers of meaning, in keeping with the adage, "There are seventy faces to the Torah."[2]

One such alternate reading is applied to the first of the "four expressions of redemption" quoted above. The great sage and *paytan* (liturgical poet) Rabbi Elazar HaKalir suggests that the Hebrew words *ve'hotzeiti etchem*, "I will take you out," can also be read as *ve'hutzeiti itchem*, "I will be taken out with you"—implying that G-d Himself is also imprisoned in Egypt, and awaits redemption together with His people.[3]

This is also the deeper meaning of a phrase that appears frequently in the prayer book, referring to the festival of Passover as "the time of our liberation." On the most basic level, the plural "our" refers to us, the people of Israel. But on another level of interpretation, "our liberation" is the joint liberation of G-d and of Israel.[4]

The essence of the human soul is "literally a part of G-d above."[5] As long as we are enslaved, as long as our soul's deepest yearnings are stifled and denied actualization, G-d, too, is not free. In the words of the prophets, "In all their distresses, He is distressed";[6] "I am with him in his affliction."[7]

---

[2] *Midrash Rabbah, Bamidbar* 13:15; *Zohar* 3:152a; et al. See also Talmud, *Sanhedrin* 34a.
[3] *Siddur, Hoshaanot* prayers. See the essay, "The Essence of Existence," on pp. 16–20 above.
[4] See *Likutei Torah, Shemini Atzeret* 88d.
[5] *Tanya*, chapter 2.
[6] Isaiah 63:9.
[7] Psalms 91:15. Also see *Sifri*, Deuteronomy 32:34.

Religious Ritual or Social Convention?

In general, the Torah's commandments fall under two categories: (a) "Between man and man"—social laws that govern relations between individuals and communities. (b) "Between man and G-d"—laws that outline our duties to our Creator.[8] On Passover, as befits the "season of *our* liberation," the two categories fuse into one: "between man and G-d" is synonymous with "between man and man," and vice versa.

Hence the unique format of the *seder* as a hybrid of religious ritual and social get-together. The purpose of the *seder* is to "remember the day on which you left Egypt"[9] and reaffirm our commitment as G-d's people. To this end, we eat the matzah and the *maror* and retell the story of the Exodus. Yet the entire *seder* is constructed as a dialogue, as answers to questions posed by the "four children"—the wise child, the wicked child, the simple child, and "the child who does not know how to ask."[10]

In other words, one remembers the Exodus not in meditative communion with G-d, but by fulfilling the commandment to "tell your child."[11] This includes "your child" in the broader sense of the term—any individual whom you are in a position to teach and enlighten,[12] including "children" who are antagonistic or indifferent to the essence of Passover.

The freedom attained on Passover reveals the superficiality of the dividing line between the social and religious spheres of life.

---

8 See Talmud, *Yoma* 85b and *Kidushin* 40a; et al.
9 Exodus 13:3.
10 Passover *Haggadah*.
11 Exodus 13:8.
12 "Your children are your disciples" (Rashi, Deuteronomy 6:7); "Whoever teaches another's child Torah, it is as if he had given birth to him" (Talmud, *Sanhedrin* 19b).

On the day that G-d became free through the redemption of the human soul, it is most obvious that no relationship can be forged with G-d that does not include a commitment to one's fellow man.

TOMORROW'S CHILD

It shall come to pass that your child will ask you, tomorrow, to say: "What is this?" You shall say to him: "With a mighty hand, G-d took us out of Egypt..."

Exodus 13:14

"Your child will ask you, tomorrow"—there is a tomorrow that is immediate, and there is a tomorrow that is a long way off.

Rashi, ad loc.

On the most basic level, Rashi is explaining the plain meaning of the verse. The child who will observe the Passover rituals and ask, "What is this?", is obviously not the child of an immediate tomorrow. Such a child would have witnessed the miracles of the Exodus themselves, and would have firsthand knowledge of the significance of these *mitzvot*. So the "tomorrow" of which the Torah speaks is of a more distant time and generation—a generation for whom the liberation from Egyptian slavery is a long-ago "historical event," and who need to be educated on its relevance to their lives.

But there is also a deeper significance to Rashi's words. The statement, "There is a tomorrow that is immediate, and there is a tomorrow that is a long way off," can also be understood as referring to two types of future generations, differentiated not by time but by mindset and attitude.

There are children who are of an immediate tomorrow: children who are of the same epoch as our own; children who are the continuum tomorrow to our today. They ask, as children are wont to ask, questioning the what, how, and why of the truths we convey to them. But we both inhabit the same world, and our dialogue with them is predicated on the same set of axioms. Doubtless we will answer this child, relate to them the origins of our heritage, and explain to them the significance of our observances.

But there are also children who are of a far-off tomorrow. Children who inhabit a distant world, who speak a distant language and relate to distant values. Children for whom a vast gulf separates their tomorrow from our today. Children whose questions are of a different nature entirely: challenging, alien, hostile. What is one to do with such a child, with such a questioner?

Speak with them, says the Torah, answer them, for they are *your* children. He or she is a child of your people, and a child of your making—for perhaps, just perhaps, you share in the responsibility for the fact that this child is wandering in the time-warp of a disconnected tomorrow?

In our own day, this "far off tomorrow" has become a painful reality. How many Jewish children inhabit such alien tomorrows? How many Jewish children are mired in bizarre "Egypts," receding, with horrifying speed, to tomorrows of increasing distance and disconnection? When such a Jewish child comes with their questions—the apathetic-bitter questions of a rootless generation—remember, he or she is your child. Devote your heart, soul, and life to them, and illuminate their way back to their holy source.

PARASHAH
SIXTEEN

BESHALACH

Exodus 13:17–17:16

A sea splits

THE MOUNTAIN AND THE SEA

G-d said to Moses: "Why do you cry out to Me? Speak to the Children of Israel, and they should travel forward."

Exodus 14:15

We all know the feeling: we wake up one morning to the realization that the world is not as we would like it to be.

A common experience, to be sure, but many and diverse are the ways in which we might react. One person embarks upon a quixotic crusade to change the world. A second gives up the world for lost and retreats into whatever protective walls they can erect around themselves and their loved ones. A third takes a "pragmatic" approach, accepting the world for what it is and doing their best under the circumstances. A fourth recognizes his or her inability to deal with the situation, and looks to a higher power for guidance and aid.

The Four Factions

Our ancestors experienced just such a rude awakening on the seventh day after their liberation from Egypt.

Ten devastating plagues had broken the Egyptians' resistance and compelled them to free the Children of Israel. After two centuries of exile and slavery, the Israelites were headed toward Mount Sinai and their covenant with G-d. Indeed, this was the stated purpose of the Exodus; as G-d had said to Moses, "When you take this people out of Egypt, you will serve G-d on this mountain."[1]

But suddenly the sea was before them, and Pharaoh's armies were closing in from behind. Egypt was alive and well; the sea, too, seemed oblivious to the destiny of the newly-born nation.

How did they react? The Midrash[2] tells us that the people were divided into four camps. There were those who said, "Let us throw ourselves into the sea." A second group said, "Let us return to Egypt." A third faction argued, "Let us wage war on the Egyptians." Finally, a fourth camp advocated, "Let us pray to G-d."

This, says the Midrash, is the meaning behind the rather elaborate reply that Moses gives to the people when they confront him over their predicament. As the Torah relates, Moses says to the people:

> *Fear not; stand by and see the salvation of G-d which He will do for you today. For as you have seen Egypt this day, you shall not see them again, forever. G-d shall fight for you, and you shall be silent.*[3]

Moses, the Midrash explains, is rejecting all four options. "Fear not; stand by and see the salvation of G-d" is Moses' response to those who had despaired of overcoming the Egyptian threat and wanted to plunge into the sea. "As you have seen Egypt this day, you shall not see them again" is addressed to those who advocated surrender and return to Egypt. "G-d shall fight for you" is the

---

1   Exodus 3:12.
2   *Mechilta* on Exodus 13:18.
3   Exodus 14:13–14.

answer to those who wished to battle the Egyptians. And "you shall be silent" is Moses' rejection of those who said: This is all beyond us; all we can do is pray.

What, then, is the Jew to do when caught between a hostile mob and an unyielding sea? "Speak to the Children of Israel," said G-d to Moses, "and they shall travel forward."[4]

The Tzaddik in a Fur Coat

The road to Sinai was full of obstacles and challenges. The same is true of the road from Sinai, our three-thousand-year journey devoted to the implementation of the ethos and ideals of Torah in our world.

Now, as then, there are several possible responses to an adverse world. There is the "Let us throw ourselves into the sea" approach of those who despair of their ability to grapple with, much less impact, the world out there. Let us plunge into the sea, they say—the "sea of the Talmud," the sea of piety, the sea of religious life. Let us sever all contact with an apostate and promiscuous world. Let us build walls of holiness to protect ourselves and our own from the alien winds that storm without, so that we may foster the legacy of Sinai within.

An old chassidic saying refers to a such-minded individual as a *tzaddik in peltz*—"a holy man in a fur coat." There are two ways to warm yourself on a cold winter day: you can build a fire or wrap yourself in furs. When the isolationist *tzaddik* is asked, "Why do you think only of conserving your own warmth? Why don't you build a fire that will warm others as well?" he replies, "What's the use? Can I warm the entire world?" If you persist, pointing out

---

4   Ibid., verse 15.

that one small fire can thaw several frozen individuals, who may, in turn, create enough fires to warm a small corner of the universe, he doesn't understand what you want of him. He is a *tzaddik*, remember, a perfectly righteous individual. There is no place for partial solutions in his life. "It's hopeless," he sighs with genuine sadness, and retreats into his spiritual Atlantis.

The Slave and the Warrior

A second camp says, "Let us return to Egypt."

Plunging into the sea is not an option, argues the Submissive Jew. This is the world in which G-d has placed us, and our mission is to deal with it, not escape it. We'll just have to lower our expectations a little.

This Exodus thing was obviously a pipe dream. How could we presume to liberate ourselves from the rules and constraints that apply to everyone else? To be G-d's "chosen people" is nice, but let us not forget that we are a minority, dependent on the goodwill of the Pharaohs who hold sway in the real world out there.

Certainly, it is our duty to influence the world. But then again, a Jew has many duties: it is our duty to pray three times a day, to give charity, and to observe Shabbat. So we'll do the best we can under the circumstances. Yes, it's not easy to keep all these laws while making sure not to antagonize our neighbors, but who ever said that being a Jew is easy?

A third response to an uncooperative world is that of the Fighting Jew. The Fighting Jew understands that it is wrong to escape the world, and equally wrong to submit to it. So he takes it on, both barrels blazing.

The Fighting Jew strides through life with a holy chip on his shoulder, battling sinners, apostates, Jew-haters, un-Jewish Jews, and non-fighting Jews. Not for him is the escapism of the first camp or the subservience of the second—he knows that his cause is just, that G-d is on his side, that ultimately he will triumph. So if the world won't listen to reason, he'll knock some sense into it.

THE SPIRITUALIST

Finally, there is the Jew who looks at the world, looks at the first three camps, shakes her head, and lifts her eyes to the heavens. She knows that turning one's back on the world is not the answer, nor is surrendering to its dictates and conventions. But she also knows that "The entirety of Torah was given to make peace in the world,"[5] that "Its ways are ways of pleasantness, and all its paths are peace."[6]

"You hope to peacefully change the world?!" say the other three camps. "When was the last time you looked out the window? You might as well try to empty the oceans with a teaspoon!"

"You're absolutely right," says the Praying Jew. "Realistically, there's no way it can be done. But we are not subject to this 'reality' that you are so impressed with.

"Do you know what the common denominator is between all three of you? Your assessments and strategies are all based on the natural reality. But we inhabit a higher reality. Is not the very existence of the Jewish people a miracle? Ours is the world of the spirit, the world of the word."

"So basically your approach is to do nothing," they counter.

"Again you are employing the standards of the material world," answers the Praying Jew, "a world that views prayer as 'doing nothing.' But a single prayer, coming from a caring heart, can achieve

---

5   *Mishneh Torah, Laws of Chanukah* 4:14.
6   Proverbs 3:17; see Talmud, *Gittin* 59b.

more than the most secure fortress, the most flattering diplomat or the most powerful army."

Travel Forward

And what does G-d say? "Speak to the Children of Israel, *and they shall travel forward.*"

True, it is important to safeguard and cultivate all that is pure and holy in the Jewish soul, to create an inviolable sanctum of G-dliness in one's own heart and one's own community. True, there are times when we must deal with the world on its own terms. True, we must battle evil. And certainly we must acknowledge that we cannot do it on our own.

Each of the four approaches has its time and place. But neither of them is the overall vision that guides our lives and defines our relationship with the world we inhabit. When we are headed toward Sinai and are confronted with a hostile or indifferent world, our most basic response must be to move forward.

Not to escape reality, not to submit to it, not to wage war on it, not to deal with it only on a spiritual level, but to move forward. Do another *mitzvah*, ignite another soul, take one more step toward your goal. Pharaoh's charioteers are breathing down your neck? A cold and impregnable sea bars your path? Don't look up; look forward. See that mountain? Move toward it.

And when you move forward, you will see that insurmountable barrier yield and that ominous threat fade away. You will see that despite all the "evidence" to the contrary, you have it within your power to reach your goal. Even if you have to split some seas.

THE AMPHIBIAN SOUL

The Children of Israel entered within the sea, on dry land.   Exodus 14:22

Every creature that exists on land has its equivalent in the sea.   Talmud, Chulin 127a

Land and sea mirror each other, yet they are vastly different worlds. Both are life-supporting environments, providing sustenance and shelter to a myriad of creatures. Both are complex ecosystems, complete with the great variety of minerals, vegetation, and animals which form a multi-linked chain of life. But despite their similarities, land and sea are different in many ways, particularly in the manner in which the creatures who populate them relate to their environment.

Our sages have said that the human being is "a miniature universe,"[1] a microcosm of the entire created existence. The human being thus includes both these worlds—each of us has both a terrestrial and an aquatic aspect to our psyche and personality.

The Secret of the Deep

Creatures of the land are to be found upon the land. Some species burrow under for a certain part of the day or year, and there

---

[1] *Midrash Tanchuma, Pekudei* 3.

are even species who rarely, if ever, show themselves above ground. But on the whole, land creatures live their lives on the surface of the earth. In fact, there is nothing to prevent them from severing all direct contact with the land for extended periods of time (modern man has all but done so).

Not so the creatures of the sea, who live submerged within their environment. For most sea-dwelling animals, this submersion is a matter of life and death: a fish out of water is not only a creature out of its element, but a creature who cannot survive for more than a short while.

The creatures of the land are no less dependent upon the land than their sister creatures of the sea are dependent upon the sea; ultimately, without the land and its resources, a land animal cannot live. The difference, however, is in how this truth is reflected in their day-by-day and minute-by-minute existence. With the sea creature, this dependence is constant and obvious. The sea animal cannot separate itself from its sustaining environment; its life and its life-source are inexorably bound together.[2] The land creature, on the other hand, can receive its nourishment from the earth and then forget about it, even deny it. Conceivably, a land creature can live an entire lifetime without acknowledging, or in any way demonstrating, from where its sustenance is derived.

This is the significance of the "land" and "sea" personalities within us. There is a part of us that is disconnected from our

---

2 A sea creature's utter identification with its environment is also reflected in Torah law. When a person immerses in a *mikvah* to attain ritual purity, nothing must interpose between the person and the *mikvah*'s waters; if the slightest particle of any substance adheres to their body, the immersion is invalid. Yet this rule does not apply to anything which grows in water; the body of a fish, for example, or any product thereof, is not considered an "interposition" (*chatzitzah*) but an integral part of the waters themselves.

purpose and source—a "land" self that is oblivious to the fact that our soul is a "part of G-d above";[3] that we are granted life anew, each and every moment of time, by our Creator; that our existence has meaning only in the context of its role in the divine purpose. This "land self" defines its existence in the narrow terms of personal ego and its individual desires and aspirations.

But we also possesses a "sea" persona—a spiritual self that transcends ego and individuality to attune its every deed and thought to the higher goals for which we were created. When this self asserts itself, nothing about us is separate from our connection to our Source. Like a fish in water, our every living moment is an attestation to our utter dependence upon, and devotion to, our source of nourishment and life.

The kabbalistic masters tell us that there are *tzaddikim* (righteous individuals) who live their entire lives as "fishes of the sea," wholly submerged within a perpetual awareness of and subjugation to the divine reality. Such an individual was Moses, whose name expresses the "aquatic" nature of his soul.[4] Thus the Torah attests that "Moses was the most humble man on the face of the earth."[5] Moses was certainly aware of his own greatness; certainly he knew that he was the single human being chosen by G-d to serve as the conveyor of the divine wisdom and will to humanity. Yet Moses did not view his qualities as his "own" attainments, for he had utterly nullified and submerged his self within the sea of the divine reality. His own life was merely the divine plan being

---

[3] Job 31:2; *Tanya*, chapter 2.
[4] "She called his name Moses and said: Because I drew him from the water" (Exodus 2:10).
[5] Numbers 12:3.

realized through an egoless vehicle; his teachings, the "divine presence speaking from his throat."[6]

Land Fish

This is not to say that our "terrestrial" self—our sense of identity and individuality—is to be uprooted or suppressed. Selfhood is not, in and of itself, a negative trait; it is only that, left to its own devices, it is prone to develop some very negative attributes. If we fail to develop an "aquatic" consciousness and behavior—if we lose sight of the source and goal of life—our self is sure to turn selfish, its self-identity translating into self-centeredness, its individuality becoming disconnectedness and rootlessness.

Only when we have submerged ourselves within the sea of the divine reality can we exploit our ego as the positive force it inherently is. Only then can we properly harness our unique worth as an individual to optimally realize our mission in life.

This is the ideal expressed in Jacob's blessing to his grandchildren, Manasseh and Ephraim—"They shall swarm as fish[7] in the midst of the land."[8] The ultimate challenge is for us not just to be a "fish," but to be "a fish in the midst of the land."

Day Seven

Therein lies the deeper significance of the splitting of the sea seven days after our Exodus from Egypt. In recounting the miracle, the Torah describes the Children of Israel coming "within the sea, on

---

6   *Zohar* 3:232a.
7   *Ve'yidgu*, from the word *dag*, "fish."
8   Genesis 48:16.

dry land." Following our redemption, in both the physical and spiritual sense, from Egypt and its pagan culture, we were empowered to enter "within the sea"—to immerse ourselves within the sea of the all-pervading universal truth of truths—and at the same time walk "on dry land" as distinct and unique beings.

Our sages tell us that the splitting of the sea was but the first step of a process that spans the whole of our history; that the song which Moses and the people of Israel sang upon traversing the sea is but the first stanza of a song that culminates in the era of Moshiach, the end goal of creation.⁹ The splitting of the sea was the precedent that enables and directs our centuries-long quest for that perfect synthesis of land and sea that will be fully realized in the messianic age, when "the land will be filled with the knowledge of G-d as the waters cover the sea."¹⁰

---

9 See Talmud, *Sanhedrin* 91b; *Midrash Tanchuma, Beshalach* 10.
10 Isaiah 11:9.

ON THE ESSENCE OF LEADERSHIP

Israel saw G-d's mighty hand ... and they believed in G-d and in Moses His servant...
Then sang Moses and the Children of Israel this song to G-d, saying: I shall sing to G-d for He is most exalted... Exodus 14:31; 15:1

"Then sang Moses and the Children of Israel"— Moses being the equivalent of the Children of Israel, and the Children of Israel being the equivalent of Moses. Midrash Mechilta, ad loc.

What is leadership?

We expect our leaders to be wise: to be able to discern right from wrong and make the proper decisions on issues that affect our lives; to provide us with a vision of where we stand and where we are headed, and guide us toward the realization of our goals.

We expect our leaders to be caring and committed: to empathize with our needs and aspirations and devote themselves to their fulfillment.

We expect our leaders to be strong: calm and decisive in times of crisis, capable warriors and diplomats in the furtherance of our aims.

We expect our leaders to be individuals of high moral character and integrity, bearers of an ethical standard for young and old to emulate.

But the most important—and probably the most overlooked—function of the leader is to unite us. To knit diverse individuals into a single people, and inspire diverse—and often conflicting—wills to coalesce into a common destiny.

A Chorus in Three Versions

One of the first things we did together as a people was sing.

The nation of Israel was born on the fifteenth of *Nissan* in the year 2448 from creation (1313 BCE)—the day that G-d "extracted a nation from the bowels of a nation,"[1] freeing the Children of Israel from Egyptian slavery. Seven days later, the Israelites witnessed the destruction of their former enslavers when the sea split to allow them passage and drowned the pursuing Egyptians. The Torah relates how, upon beholding the great miracle,

> *Moses and the Children of Israel sang this song to G-d, saying:*
> *I shall sing to G-d for He is most exalted;*
> *Horse and rider He cast in the sea.*
> *G-d is my strength and song; He is my salvation*
> *This is my G-d, and I shall glorify Him*
> *The G-d of my fathers, and I shall exalt Him...*[2]

---

[1] Deuteronomy 4:34.
[2] Exodus 15. Rabbi Chaim ibn Attar points out in his *Ohr HaChaim* commentary that the words, "I shall sing," are in first person singular, implying that the people of Israel sang this song "as a single person, without difference and separation."

This song, known as *Shirat HaYam*—"Song at the Sea"—goes on to describe the great miracles that G-d performed for His people, G-d's promise to bring them to the Holy Land and reveal His presence among them in the Holy Temple in Jerusalem, and Israel's goal to implement G-d's eternal sovereignty in the world. Its forty-four verses express the gist of our relationship with G-d and our mission in life, and thus occupy a most important place in the Torah and in Jewish life.

Our sages also focus on the prefatory line to the Song at the Sea, in which the Torah introduces it as a song sung by "Moses and the Children of Israel." Moses was obviously one of the "Children of Israel," so the fact that the Torah singles him out implies that Moses took a leading role in the composition and delivery of this song. Indeed, the nature of Moses' role is a point of much discussion by the sages; the Talmud[3] relates no fewer than three different opinions on how Moses led his people in their song of praise and thanksgiving to G-d:

(a) According to Rabbi Akiva, it was Moses who composed and sang the *Shirat HaYam*, while the people of Israel merely responded to each verse with the refrain, "I shall sing to G-d." Moses sang, "For He is most exalted," and they answered, "I shall sing to G-d"; Moses sang, "Horse and rider He cast in the sea," and they answered, "I shall sing to G-d"; and so on with all forty-four verses of the song.

(b) Rabbi Eliezer is of the opinion that the people *repeated* each verse after Moses. Moses sang, "I shall sing to G-d for He is most exalted," and they repeated, "I shall sing to G-d for He is most exalted"; Moses sang "Horse and rider He cast in the sea," and they repeated, "Horse and rider He cast in the sea"; and so on.

---

3 Talmud, *Sotah* 30b.

(c) A third opinion is that of Rabbi Nechemiah, who posits that Moses simply pronounced the opening words of the song, following which the people of Israel all sang the entire song together. In other words, each of them, on their own, composed the entire—and very same—forty-four verses![4]

Submission vs. Identification

These three versions of how Moses led Israel in song express three different perspectives on unity—particularly the unity achieved when a people rallies under the leadership of their leader.[5]

Rabbi Akiva describes an ideal in which the members of a community abnegate their individuality to the collective identity embodied by the leader. Moses alone sang the nation's gratitude to G-d, their experience of redemption, and their vision of their future as G-d's people. The people had nothing further to say as individuals, other than to affirm their unanimous assent to what Moses was expressing.

At first glance, this seems the ultimate in unity: more than two million[6] hearts and minds yielding to a single program and vision. Rabbi Eliezer, however, argues that this is a superficial unity—an externally imposed unity of the moment, rather than an internal, enduring unity. When people set aside their own thoughts and

---

4   Rashi on Talmud, ad loc.; *Mechilta* on Exodus 15:1.
5   See Rashi on Numbers 21:21: "Moses is Israel and Israel is Moses.... For the leader of the generation is as the entire generation, for the leader embodies them all." See also *Mechilta* on Exodus 15:1 (quoted at the beginning of this essay) and *Tanya*, end of chapter 2.
6   The census taken one year after the Exodus counted 600,000 males between the ages of 20 and 60; a rough demographic estimate makes for a total of 2–3 million people.

feelings to accept what is dictated to them by a higher authority, they are united only in word and deed; their inner selves remain different and distinct. Such a unity is inevitably short-lived: sooner or later their intrinsic differences and counter-aims will assert themselves, and fissures will begin to appear also in their unanimous exterior.

Rabbi Eliezer therefore asserts that if the people of Israel achieved true unity under the leadership of Moses at the Sea of Reeds, then it must have happened this way: that the people of Israel *repeated* each verse that issued from Moses' lips. Yes, they all submitted to the leadership of Moses, and saw in him the embodiment of their collective will and goals; but they did not suffice with a "blind" affirmation of his articulation of Israel's song. Rather, they repeated it after him, running it through the sieve of their own understanding and feelings, finding the roots for an identical declaration in their own personality and experience. Thus, the very same words assumed two million nuances of meaning, as they were absorbed by two million minds and articulated by two million mouths.

This, maintains Rabbi Eliezer, is the ultimate unity. When each repeats the verses uttered by Moses on their own, relating to them in their individual way, the singular vision of Moses has permeated each individual's being, uniting them in word as well as in essence.

Ultimate Unity

Rabbi Nechemiah, however, is still not satisfied. If Israel repeated these verses after Moses, argues Rabbi Nechemiah, this would imply that their song did not stem from the very deepest part of themselves. For if the people were truly one with Moses and his articulation of the quintessence of Israel, why would they need to hear their song from his lips before they could sing it themselves?

No, says Rabbi Nechemiah, the way it happened was that Moses pronounced the opening words of the song, following which each and every Jew, including "the infant at his mother's breast and the fetus in the womb,"⁷ sang the entire song themselves. Yes, it was Moses who achieved the unity of Israel, as evidenced by the fact that their song could not begin until Moses sang its opening words. Were it not for Moses' leadership, the people could not have risen above the selfishness that mars the surface of every character. Had not the people of Israel abnegated their will to his, they could not have uncovered the singular core of their own souls. But once they made that commitment, once they unequivocally responded to Moses' opening words, each *independently* conceived and articulated the very same experience of the historic moment in which they stood.

Each and every individual Jew, from the octogenarian sage to the unborn infant, expressed their deepest feelings and aspirations with the very same 187 words. For in Moses they had a leader in whom the soul of Israel was one.⁸

---

7   Talmud, *Sotah* 30b.
8   Based on an address by the Rebbe delivered on *Shevat* 11, 5748 (January 30, 1988), at a gathering marking the passing of the previous Lubavitcher Rebbe, Rabbi Yosef Yitzchak Schneersohn, on the tenth of *Shevat*, 5710 (1950), and the Rebbe's formal assumption of the leadership of Chabad-Lubavitch on the same date, one year later.

BRINGING G-D HOME

This is my G-d, and I shall make a home for Him;
the G-d of my fathers, and I shall exalt Him.

Exodus 15:2

There are two basic tools by which we relate to the divine reality: faith and reason. Each of these avenues contributes something unique to the relationship, so that, together, they complement and fulfill each other.

Our rational conception of G-d, defined by the limits of the human mind and of intellect *per se*, cannot encompass G-d's infinite and undefinable truth. Faith suffers no such limitation, being the unequivocal, unqualified acceptance of a truth greater than ourselves.

On the other hand, what we understand is real to us, whereas what we believe can be abstract and not personally meaningful. The Talmud describes a situation in which, "A thief, at the mouth of his tunnel, calls on G-d."[1] The thief obviously believes in G-d, since his instinctive reaction to his fear of capture is to call on Him; yet this does not prevent him from transgressing the divine command, "Do not steal," and even to appeal to G-d to assist his doing so.

Hence the need for both faith and reason. Where reason falls short of grasping the full extent of the divine infinity, faith fills the

---

[1] Talmud, *Berachot* 63a.

gap with its acceptance of G-d as G-d is, regardless of the degree to which G-d is understood. And when faith fails to make it relevant, the mind personalizes our perception of G-d and makes the divine reality real to us.

Exalted and Mine

This the deeper meaning of a key verse of the "Song at the Sea" sung by Moses and the Children of Israel upon their liberation from Egypt. The verse reads, "This is my G-d, and I shall make a home for Him; the G-d of my fathers, and I shall exalt Him."

When "this is *my* G-d," when my perception of G-d is personalized by my own understanding and appreciation of His truth, then, "I shall make a home for Him"—G-d's truth dwells within me and is an integral part of my being. The Hebrew word *anvehu* ("I shall make a home for Him") can also be read as an acronym of the words *ani v'hu*, "I and He," to say: with my rational understanding of G-d, I internalize His truth so that I and He are united.

On the other hand, when G-d is "the G-d of my fathers"—when I relate to G-d with the faith which I inherited from[2] and with which I was inculcated by my progenitors—this brings me to "exalt Him." This is a more exalted perception of the divine than "*my* G-d," as it is not limited to who and what I am and what my faculties can generate. But for that very reason, it is exalted beyond my everyday self, beyond the plane of my daily reality, necessitating my internalization of the divine truth through study and understanding.

---

2   See *Tanya*, chapter 18.

THE MANNA EATERS

Behold, I will rain down to you bread from heaven.

Exodus 16:4

The Torah was given to be expounded only to the eaters of the manna.

Midrash Mechilta, Beshalach 17

Whenever the sublime is brought down to earth, it seems to lose something in the translation. Somehow, when theory comes into practice, or when great inspiration is applied to everyday life, the result is less pure than the original.

But then there is the manna.

The manna was the "bread from heaven" that sustained us in our first generation as a nation, as we traversed the Sinai desert and acquired the wisdom of Torah. Indeed, our sages have said that "the Torah was given to be expounded only to the eaters of the manna."

What is the meaning of this statement? While the Torah relates that Moses and Aaron preserved a jar of manna for posterity,[1] the heavenly bread has not been part of our actual diet for more than 3,000 years. Does this mean that post-manna generations are incapable of expounding the Torah? Or is there some way that we, today, can also be manna eaters?

---

1 Exodus 16:33–34.

Flawless Digestion

The Torah describes the manna as the perfect food. Each individual's daily portion was exactly what he or she needed—not a morsel less or more. In addition, the manna encapsulated a person's nutritional needs so concisely that there was no waste—the body's limbs and organs absorbed and utilized it in a complete and optimum manner.[2]

Food is a prime example of the "waste" that accompanies the transition from spirit to substance. In one of the profound wonders of nature, the Creator has imbued physical foodstuffs with the power to sustain life. But because these vitalizing energies have been incarnated within physical bread and meat, and reach the body via the physical process of digestion, the transformation is not perfect. Although food is the material embodiment of a spiritual life-force, it is not a perfect embodiment; its coarser elements are nutritionally useless and are rejected by the body.

There is bread for the body, and there is bread for the soul. The book of Proverbs, calling upon us to nourish our lives with the divine wisdom of Torah, enjoins: "Come, partake of My bread."[3] The soul, too, has its nutritional needs, requiring a diet of wisdom, knowledge, and inspiration to sustain, develop, and vitalize its spiritual vision and endeavors. As is the case with the body, the soul becomes what it eats, metabolizing the stimuli it ingests and digests to make it the very substance of its being.

It might be argued that when the lofty concepts of Torah are brought down to earth and applied to our everyday existence, a certain degree of "waste" is inevitable; that certain aspects of the Torah's message and medium will prove archaic and superfluous in

---

2   Ibid., verse 18; Rashi on Numbers 21:5.
3   Proverbs 9:5.

the course of the digestive process, as is the fate of every attempted translation from the spiritual to the material. Comes the manna to teach us: this is only true of "bread from the earth," of *human* attempts to apply the sublime to the pedestrian. But the Torah is divine "bread from heaven"—a perfect, utterly efficient embodiment of the divine wisdom and will.

License to interpret the Torah is thus granted only to "the eaters of the manna"—to those who appreciate that there is no waste or selectivity in the Torah's timeless application to the human experience; that the Torah is perfect food for life, to be flawlessly "digested" by every age and culture; that it permeates and vitalizes every limb and organ of the universe, yet is never coarsened or compromised by its application to the nitty-gritty of physical life.

REASON, DOUBT, FAITH, AND MEMORY

The entire community of the Children of Israel journeyed... and they camped in Rephidim....

[Moses] named the place "Challenge and Strife," because of the strife of the Children of Israel, and their challenging of G-d, saying: Is G-d amongst us or not?

Then came Amalek and attacked Israel in Rephidim.

Exodus 17:1–8

The Jewish people had just experienced one of the greatest manifestations of divine power in history. Ten supernatural plagues had compelled the mightiest nation on earth to free them from their servitude. The sea had split before them, and manna had rained down from the heavens to nourish them. How could they possibly question, "Is G-d amongst us or not"?

Yet such is the nature of doubt. There is doubt that is based on rational query. There is doubt that arises from the doubter's subjective motives and desires. But then there is doubt pure and simple: irrational doubt, doubt more powerful than reason. Doubt that neutralizes the most convincing arguments and the most inspiring experiences with nothing more than a cynical shrug.

Such was the doubt that left the Jewish people susceptible to attack from Amalek. "Amalek," in the spiritual sphere, is the essence of baseless, irrational indifference. In the words of the Midrash:

> *To what is the incident [of Amalek] comparable? To a boiling tub of water which no creature was able to enter. Along came one evildoer and jumped into it. Although he was burned, he cooled it for the others.*
>
> *So, too, when Israel came out of Egypt, and G-d rent the sea before them and drowned the Egyptians within it, the fear of them was upon all the nations. But when Amalek came and challenged them, although he received his due from them, he cooled the awe of them for the nations of the world.*[1]

Truth can refute the logical arguments offered against it. Truth can even prevail over a person's selfish drives and desires, for intrinsic to the nature of man is the axiom that the "mind rules over the heart"—that a person has the capacity to so thoroughly appreciate a truth that it is ingrained in their character and implemented in their behavior.[2] But our rational faculties are powerless against the challenge of an Amalek who leaps into the boiling tub, who brazenly mocks the truth and cools our most inspired moments with nothing more than a dismissive "So what?"

This is why Amalek and what it represents constitutes the arch enemy of the Jewish people and of our mission in life. As Moses proclaimed, "G-d has sworn by His throne; G-d is at war with Amalek for all generations."[3] The Torah establishes three distinct

---

1   *Midrash Tanchuma, Ki Teitzei* 9. The Hebrew word *karcha*, "he encountered you," employed in Deuteronomy 25:18 to describe Amalek's attack on Israel, also translates as "he cooled you."
2   *Zohar* 3:224a; *Tanya*, chapter 12.
3   Exodus 17:16.

mitzvot devoted to remembering Amalek's deed, eradicating his memory, and not forgetting the challenge that Amalek poses:

> *Remember what Amalek did to you on the road, on your way out of Egypt. That he encountered you on the way, and he cut off those lagging to your rear, when you were tired and exhausted; he did not fear G-d. Therefore ... you must obliterate the memory of Amalek from under the heavens. Do not forget.*[4]

Amalek attacked us "on the road, on your way out of Egypt," as we were headed toward Mount Sinai to receive G-d's Torah and our mandate as G-d's people. Here, too, history mirrors the inner workings of the soul. The timing of the historical Amalek's attack describes the internal circumstances under which the pestilence of baseless doubt rears its head—when we are on the road, after having achieved our own personal "Exodus from Egypt."

The Personal Exodus

In the Passover *Haggadah* we say: "In every generation, a person should see himself as if he himself came out of *Mitzrayim*."

Mitzrayim, the Hebrew word for Egypt, means "narrow straits." On the personal level, this refers to what chassidic teaching calls the "narrow strait of the neck" which intersects between the mind and the heart. For just as, physically, the head and the heart are joined by the narrow passageway of the neck, so it is in the spiritual-psychological sense.

The mind, as mentioned earlier, possesses an innate superiority over the heart; yet it is a most difficult and challenging task

---

4   Deuteronomy 25:17–19.

for a person to exercise this superiority. It is no easy task to make our feelings and desires conform with what we know to be right. This is the "Exodus from *mitzrayim*" that is incumbent on each and every one of us: to negotiate the narrow strait of our internal "neck" and overcome the material enticements, the emotional subjectivity, and the ego and self-interest which undermine the mind's authority over the heart and impede its influence on our character and behavior.[5]

The Final Challenge

Then, once we achieve our personal Exodus, there remains one final challenge: the challenge of Amalek.

As long as we are still imprisoned in our personal *mitzrayim*, we face many challenges to our integrity. As long as we have not succeeded in establishing our mind as the axis on which all else revolves, our base instincts and traits—such as greed, anger, the quest for power and instant gratification—may get the better of us. But once we achieve this personal Exodus, once we establish our knowledge and understanding of the truth as the determining force in our life, the battle is all but won. We may be confronted with negative ideas and rationalizations, but free of the distortions of self-interest, the truth will triumph. We may be tempted by negative drives and desires, but if in our life the mind rules the heart, it will curb and ultimately transform them.

But there remains one enemy which threatens also the post-Exodus individual: Amalek. Amalek "knows his Master and

---

[5] See the essay, "When to Weep," in vol. I (Genesis) of *The Inside Story*, pp. 391–398.

deliberately rebels against Him."⁶ Amalek does not challenge the truth with arguments, or even with selfish motivations—he just disregards it. To the axiom, "Do truth because it is true,"⁷ Amalek says "So what?" Armed with nothing but his chutzpah, Amalek jumps into the boiling tub and contests the incontestable. And in doing so, he cools its impact.

Memory of the Soul

How is one to respond to Amalek? How is one to deal with the apathy, the cynicism, the senseless doubt within? Amalek is irrational and totally unresponsive to reason; the answer to Amalek is likewise suprarational.

In his *Tanya*, Rabbi Schneur Zalman of Liadi discusses the faith in G-d that is integral to the Jewish soul. Faith is not something that must be attained; it need only be uncovered, for it is woven into the very fabric of the soul's essence. Faith, continues Rabbi Schneur Zalman, transcends reason. Through faith, a person relates to the infinite truth of G-d in its totality, unlike the perception achieved by reason, which is defined and limited by the finite nature of the human mind.

Thus Rabbi Schneur Zalman explains an amazing phenomenon: throughout Jewish history, many thousands of Jews have sacrificed their lives rather than renounce their faith and their bond with the Almighty, including many who had little conscious knowledge and appreciation of their Jewishness and did not practice it in their daily lives. At their moment of truth, when they perceived that their very identity as Jews was at stake, their intrinsic

---

6   See *Torat Kohanim*, Leviticus 26:14; *Derech Mitzvotecha* 95a.
7   See *Mishneh Torah, Laws of Repentance*, 10:2.

faith—a faith that knows no bounds or equivocations—came to light and overpowered all else.⁸

Our response to Amalek is to remember. To call forth our soul's reserves of suprarational faith, a faith which may lie buried and forgotten under a mass of mundane involvements and entanglements. A faith which, when remembered, can meet his every moral challenge, rational or not.

---

8   *Tanya*, chapter 18.

PARASHAH
SEVENTEEN

YITRO

Exodus 18:1–20:23

Revelation and law

CAPTAINS OF THOUSAND

Why was he called Yitro? Because he added a chapter to the Torah—[the chapter] "You should see [to choose] from the people…"

Midrash Rabbah, Shemot 27:8

In the Torah section of *Yitro* (Exodus 18:1–20:23), we read of the most important event in Jewish history, the event that defines our Jewishness to this very day: the revelation at Mount Sinai, where G-d proclaimed the Ten Commandments and gave us the Torah.

Ostensibly, the name *Yitro* derives from the opening lines of the Torah section, which begins by relating that "Jethro [*Yitro*, in the Hebrew], the priest of Midian and the father-in-law of Moses, heard of all that G-d did for Moses, and for His people Israel," and came to join Moses and the people of Israel at their encampment at the foot of Mount Sinai.[1]

Yet the name of a thing, particularly the name of a section of Torah, always expresses its essential quality.[2] We would therefore have expected that the name of the section that describes the giving of the Torah would reflect the specialness of that event. Instead, it is named after a seemingly minor character in the

---

1   Exodus 18:1–5.
2   See the essay, "The Soul of Evil," on pp. 70–75 above. Also see the essays, "A Legacy of Laughter," "Life After Life," and "The Human Story in Twelve Words," in vol. I (Genesis) of *The Inside Story*.

biblical narrative, whose role in the events described in our section actually take place several months *after* the revelation at Sinai.³ Obviously, Jethro and what he represents expresses something very fundamental about the revelation at Sinai and the manner in which the Torah—the "wisdom and will of G-d"⁴—was communicated to us to guide and instruct our lives.

Jethro's Addition

The Torah was communicated to us through Moses; indeed, the prophet Malachi goes so far as to refer to the word of G-d as "The Torah of Moses."⁵ On several occasions, however, other individuals are given credit for the revelation of a particular section. The book of Numbers (9:6–14) relates how the laws of the "Second Passover" came as G-d's response to a group of people who were ritually impure, but refused to reconcile themselves with the fact that they could not participate in the Passover offering; the sages tell us that these laws "ought to have been related by Moses, like the rest of the Torah; but these people merited that it be revealed

---

3   Jethro's arrival in the Israelite camp and the administrative plan he proposed to Moses are described in the 18th chapter of Exodus, while the revelation at Sinai is recounted in chapters 19, 20, and 24. However, according to a majority of the commentaries, Jethro's proposal was made on the 11th of *Tishrei* (the day after the Second Tablets were given on Yom Kippur), more than four months after the revelation at Sinai on the sixth of *Sivan* of the previous year. According to one opinion, Jethro's arrival in the camp was also after the giving of the Torah. This is in keeping with the rule that "there is no earlier and later in Torah"— i.e., that Torah's narratives do not necessarily appear in chronological order. See *Mechilta* on Exodus 18:13; Rashi, ad loc.; Talmud, *Zevachim* 116a and *Pesachim* 6b. See, however, a dissenting view in *Daat Zekeinim MiBaalei HaTosafot* on Exodus, ad loc.
4   See *Tanya*, chapter 4 and 5.
5   Malachi 3:22.

by their initiative."[6] The same is said regarding the laws of inheritance (Numbers 27:6–11) whose revelation was prompted by the daughters of Zelophehad;[7] the penalty for desecrating Shabbat (Numbers 15:35–36) prompted by the "wood gatherer";[8] and so on.

Jethro, Moses' father-in-law, is also credited with a section of Torah. Indeed, his name, *Yitro* in the Hebrew, means "his addition," and was given him "because he added a chapter to the Torah." In this, the case of Jethro is unique. In all other instances, nothing was "added" to the Torah—these were laws that would have been included in the Torah in any case, for without them the Torah is not complete; it was only that instead of being communicated directly to Moses, as was the rest of the Torah, certain individuals had the merit to be involved in the process of their revelation. Only Jethro's section is referred to as an "addition," implying that it would not have been part of the Torah were it not for his initiative. In other words, the Torah was complete without this section, and Jethro added something to it.

On the other hand, the statement that this section was *added* to the Torah implies that, as a result of its addition, it is now part of Torah—no less so than its other laws, principles, and narratives.

What was Jethro's addition? What did it contribute to the manner in which we apprehend the divine wisdom and apply it to our lives?

Delegated Authority

As related in the eighteenth chapter of the book of Exodus, following Jethro's arrival in the Israelite camp he was shocked to discover

---

6   *Sifri*, Numbers 9:8.
7   Talmud, *Bava Batra* 119a.
8   Ibid.

that Moses was serving as a one-man educational and judicial system for a community of more than two million souls.[9] "Why do you sit alone," he asked his son-in-law, "and the entire people stand about you from morning till evening?"

Moses replied: "The people come to me to seek G-d. When they have a matter of dispute they come to me, and I judge between a man and his fellow. I teach them the laws of G-d and His instructions."

Said Jethro: "It is not good, this thing that you are doing. You will wither away, both you and this people who are with you... you cannot do this alone." Jethro went on to suggest that Moses should select from among the people "able men, who fear G-d, men of truth, who abhor profit," and appoint them as arbiters and judges. Moses should continue to teach the people "the laws and the instructions ... the path they should follow and the deeds they should do." But the application of these laws to the daily life of the camp—the resolution of questions and the settlement of disputes—should be delegated to these appointees. "They shall judge the people at all times; the great matters they shall present to you, and the minor things they shall arbitrate themselves."

The Torah concludes its account of this incident by saying that "Moses listened to the voice of his father-in-law and he did all that he said." He implemented Jethro's plan, appointing "captains of thousand, captains of hundred, captains of fifty, and captains of ten." The people were themselves entrusted with the application of the divine law to their daily lives, while Moses confined his role to teaching them the laws and deciding the most difficult issues.[10]

---

9   A census taken several months later counted 603,550 males between the ages of 20 and 60, excluding the tribe of Levi.
10 Exodus 18:14–26.

A Reluctant Mouthpiece

This was not the first time that such a "delegation of authority" had been suggested to Moses, contrary to his initial desires. A similar thing had occurred four months earlier,[11] when the people of Israel assembled at the foot of Mount Sinai to receive the Torah from G-d.

At Sinai, the divine voice pronounced the first two of the Ten Commandments ("I am G-d your G-d..." and "You shall have no other gods before Me..."). But, as Moses later recounts the events of that day, the people approached Moses and argued that they were incapable of receiving a direct communication from G-d. "You approach," they begged Moses, "and hear all that G-d our G-d will say. You tell us all that G-d our G-d will say to you, and we will listen and do."[12]

Moses was deeply disappointed to hear this, as it was his desire that the people should receive the entire Torah directly from the mouth of G-d.[13] But G-d said to him:

> *I have heard the words that the people have spoken to you; they have spoken well... Go and say to them: "Return to your tents." And you remain here with Me, and I will relate to you the commandments, the statutes, and the laws that you shall teach them...*[14]

One way of understanding this exchange is that Moses misjudged the people's capacity for divine revelation, assuming that they could receive the Torah directly from G-d, but G-d confirmed the people's own contention that this was beyond their capability.

---

11 See footnote 3 above.
12 Deuteronomy 5:20–24; also see Exodus 20:16–18.
13 See Rashi's commentary to Deuteronomy 5:24.
14 Deuteronomy 5:25–28.

This explanation, however, is not consistent with what we know about Moses and his relationship with the people of Israel.

Moses was not only a great and holy man; he was Israel's leader—the greatest leader we have ever known. He was a "faithful shepherd"[15] to his people, feeding their bodies and nourishing their souls, sensitive to the individual needs of every member of his flock.[16] Accordingly, the deeper significance of the exchange between between the people and Moses at the foot of Mount Sinai is not that Moses "overestimated" his people when he desired that they receive the Torah directly from G-d. On the contrary: he perceived their true and ultimate potential, and as a true leader, he endeavored to actualize it. In Moses' eyes, the people of Israel were capable of assimilating the highest revelations, and under his leadership, they could have achieved this.

But the people did not want to relate to G-d on this level. They wanted to receive the Torah with their own, *self-actualized* faculties, not with the sublime powers that Moses could summon forth from the depths of their souls. They wanted that their experience of Torah should be true to how they are to themselves, rather than to how Moses sees them.

G-d agreed. After having been exposed to the divine essence of Torah (as contained within the first two commandments), they would receive the Torah not as a supernal voice from Heaven, but as ideas formulated in a human mind, as words articulated by a human mouth and put in writing by a human hand. They would receive the Torah via the mind, mouth, and pen of Moses.

---

15   *Raaya meheimna.* Also translated, "shepherd of faith," in the sense that Moses is Israel's conduit of faith, the one who inculcates them with their knowledge and recognition of G-d, as a shepherd who feeds his flocks their vital needs (see *Tanya,* ch. 42).

16   See *Midrash Rabbah, Shemot* 2:2. Also see the essay, "The Runaway Kid," p. 13 above.

The Outsider's View

The dialogue between Moses and Jethro, which resulted in Jethro's "addition" to the Torah, bears many similarities to the above-discussed dialogue between Moses and the people following the revelation at Sinai. In fact, it is basically the same debate, albeit in regard to different aspects of Torah. The debate between Moses and the people was regarding the dynamics of the *communication of the Torah from G-d to us*, while the debate between Moses and Jethro was regarding the dynamics of the *application* of Torah to our everyday lives.[17]

Having learned the divine laws from Moses, how were they to be implemented in the people's daily lives? How were they to be translated into guidance for raising a child, righting a troubled marriage, or resolving a dispute between neighbors?

One might go to Moses. He received these laws from G-d; his knowledge and understanding of them is absolute. His application is certain to be the most authentic, unequivocal rendition of the divine law.

It is true that Moses is a million miles away from the petty neighbors' dispute he is being troubled to resolve. But it is also true that the two litigants standing before Moses are certain to be elevated by the experience. In the presence of Moses, they, too, are capable of rising above the pettiness of their conflict. In the presence of Moses, they, too, are capable of relating to the pure

---

17 Otherwise stated, the first debate was in regard to the nature of the "Written Torah," and the second debate was in regard to the nature of the "Oral Torah." Because of Jethro's "addition," the process that generates the Oral Torah was made an integral part of the Written Torah itself, meaning that the two are not distinct elements, but a single, integrated continuum.

principle being expounded, and of applying it to their relations back in their neighborhood.

This was how it was done until Jethro proposed his plan.

Jethro was an outsider—a convert to Judaism who, by most accounts, was not even present at the revelation at Mount Sinai.[18] Moses saw the people of Israel from the inside—in the light of their highest potentials, from the perspective of the inner core of their souls as they are one with his own soul in the singular soul of Israel. Jethro saw them from the outside—from the vantage point of their everyday selves, their petty cares and conflicts. He saw them as they are apart from Moses, while Moses saw them only as they are in the presence of Moses.

So Jethro suggested to Moses that the people of Israel learn to govern themselves, to arbitrate their disputes, to apply the laws of Torah to their lives. Moses was to remain the source of these laws; but their implementation was to be achieved by a multi-tiered body of magistrates and counselors at every level of the community—"captains of ten, captains of hundred, and captains of thousand." In this way, the divine law would permeate their lives on every level, not only at the apogee of their being.

This is what Jethro "added" to the Torah. Without his addition, the Torah was complete. Indeed, there was no real need for Jethro's system, for Moses could always be counted on to raise the lives of his people to the level on which he expounded the word of G-d. But their understanding and practice of Torah would have remained something that Moses had empowered them to attain, not something they had attained on their own. Jethro's system made the Torah the personal achievement of every individual.

---

[18] See sources cited in note 3 above.

More significantly, Jethro's initiative was accepted and implemented by Moses, *and written into the Torah*. Were it not for Jethro, the Torah would have remained a guide to life for Moseses and Moses-elevated Jews. After Moses' passing, a system such as Jethro's would have been established, to "bring down" Moses' Torah to a lesser generation. But this process would have been a mechanism that is not itself part of the Torah.

Jethro, however, insisted that Moses delegate of his capacity to interpret the Torah to the sages of his generation, and by extension, to the sages of all generations. Because it was *Moses* who established this system, it was incorporated as a section in Torah, making it an integral part of G-d's original communication to us. Because of Jethro, when we study Torah today, using our own finite capabilities to understand it and apply it to our lives, we are not relating to some "lesser" version of Torah, but to the divine wisdom as transmitted to us through Moses.[19]

---

[19] This is the meaning of the statement by the sages, "Everything that a qualified student of Torah is destined to innovate was already given to Moses at Sinai" (Jerusalem Talmud, *Pe'ah* 2:4; see glosses of Gra, ad loc.). The Talmud refers to the student's achievement as an "innovation" (*chidush*, in the Hebrew), yet says that it was already given to Moses! In other words, for an interpretation to be an authentic part of Torah, it must derive from the authority of Moses; yet Moses transmitted the Torah to us in such a way that enables our understanding of it to be our "own" achievement. See also *Tanya*, chapter 42.

SHARDS OR SPARKS?

G-d spoke all these words, to say.

Exodus 20:1

Scripture, Mishnah, Talmud, and aggadah—*even what a proficient pupil is destined to innovate—was already said to Moses at Sinai.*

Jerusalem Talmud, Pe'ah 2:4

Quoting the verse (Jeremiah 23:29), "My words are like fire, and like a hammer that shatters a rock," the Talmud expounds:

> Just as a hammer divides into many sparks, so does a single verse of Torah yield many meanings.[1]

This teaching itself is no exception; it, too, spawns several interpretations by the sages.

Rashi understands the metaphor to mean, "Just as a hammer divides *the rock* into many sparks..." According to this, the "sparks" the Talmud speaks of are the rock-fragments of the shattered stone. In other words, the Torah itself is the "rock" that breaks up into different fragments, each representing a different meaning of its words. This interpretation is in keeping with the wording of the

---

[1] Talmud, *Sanhedrin* 34a and *Shabbat* 88b.

verse on which the metaphor is based, which likens the word of G-d to "a hammer that shatters a rock."[2]

Others understand the word "sparks" in the literal sense—i.e., the sparks that are generated by the hammer when it strikes a rock. According to this interpretation, the word "shatters" is to be understood in the sense of "scatters."[3] In other words, the Torah is the "hammer" which, upon striking the rock, lets fly many sparks, representing its divergent meanings.

When the Hammer Strikes the Rock

What is the deeper significance of these variant interpretations?

Often, a student of Torah might be inclined to favor one mode of Torah study over the others. A certain type of mind might tend to a literal approach to Torah's narratives, and be interested primarily in what actually happened historically, and what the Torah is saying on the most basic, pragmatic level. Another might adopt an exclusively "Talmudic" stance, with an eye only to the legal dimension of Torah. A third is drawn most strongly to the philosophical implications of the texts, while a fourth is inspired by the mysticism of its kabbalistic interpretations.

In this sense, G-d's word is as a hammer that shatters a rock, breaking it into fragments of diverse sizes and shapes. Each of us can find the particular fragment that most appeals to him- or herself, the one that best fits the form and texture of their own nature and aptitudes.

---

2   Rashi on Talmud, *Shabbat*, ad loc.
3   Maharal, *Divrei Dovid*, and *Nimukei Shmuel* on Rashi, Exodus 6:9. For yet a third interpretation, see Tosafot on Talmud, *Shabbat* 88b and *Sanhedrin* 34a.

However, we should remember that G-d's word is also as a hammer that lets fly sparks—a spray of unquantifiable pinpoints of energy.

When the hammer of divine wisdom strikes the rock of reality, the sparks fly off in all directions. Some ascend to the esoteric heights, others cascade down to the pragmatic ground; still others meander off to philosophical, psychological, inspirational, and countless other points of the cosmic compass. But can one measure sparks against each other? Can one say that any one spark is greater, brighter, or more relevant than its fellows?

SIGHTING THE SOUNDS

All the people saw the sounds and the flames and the mountain smoking; the people saw and trembled, and stood afar.
Exodus 20:15

Rabbi Ishmael says: They saw what is seen and heard what is heard. Rabbi Akiva says: They saw what is heard and heard what is seen.
Midrash Mechilta, ad loc.

Thirty-three centuries ago, the entire Jewish nation witnessed the revelation of G-d at Mount Sinai. Centuries later, two Talmudic sages, Rabbi Akiva and Rabbi Ishmael, offered somewhat differing accounts of the experience.

One difference between them concerns the manner in which the revelation at Sinai was perceived by our senses. After recounting the proclamation of the Ten Commandments at Sinai, the Torah relates: "All the people saw the sounds and the flames and the mountain smoking; the people saw and trembled, and stood afar."

What does it mean that they "saw the sounds"? According to Rabbi Akiva, the manner in which we perceived the sights and sounds of Sinai was radically different from the way in which such stimuli are ordinarily assimilated. At Sinai, our senses of sight and hearing reversed their roles—we "saw what is [ordinarily] heard, and heard what is [ordinarily] seen." Not so, says Rabbi Ishmael.

At Sinai, we experienced the greatest divine revelation of all time in the same manner in which we ordinarily relate to reality: we "saw what is seen and heard what is heard." According to Rabbi Ishmael, the word "saw" in the verse refers to the "flames" and the "smoking mountain" mentioned later in the sentence.

But both interpretations of the verse raise as many questions as they answer. Regarding Rabbi Akiva's description of an extraordinary transmutation of our senses, we can ask: Amazing, but why? We know that, as a rule, the Creator is loath to suspend the natural order of things; miracles are rare, and come only to achieve a specific end.[1] How would Rabbi Akiva explain the purpose for such a nature-trouncing feat?

As for Rabbi Ishmael's view, it raises the question as to what this verse is coming to tell us in the first place. The Torah has already described the thunder, the *shofar* blast, the lightning, the fire, and the smoke which accompanied G-d's descent upon Sinai.[2] Need we be told that the people of Israel saw these sights and heard these sounds?

"Seeing" versus "Hearing"

As tools of perception, sight and hearing differ in two significant ways.

Sight is a very physical experience: we see the thing itself—its mass, its immanence, the brute fact of its being. Hearing, on the other hand, registers stimuli of a more metaphysical nature. We see a wall, but we hear music, emotional inflections, ideas. This is even more so regarding the other meaning of "to hear" which is

---

[1] *Derashot HaRan*, 8. See also Genesis 8:22; Talmud, *Shabbat* 53b.
[2] Exodus 19:16–19.

"to comprehend" (in Hebrew, the word *shemi'ah* means both "hearing" and "comprehension"). We hear and understand things that are too ethereal to be captured by the physical eye.

A second difference is the manner in which sight and hearing affect us—the extent to which they impress their findings upon our mind and heart. Sight is the most convincing of faculties: once we have seen something with "our own eyes," it is virtually impossible for other sensory evidence or rational proofs to refute what we now know. Hearing and comprehension, on the other hand, are far less vivid impressers of the information they convey. They will convince us of certain truths, but not as unequivocally as do our eyes. What we hear and understand are facts which have been "proven" to us; what we see is reality.

(This difference is also reflected in Torah law. The Talmud[3] rules that a judge who has witnessed a crime cannot sit in judgment over the case. Why not? Is not the entire point of the trial that the judge should learn the truth? Here we have a judge who knows what happened, not through second-hand information received from witnesses, but by the testimony of his own eyes! Explains the Talmud: "Since he has seen the accused commit the crime, he is incapable of seeing him in the right." A judge must consider more than what the accused did or did not do; he must also examine issues such as intent and culpability. When the judge merely *hears* from witnesses that the accused committed a criminal act—even if he is convinced that they are telling the truth—he can still maintain the proper distance to objectively consider the other factors which may absolve the accused from guilt. But when he himself *sees* what happened, the fact of the accused's criminal deed is not only known but also real to him, making it extremely

---

3   Talmud, *Rosh Hashanah* 26a.

difficult for him to override this unequivocal reality with logical considerations.)

These two differences between sight and hearing are interconnected. We are physical beings inhabiting a physical reality. The physical is real to us, while the conceptual and metaphysical are foreign and insubstantial. So sight, which perceives physical objects, is definitive and absolute, whereas the intangibles perceived via the ear and mind are, at most, "proven facts," always subject to reassessment and reconsideration.

Seeing G-dliness, Hearing the World

The story is told of the mystic who tells the philosopher: "Do you know the difference between you and me? You are constantly thinking about G-d, while I am forever thinking about myself."

The philosopher was very pleased with the compliment. But one day it dawned on him what the old sage had meant. The philosopher is convinced that he, the thinker, exists, and doesn't give it a second thought. So he ponders the existence of G-d: Does G-d exist? What is G-d? How does His existence affect us? To the mystic, however, G-d is the very essence of reality. But where does that leave *us*? What possible legitimacy can our finite and transitory existence have within the all-transcending, all pervading reality of G-d? The divine truth a given, the mystic ponders his own subjective reality: Do I exist? What significance, if any, is there to my existence? Why do I exist?

This is what Rabbi Akiva means when he says that at Sinai we "saw what is heard, and heard what is seen." Ordinarily, it is our physical existence that is "seen" and real to us. Of course, we understand that all this has a Creator and a purpose. There is proof of it in the majesty and complexity of the universe; every throb of life bespeaks it, and every stirring of conscience in the soul of man. But this higher reality is merely "heard" in our world—deduced, sensed, even experienced—but never perceived with the unequivocal realness of sight. To us, reality is the physical; everything else is merely a concept.

But not at Sinai. At Sinai our eyes were opened, and we "saw the G-d of Israel."[4] We saw what is heard, what is ordinarily abstract and "spiritual." And we heard what is seen: our formidable world, so real and tangible, was suddenly a distant echo, a concept. For if G-d is Reality, if the essence of existence is the infinite and omnipresent divine truth, what is our world? Just an illusion? But no, there must be a world—otherwise, what is the significance of creation? Of the Torah and its commandments? All this tells us that our world does exist—it *proves* it to us. What is ordinarily a given is now a substantiated theory.

Holding Our Ground

Rabbi Ishmael disagrees. As he sees it, the revelation at Sinai did not come to turn our natural reality upside down. The function of Torah is not to overwhelm and negate our world, but to enable us to deal with it, on its own terms, and uncover its potential to reflect the goodness and perfection of its Creator.

This, maintains Rabbi Ishmael, is an even greater miracle than for the material reality to evaporate the moment G-d introduces Himself. That would be the most obvious and "natural" thing to happen. But at Sinai we achieved an even greater feat: we held our ground. Brought face-to-face with the Divine, we refused to make this an otherworldly experience, a refutation of our finite

---

4 Exodus 24:10.

and subjective existence. Instead, we insisted on applying the revelation to *our* reality. We saw and heard G-dliness, but on our terms, seeing what is seen and hearing what is heard. The physical remained real and the spiritual remained abstract, and both were permeated with the vision of their divine essence and purpose.

Responding to the Commandments

The Midrash relates a second difference of opinion between Rabbi Akiva and Rabbi Ishmael regarding the revelation at Sinai, pertaining to how we responded to G-d's proclamation of the Ten Commandments.

The Torah relates that "G-d spoke all these words, to say: 'I am G-d your Lord... You shall have no other gods before Me...'"[5] The Midrash is puzzled by the Torah's use of the word *leimor*, "to say." What does it mean that "G-d spoke all these words, to say"? Throughout the Torah, dozens of laws are preceded by the phrase, "G-d spoke to Moses, to say..."; but in those instances, Moses is being instructed to convey those divine directives to the Jewish people. Obviously, *leimor* cannot be so interpreted in our case, as all of Israel were present at Sinai. Explains the Midrash: "to say" means that the people responded to each of the Ten Commandments, affirming their commitment to its observance.

What did they say?

> They says "yes" to the yeses, and "no" to the nos. This is the opinion of Rabbi Ishmael.
>
> Rabbi Akiva says: They said "yes" to the yeses, and "yes" to the nos.[6]

---

5 Ibid., 20:1–3.
6 *Mechilta*, ad loc.

The Ten Commandments include "positive commandments," such as, "Honor your father and your mother" and "Remember the day of Shabbat," as well as "negative commandments" or prohibitions, such as "Do not murder" and "Do not steal." According to Rabbi Ishmael, when we heard G-d proclaim the commandments, we responded "Yes," to the positive commandments (i.e., "Yes, we will do so"), and "No" to the prohibitions (i.e., "No, we will not do so"). Rabbi Akiva disagrees. According to his understanding of the dialogue between G-d and us at Sinai, we said "Yes" to each of the positive commandments, and "Yes" (i.e., "Yes, we will obey") to the prohibitions.

But what is the point of their disagreement? In either case, our response was to declare our readiness to uphold both the positive and negative commandments of G-d. What difference does it make if we said the word "yes" or the word "no," if the meaning of both these responses is the same?

The Positive No

There are two ways of relating to the divine commandments in the Torah. One approach is to view them through the lens of human experience: to appreciate the wisdom gained from Torah study, the spiritual elevation achieved by prayer, the tranquility experienced on Shabbat, the educational potential of a Passover *seder*, the social value of charity. On the "negative" side, we can appreciate the importance of the *mitzvot* that prohibit theft, gossip, promiscuity, food harmful to the body and psyche, and so on. Indeed, our sages have said that "The *mitzvot* were given in order to refine humanity."[7]

---

[7] *Midrash Rabbah, Bereishith* 44:1.

But is any of this truly relevant? After all, these are G-d's commandments. What greater achievement can there possibly be than to carry out G-d's will? From this perspective, all *mitzvot* are equal, for all else pales to insignificance before this one monumental fact. In the words of Rabbi Schneur Zalman of Liadi, "had we been commanded to chop wood," this would be no less a *mitzvah* than the most enlightening, fulfilling, and character-refining of G-d's commandments.[8]

This is why Rabbi Akiva maintains that we responded "Yes" to the positive commandments and "Yes" to the prohibitions. At Sinai, Rabbi Akiva is saying, there was no such thing as a "negative" *mitzvah*.

Indeed, one who views the *mitzvot* in terms of their beneficial effects on their personal life and on society, will distinguish between the positive commandments and the prohibitions. To give a million dollars to charity is to *do* something. But what is accomplished by refraining from eating nonkosher foods? To eat that cheeseburger would be detrimental to one's spiritual health; but to not eat it is to do—nothing. But at Sinai, says Rabbi Akiva, we were beyond all that. We saw what is heard and heard what is seen. The material world, with its "issues" and pretensions for significance, was but a figment of the imagination. Reality was G-d. From such a vantage point, who would think of G-d's expressed will in terms of moral and social utility?

To one who stands at Sinai, says Rabbi Akiva, the definition of *mitzvah* is an opportunity to fulfill G-d's will. Everything else is of secondary, "hearable" significance. When you give a million dollars to charity, you are doing something: you are fulfilling G-d's will. When you refrain from eating a forbidden food, you are

---

8   *Likutei Torah, Shelach* 40a.

doing something: you are fulfilling G-d's will. Every *mitzvah* is a positive act, the same positive act, the ultimate positive act—the implementation of a divine desire. Every *mitzvah* elicits the same *positive* response: "Yes, we will."

On Our Terms

Rabbi Ishmael disagrees. Assembled at Sinai, we obviously knew that the ultimate significance of the *mitzvah* is that it is G-d's will. But we knew this as a sublime truth, as a concept that is "heard" and understood but remains beyond our tangible grasp. Our reality was the physical existence, and the point of revelation at Sinai was not to overturn our perspective but to perfect the one we had. What was real to us—what we "saw"—was the way in which the *mitzvot* sanctify our everyday lives and create a world that is at peace with itself and its Creator.

So there *are* differences between *mitzvot*—most significantly, the difference between "do" and "don't," as befits dealing with a world polarized by good and evil. There are *mitzvot* with which we develop the positive in our world, and those which guide us in the rejection of the negative; *mitzvot* which cultivate the light, and *mitzvot* which combat the darkness.

At Sinai, says Rabbi Ishmael, we heard what is heard and saw what is seen. True, we understood that the essence of a *mitzvah* is beyond anything our finite physical selves can relate to. But our primary response to G-d's commandments was to embrace them as the foundation of our lives—lives defined by the yes and no of our reality.

A GIFT AND A TEST

In order to test you, G-d came...

Exodus 20:17

The giving of the Torah at Mount Sinai was many things. It was a divine revelation, the first (and thus far, only) time that G-d enabled us to apprehend His very being; it was the making of a nation, the people of Israel; it was the communication of the divine blueprint for creation to mankind; it was, say the chassidic masters, a foretaste of the messianic World to Come.[1] But why was it a test?

If we examine the different contexts in which the Torah uses the term *nisayon* ("test"),[2] we discover that the tests in our lives come in various forms:

Inevitably, there are the "temptation" tests. The financially profitable but morally dubious business deal; the verily deserved insult on the verge of one's lips. In these and countless other ways, our integrity is constantly tested.

There are tests of travail and tribulation. How do we react to the troubles in our life? Do we lose hope, or do we trust in the Almighty that all is for the best? Poverty, illness, even the front-page news will often undermine our sense of G-d's goodness and of the G-dliness of life.

---

1 See *Tanya*, chapter 36.
2 E.g., Genesis 22:1; Exodus 15:25; ibid., 16:4; Deuteronomy 8:16; ibid., 13:4; Psalms 26:2; Job 4:2.

There are tests of faith, when our thoughts and experiences clash with what we know to be right and true, and we are challenged to affirm the beliefs and convictions that reside at the very core of our souls.

Certainly the most prodigious of the lot are the "martyrdom" tests. We are awed by those who did not bow before the crusader's sword or the inquisitor's tortures. Who chose to die true rather than live a lie.

Finally, there are the innumerable tests, great and small, which come in the guise of a "gift." Indeed, the windfalls of life—an exceptional talent, an unexpected profit, an enlightening experience—can, in a certain sense, be the most challenging of tests. How will we respond to the gifts we have been granted? Will we utilize them optimally and constructively? Or will we stow away these treasures in the attics and cellars of our lives, their potential unlocked and their possibilities unrealized?

At Sinai, G-d granted us the most fundamental gift of them all: the gift of wisdom and purpose. So immediately following the greatest divine revelation of all time, Moses tells the assembled nation of Israel: "In order to test you, G-d came..."

PARASHAH
EIGHTEEN

MISHPATIM

Exodus 21:1–24:18

In the courtroom of the soul

OXEN AND SOULS

And these are the laws which you shall set before them: If you purchase a Hebrew servant... If a man strikes his fellow with a stone or with his fist... If a person's ox gores the ox of his fellow... If a person gives his friend money or utensils to watch and they are stolen from the [guardian's] home...   Exodus 21:1–22:6

The *mitzvot* (divine commandments) of the Torah are commonly divided into two categories: (a) laws that govern the relationship "between man and G‑d"; and (b) laws that legislate the proper conduct "between man and his fellow." Even the Ten Commandments, which are an encapsulation of the entire Torah, were inscribed on two separate tablets: one containing commandments such as "I am G-d your G-d," and "Remember the day of Shabbat," and the other bearing laws like "Do not murder" and "Do not steal."

Yet the two categories are deeply interrelated. The *Zohar* states that the divine statements, "I am G‑d your G‑d," and "You shall have no other gods before Me," are the essence of all 613 commandments and prohibitions of the Torah.[1] Conversely, the Talmud relates that when a man asked the great sage Hillel to teach him

---

[1] *Zohar* 2:276a. Also see Shaloh, *Torah Shebichtav*, beginning of *Parashat Yitro*; *Tanya*, chapter 20.

the entire Torah while he stood on one foot, Hillel said: "What is hateful to yourself, do not do to your fellow. This is the entire Torah—the rest is commentary."[2]

Ultimately, there is no essential difference between the Torah's "civil" laws and its "religious" laws. A crime against a fellow is also a crime against G-d, and a crime against G-d is a crime against all of G-d's creations. A kindness to a fellow human being is a kindness to the One who created us all and desires that we live in peace and harmony with each other; and a positive relationship with G-d has a positive effect on G-d's relationship with creation as a whole, and with each and every citizen of G-d's world. In the words of Maimonides:

> *A person should always view himself as equally balanced: half good and half evil. Likewise, he should see the entire world as half good and half evil. By committing a single transgression, he tips the scales for himself, and for the entire world, to the side of guilt, and brings destruction upon it. And with a single good deed, he tips the scales for himself, and for the entire world, to the side of merit, and brings it salvation.*[3]

---

2   Talmud, *Shabbat* 31a. Similarly, the Jerusalem Talmud, *Nedarim* 9:4, cites Rabbi Akiva's teaching that the precept "Love your fellow as yourself" (Leviticus 19:18) is "a cardinal principle of the Torah."

3   *Mishneh Torah, Laws of Repentance*, 3:4. At a gathering on December 28, 1968, one day after the successful conclusion of the Apollo 8 space mission, the Rebbe referred to that event as providing us a way to better understand and appreciate Maimonides's statement. The following is an excerpt from the Rebbe's talk:

Many *mitzvot* of the Torah address a person's everyday activities—what one should or should not eat, when one may work and when one should rest, and so on. The Torah empowers the *bet din* (court of Torah law) to enforce these laws, and even establishes penalties for their

Chassidic teaching takes this a step further. It teaches that every law has both a "body" and a "soul." The body of the law is its legal/practical application—the action (or non-action) mandated as a transgression. Many question why anyone but the person themselves should be concerned about what he or she does in their personal life. After all, it's not that anyone else is being hurt by these actions.

In truth, our sages tell us that, "A person is obligated to say: The entire world was created for my sake" (Talmud, *Sanhedrin* 37a). Maimonides writes that a person should always be conscious of the fact that with a single transgression, he or she can tip the balance of the entire world to the side of guilt, G-d forbid, whereas a single good deed can bring redemption to the world.

This is what is written in the books. Human nature, however, is that things are more readily understood and accepted when we see a tangible example. By divine providence, we have such an example in an event that is currently in the news.

Yesterday marked the conclusion of an event that has no known precedent in human history. A manned spacecraft approached the moon, orbited it several times, photographed both its light side and its dark side, and returned safely to earth at the exact time and place that were programmed.

In order for this mission to succeed, three adult men were told to put aside all personal preferences and follow a set of guidelines that dictated their every behavior, including their most intimate habits. They were told exactly what, how much, and when to eat; when and in what position to sleep; which shoes to wear; and so on. Should any one of them have challenged this "dictatorial" regimen, he would have been reminded that one billion dollars have been invested in this mission. Now, one billion dollars commands a lot of respect. Never mind that it's not his billion—it's only Uncle Sam's billion—still, when a person is told that one billion dollars are at stake, he will conform to all guidelines and instructions. He will do so despite the fact that he has no understanding of how many of these instructions relate to the success of his mission—that has been determined by white-haired scientists after many years of research; but he will take their word for it, and will readily accept the extensive intrusion into his private affairs.

What if what is at stake is not a billion-dollar scientific project, but the divine purpose in creation?

duty toward G-d or as the proper practice toward one's fellow. The soul of the law is its deeper conceptual/spiritual significance, its meaning in the inner life of the soul. The "body" of a law might apply only in very specific circumstances. (When was the last time your ox gored your neighbor's ox, necessitating the application of the rules governing the compensation owed to him as laid down in Exodus 21:35–36?) The "soul" of the law, however, applies at all times and in all places.

So while the more specific applications of the body of a law will place it within a certain category—e.g., as a "religious" or as a "social" precept—when approached on its soul level, the law will extend beyond its basic classification. A *mitzvah* whose bodily application is of a ritualistic nature will, on the soul level, also contain an instruction in how to behave toward a fellow. Conversely, a *mitzvah* whose literal meaning places it squarely within the Torah's civil code, will also address the internal world of the soul's relationship with G-d and its fulfillment of its mission in life.

"Three Gates" of Civil Law

Let us look at some classic examples of the Torah's civil laws, and seek to uncover glimpses of their inner, spiritual meaning.

Many of the Torah's civil laws have their source in the Torah section of *Mishpatim* (Exodus 21:1–24:18), which immediately follows the Torah's description of the revelation at Mount Sinai in the section of *Yitro* (Exodus 18:1–20:23). This, say our sages, is to emphasize that "Just as the previous ones are from Sinai, these too are from Sinai."[4] Namely, that even the most utilitarian social law is a *mitzvah*—a divine commandment, a revelation of divine will.

---

4   Rashi, Exodus 21:1; this is further emphasized by the opening verse of

The Talmud, which analyzes the biblical verses and deduces the laws encoded within them, devotes its largest tractate, *Nezikin*, to the civil laws of *Mishpatim*. Because of its size, *Nezikin* is subdivided into three parts, each of which has come to be regarded as a tractate in its own right: *Bava Kama* ("First Gate"), *Bava Metzia* ("Middle Gate"), and *Bava Batra* ("Final Gate").

Each of the three "Gates" deals with a different category of civil law. A reading of the opening lines of these three tractates will serve to illustrate the types of cases they each deal with.

The Ox, the Pit, Man, and Fire

The "First Gate," *Bava Kama*, begins:

> *There are four primary classes of damages: the ox, the pit, man, and fire.*

The Talmud goes on to discuss the laws governing a person's responsibility for these four categories of damages:

(a) Damages inflicted by one's personal property (e.g., a person's ox goring his neighbor's ox);

(b) Damages caused by hazards placed on public property (e.g., digging a hole in the middle of the street);

(c) Damage inflicted directly by the person himself; and

(d) Failure to prevent damages arising from potentially dangerous actions (e.g., a person starts a fire on his own property which spreads to that of his neighbor).

In addition to defining the four categories of damages and the numerous subcategories and particular laws they each contain,

---

Mishpatim, "And these are the laws which you shall set before them," with the prefix *vav* ("and") implying a continuation of preceding text.

Bava Kama also legislates the reparations and penalties for theft and robbery. In other words, the "First Gate" of Torah's civil law deals primarily with criminal, even violent, attacks on a fellow's property and person, addressing the most crass form of disharmony between people.

Finders and Keepers

The laws discussed in *Bava Metzia*, the "Middle Gate," include: laws pertaining to the return of lost objects; disputes arising out of loans, sales, and employment; and the responsibilities of the "four guardians" (the paid guardian, the unpaid guardian, the borrower, and the renter) for the objects entrusted to their care.

Like the first *Bava*, the "Middle Gate" also deals with disputes between people. But these are, for the most part, more benign conflicts, arising out of honest disagreement rather than malicious or blatantly irresponsible behavior. The first law discussed in this tractate is a case in point:

> *Two people are holding onto a garment. One says, "I found it," and the other says, "I found it"...*

To be sure, the laws of *Bava Metzia* hardly reflect the ideal in interpersonal relations. The court's verdict inevitably satisfies only one, and at times neither, of the claimants. But unlike the cases discussed in the "First Gate," there are no overtly anti-civil actions involved. Rather, in the course of their normal, day-to-day dealings, two people find themselves in disagreement with each other. In many cases, each party honestly believes himself to be in the right.

Partnerships and Commerce

The "Final Gate," *Bava Batra*, includes an entirely different genre of civil law: laws which come not to settle disputes, but to lay the groundwork for a socially just and harmonious existence between people. This tractate discusses the laws outlining property rights, neighbor relations and responsibilities, partnerships, commerce, inheritance, and charity. A case in point is *Bava Batra*'s first scenario:

> Partners [in a courtyard] who wish to divide, should build a wall in the middle... In everything they should follow the local custom. [When they build] with uncut stones, one gives three handbreadths and the other gives three handbreadths [of space for the wall]... With bricks, one gives one-and-one-half handbreadths and the other gives one-and-one-half handbreadths... Thus... the area and the stones belong equally to both.

This law is typical of the laws that form the backbone of the "Final Gate." Its function might be to define and divide, but this is a division that is desired by both parties and beneficial to them both. Indeed, the very wall which divides them becomes a joint undertaking, linking them and attesting to their mutual desire to live as neighbors who respect each other's rights and privileges.

The Three Gates of History

On the cosmic-historical level, the three gates of *Nezikin* can be seen as three phases in the social development of humanity, and as a barometer of Torah law's progressive influence upon society.

In the "First Gate," we encounter human society in a base and barbaric state: "law" is an institution whose function is to deal with criminal and violent behavior among its members. In the "Second Gate," we progress from criminal to non-malicious conflict. Finally, the "Final Gate" describes a strife-free society—a society in which the primary role of the law is not to deal with disputes, but to establish guidelines for a greater cooperation and a deeper unity in the community of man.

The three *Bavot* tell the story of history itself: the story of mankind's progress toward the perfect and harmonious world of Moshiach. As humanity learns to disarm and unite, beating the swords of war machinery into the plowshares of aid to the needy, we near the day when the "Final Gate" of Torah's civil and civilizing law will forever abolish conflict and animosity from the human experience.

Internal Damages

As discussed above, the social *mitzvot* of the Torah have their counterpart in the life of the soul. Thus, the "three gates" of progress from barbarism to harmonious coexistence on the social level also describe three corresponding stages in our spiritual development and our quest for connection with G-d.

In the "First Gate," we contend with "damages"—internal negative forces that actively undermine our spiritual integrity. These fall under four general categories, corresponding to the "four primary classes of damages": (a) our animal lusts and desires ("the ox"); (b) our propensity for anger and other violent emotions ("fire"); (c) the destructive effect of "passive" vices such as sloth and inertia ("the pit"); and (d) our misleadingly "sophisticated" vices, which are all the more harmful because they exploit our elevated, distinctly human talents ("man") to spiritually destructive ends.

Once these overtly destructive forces, and various type of compensations that remedy them, have been identified, we proceed to the "Middle Gate," which describes internal conflicts of a more subtle nature.

Lost Objects in the Life of the Soul

The spiritual *Bava Metzia* deals with issues such as "finding lost objects," and the responsibilities and privileges of the "four guardians."

To understand the "soul" of the laws pertaining to lost objects, we need to look at another Talmudic rule, which concerns itself with the definition of a *shoteh* ("fool")—a legal term for someone who lacks the mental capability to be held responsible for his actions:

> *What is a "fool"? One who loses everything that is given to him.*[5]

The Hebrew words for "everything that"—*kol mah*—also translate as "all the *mah*." *Mah* (literally, "what") is a kabbalistic term for our soul's capacity for receptiveness and self-abnegation. Every soul is supplied from Above with the *mah* that is the foundation for spiritual sensitivity and connection with G-d. A "fool," in the spiritual sense, is one who loses all the *mah* that has been given them—a person whose self-absorption prevents him or her from being receptive to anything that is loftier than their present comprehension and experience.

---

5   Talmud, *Chagigah* 4a.

This is the "between man and G-d" significance of the laws that deal with the recovery of lost objects. After we have cleansed our souls of the blatantly destructive traits enumerated in the "First Gate," we must labor to recover our lost *mah* and resolve the internal dissonance that occurs when our ego obstructs our spiritual development.

(*Bava Metzia* also includes the laws of "four guardians." As will be discussed in the next essay, these laws describe four types of spiritual personalities, who vary in the degree of reward they expect in return for their guardianship of the life-mission entrusted to them, and the corresponding degree of responsibility they must assume for the hazards of life. As with the "lost object" laws that appear in the first two chapters of *Bava Metzia*, the guardianship laws address the spiritual challenges of the soul that struggles to define its relationship with its Creator and with its task in life.[6])

The Partner

After the spiritually damaging elements of *Bava Kama* and the more subtle spiritual challenges of *Bava Metzia*, we progress to the "Final Gate," which introduces us to the laws of partnership.

There are several ways in which we might perceive the labor of life. We might see ourselves as servants of an autocratic master. The "servant" personality does the right thing, but solely as a duty. A more spiritually engaged life is that lived by the "employee" personality, who labors for the reward he or she anticipates in return for their toil.

Finally, we can progress to the point that we experience life as a partnership with G-d. As G-d's partners, we develop our self and

---

6 See "The Four Guardians," pp. 183–189 below.

world in accordance with the divine will not only because we must, nor merely for the rewards of a life of righteousness and spiritual fulfillment, but as an intensely personal enterprise. Life becomes our joint venture with G-d, equally driven by the Creator's vision and desire, and by our own initiative and ambition.[7]

The spiritual version of the "Final Gate" describes this venture. As in any joint enterprise, there is need for "walls" that delineate the terms of the partnership (hence the opening law of *Bava Batra*, quoted above, "Partners who wish to divide..."). The domain of each partner must be defined, as well as their rights and responsibilities. These walls are of several types: some are wholly divine institutions ("uncut stones"); others are products of man's development of divinely provided resources ("brick").[8]

But while these walls divide and define, they are not divisive walls. There are no saboteurs in this relationship (as in the "First Gate"), nor even benign conflict (as in the more spiritually mature "Second Gate"). Rather, these are uniting walls, jointly constructed edifices that galvanize our relationship with G-d and empower us to execute our part in the partnership.

---

[7] For a detailed discussion of the "servant," "employee," and "partner" modes of life, see the essay, "Working Conditions," in vol. 3 (Leviticus) of *The Inside Story*.

[8] See the essay, "The Brick Factory," pp. 5–7 above.

THE FOUR GUARDIANS

If a person gives his friend money or utensils to watch, and they are stolen from the [guardian's] home... If a person borrows [something] from his friend, and it breaks... If he is a renter...

Exodus 22:6–14

In the twenty-second chapter of Exodus, the Torah puts forth the laws of the "four guardians." The basic issue at hand is: To what degree is a person responsible for another person's object that has been placed in his or her care?

The Talmud (primarily in the third, seventh, and eighth chapters of *Bava Metzia*) analyzes the relevant biblical verses and concludes that there are four classes of guardian:

(a) *The unpaid guardian.* One who takes care of another's property purely as a favor and is receiving no compensation for his trouble. Although he is duty bound to care for the object, his responsibility in case of mishap is minimal. If the object is damaged or lost as a result of his negligence, he must pay; but as long as he has provided the reasonable care to which he had obligated himself, and takes an oath to that effect, he is absolved from payment.

(b) *The paid guardian.* Since he is being paid (or otherwise compensated) for his services, the level of care he is expected to provide, and his responsibility in the case of mishap, are greater. Here the Torah differentiates between "avoidable damages," such as loss or theft, and "unavoidable damages" such as armed robbery and natural death. The paid guardian is responsible for the former, and absolved by oath of the latter.

(c) *The borrower.* His is the highest level of liability. He is responsible to return what has been given to him intact, or make good on its value, regardless of the degree of his fault in the case of damage. Even if the borrowed object is destroyed by a lightning bolt, the borrower must pay.[1]

(d) *The renter.* The Torah also mentions a fourth case in which a person is responsible for the property of his fellow: the case of the renter who pays for its use. But the text is unclear on the level of his responsibility. The Talmud cites two opinions on the status of the renter: Rabbi Judah rules that he is like the unpaid guardian, who is responsible only for outright negligence; Rabbi Meir is of the opinion that the renter's obligations are identical to those of the paid guardian, and he is liable also for "avoidable damages" such as loss and theft.

Two Views on the Renter

An examination of the arguments offered by Rabbi Judah and Rabbi Meir, and the discussion of their opinions by later generations of Talmudic sages, presents the following two views on the renter:

According to Rabbi Judah, the payment given by the renter is in return for, and of equivalent value to, the right of use he enjoys. So the fact that the renter benefits from the possession of his fellow's property, and the fact that the owner is paid, should have no

---

[1] The only cases in which the borrower is absolved from payment are: (a) if the damage resulted from his normal use of the object; (b) if the object's owner was with him at the time of the loss.

bearing on the level of the renter's responsibility, as they cancel each other out. In the final analysis, the renter receives nothing in return for the care he is providing for the object, making him, in effect, an unpaid guardian.

To Rabbi Meir, however, the primary issue is not how much a guardian receives in return for his trouble, but why the object is in his possession in the first place. The question of payment or non-payment is secondary. In the case of the first two guardians, the object has entered their domain *for the sake of the owner*. So the responsibility of the guardian is minimal. In the case of the unpaid guardian it is limited to outright negligence; in the case of the paid guardian, the fact that there is also some benefit for the guardian means that the level of responsibility should be raised a notch.

But in the case of the borrower and the renter, says Rabbi Meir, the opposite is true: the object has left its owner's domain *for the sake of the guardian*. So the responsibility is total. The addition of the other, secondary factor, that of payment, has a similar effect as in the case of the paid guardian: because the renter pays for the favor, his level of responsibility is lowered a notch. As Rabbi Meir sees it, the paid guardian is basically an unpaid guardian who has been paid to be slightly more responsible, while the renter is basically a borrower who has paid to reduce his responsibility.[2]

---

2   This explains why the Talmud states that there are *four* types of guardians. Obviously, the four cases enumerated above—the unpaid guardian, the paid guardian, the borrower, and the renter—are not the only cases in which one person has another person's object under his care and responsibility. The scenarios leading to such a situation are virtually endless. But they all fall under one of the four categories. Indeed, the Talmud considers many other situations—e.g., a person who finds a lost object and is caring for it until the owner can be located, a person who is holding on to a fellow's object as collateral for a loan, and so on.

The Soul of the Law

The Torah has been likened to the human being.[3] Man is a synthesis of body and soul; Torah, too, possesses a tangible, "physical" aspect—the laws and directives which deal with our physical existence—as well as a conceptual, "spiritual" dimension. And just as the human body and soul combine and integrate to form a single entity, so it is with the body and soul of Torah. On the one hand, the most sublime concepts of the Torah's "soul" have their practical applications in everyday life; on the other hand, every limb and cell of its "body"—every nuance of the Torah's legal code and pragmatic guide to daily living—also addresses the internal world of the human psyche, our relationship with the Creator, and the purpose of our existence.

In each case the Talmud determines which of the four categories the said "guardian" belongs to.

This raises the question: Why, then, do we say that there are *four* categories of guardians? Why is the "renter" regarded as a category unto itself, if the laws that govern a renter's culpability are identical either with those of an unpaid guardian (according to Rabbi Judah) or with those of a paid guardian (according to Rabbi Meir)?

The truth is, that according to Rabbi Judah there really are only three categories of guardian. The renter is just another case of an unpaid guardian. According to Rabbi Meir, however, the "paid guardian" and the "renter" are fundamentally different types; the fact that they are technically culpable for the same set of circumstances is entirely incidental. In essence, the paid guardian has more in common with the unpaid guardian, and the renter has more in common with the borrower, than the two have in common with each other. In the words of the Talmud, according to Rabbi Meir, "There are four guardians, though their laws are three."

Indeed, the classification of "four guardians" is attributed solely to Rabbi Meir. According to Rabbi Judah, there are only three types of guardians, the renter being a form of unpaid guardian (see Talmud, *Bava Metzia* 93a).

3   See *Zohar* 3:152a.

Our role in creation is that of a guardian. In the words of the book of Genesis, "G-d took the man and placed him in the Garden of Eden, to work it and to keep it."[4] The Creator entrusted His world to our care, charging us with the responsibility of safeguarding and developing the resources and potentials He has granted and made available to each individual.

Thus, the inner "soul" aspect of the laws of guardianship address some of life's most central questions. Whose life is it, anyway? Do we possess an inherent right to its blessings, or must we earn these rights? What are our responsibilities towards our Creator, and what are the rewards we might anticipate in reciprocation for our efforts on His behalf? Is it enough to "do our best" and expect life's blessings to flow to us, or is reward measured by achievement?

Four Perspectives

The "Four Guardians" (using Rabbi Meir's model) represent four approaches to life. The first is the altruistic "unpaid guardian." This is a person who exemplifies the ideal, "I was not created, but to serve my Creator."[5] He or she sees their life, their talents, and their possessions as divine property that has been placed in their trust. Nor do they feel that G-d owes them anything in compensation for their efforts.

On the other extreme is the "borrower"—the person who believes that what they have, has been given them for their own benefit. To such a person, the purpose of life is self-fulfillment and self-realization. The "borrower" does acknowledge who the ultimate owner is, and accepts his or her obligations as a guardian;

---

4   Genesis 2:15.
5   Talmud, *Kidushin* 82b.

but they do not feel that they owe anyone anything for their use of life's blessings.

The paid guardian and the renter occupy the middle ground between these two extremes, although on the core issue of "Why are we here?" they differ as much as do the unpaid guardian and the borrower. Yet they each temper their perspective on life with the idea of "payment." The "renters" of the world (as do the "borrowers") see the purpose of it all as the fulfillment and enhancement of their own self, but they nevertheless feel that they ought to "pay" for this privilege by serving their Creator. The "paid guardians" see the fulfillment of G-d's will as the ultimate purpose of life, but reserve for themselves a little corner of self-interest: they feel that they also deserve something of "a life of my own" in return for their work as guardians in the employ of the Almighty.

Measure for Measure

Which of the four perspectives on life described above is the correct one? Which is the true reality? All of them are equally true, as the choice lies squarely with us.

Our sages tell us that G-d deals with us "measure for measure," responding to us in the manner in which we behave toward Him.[6] Thus Rabbi Israel Baal Shem Tov interprets the verse, "G-d is your shadow"[7]: just as a person's shadow moves in concert with the person's movements, so too does G-d respond to our choices and actions. However we choose to define our relationship with G-d, so does G-d relate to us.

Accordingly, it is up to us to decide which mode of "guardianship" will define our lives. We may choose the "free lunch"

---

6 Talmud, *Megillah* 12b.
7 Psalms 121:5.

approach of the borrower. But if you want to be a borrower, says G-d, you must take full responsibility, as well. If things go awry in your life, if you err and blunder, or even if circumstances beyond your control overwhelm you—that's your problem. After all, it was you who decided that it's *your* life.

Alternatively, we may take the approach of the "renter." Our basic view is still that of one who thinks that we are here for ourselves; but because we acknowledge our indebtedness to G-d and endeavor to "pay" for our use of the gifts He bestows upon us, we are relieved of some of the responsibility. We are still exposed to the hazards of life, but we need not bear their burden entirely on our own.

Or, we might assume the identity and perspective of the "paid guardian." This means that, unlike the "borrower" and "renter," we consider the purpose of our existence to be to serve G-d's will, rather than our own needs and desires. At the same time, we expect to be rewarded for our efforts. Responding "measure for measure," G-d relates to us in a similar fashion. The laws that govern our lives protect us, to a certain extent, from utter abandonment to "fate." But because we assert a certain degree of self-interest, we remain exposed to many of the uncertainties and mishaps that threaten our pitfall-prone existence.

Finally, we can embrace the unequivocal surrender of self that characterizes the "unpaid guardian." When such is our attitude, we are absolved from culpability even for the "avoidable damages." So long as we do not betray the terms of our guardianship, we need not be concerned with the threats and uncertainties that plague our world. Because we see our existence solely in terms of our service of the Creator, G-d takes full responsibility for our life.

THE RESOURCEFUL OATH

For every trespass ... for every loss that [the defendant] shall say "this is it," the two shall come before the court for an oath...

Exodus 22:8[1]

The Talmud explains that the above verse deals with the case of the *modeh bemiktzat*, a defendant who partially admits to the plaintiff's claim. For example: Two people come to court, the plaintiff claiming that the defendant owes him $1000. The defendant concedes that he indeed owes the plaintiff money, but only $500 ("This is it"). Were the defendant to deny the claim outright, the burden of proof would lie entirely on the plaintiff.[2] But because the defendant has acknowledged that there is a basis to the plaintiff's claim, he is obligated to take an oath that he owes him no more than the $500 to which he has admitted.[3]

The taking of an oath, which involves holding a sacred object (such as a Torah scroll) and evoking G-d's name, is no minor matter. Indeed, it was a common occurrence that a litigant would prefer to pay what was claimed of him rather than assume the awesome responsibility that an oath entails, even when he was certain

---

[1] As per the Talmud's interpretation of the verse.
[2] In keeping with the rule, "The one who seeks to take out from the possession of his fellow, he must bring the proof" (Talmud, *Bava Kama* 46a, derived from Exodus 24:14).
[3] Talmud, *Bava Kama* 107a.

of the veracity of his denial.[4] Thus, there is much discussion in the Talmud as to when and under what circumstances a defendant is obligated to affirm his or her arguments with an oath.

Overdue Payments and Depreciating Properties

In light of this, the famed halachic authority Rabbi Shabetai HaKohen (1621–1662), known by the acronym "Shach," explains the relevance of another issue in Torah law: Whose arguments should the court listen to first, the plaintiff's or the defendant's? In Exodus 24:14, the Torah relates how Moses, before ascending Mount Sinai where he was to spend forty days receiving the Torah from G-d, entrusted the nation's litigation matters in the hands of his brother and nephew: "To the elders he said: '...Aaron and Hur are with you. He who has a claim should approach them.'" From this the Talmud derives that it is the plaintiff ("he who has a claim") who merits the court's initial attention.[5]

When applied to a case of the "partial conceder," this procedural rule actually determines the outcome of the case. Were the defendant to be granted first say, he would no longer be a "partial conceder." For as soon as he admits to the court that he owes the plaintiff $500, this becomes an established legal fact, meaning that the plaintiff's subsequent claim of $1000 becomes, in truth, a claim for only $500—a claim which the defendant denies in full. The court would then place the entire burden of proof on the plaintiff, exempting the defendant of the dreaded oath. It is only because the plaintiff is first given the opportunity to make his claim, while the entire $1000 is still an open issue before the court,

---

4   See, for example, Talmud, *Bava Metzia* 33b (in the *mishnah*).
5   Talmud, *Bava Kama* 46b.

that defendant's denial of a *part* of this claim will obligate him to either swear or pay the claim in full.

Why, indeed, should the defendant not be given the opportunity to first establish what he freely admits to owing? Explains Shach: The defendant already had his chance to pay what he owes. Instead, he waited for the plaintiff to drag him to court, where, faced with the prospect of an oath, he suddenly wants to settle his accounts. Says the court: Now we will listen to the plaintiff's claim, which will rightfully include all that you failed to make good to date.

With this approach, Shach also explains the Talmud's ruling that "there are cases in which we first attend to the defendant, such as the case in which there is a depreciation in the value of his property."[6] If the defendant demonstrates to the court that the reason he did not immediately pay his admitted debt is that a hasty sale of his property to raise the money would have resulted is a real loss to him, the court will not fault him for the delay. In such a case, the court would agree to first establish the defendant's admission as a matter of record, and only then consider the plaintiff's claim.[7]

The Equivocal Transgressor

As we have seen,[8] the body of Torah law also has a "soul"—a deeper spiritual import. The same is true of the legal principles detailed above. "Trespasses" and "losses" may also occur in one's spiritual life, and here, too, apply these selfsame laws. The concept of the "partial conceder," the nature of his obligatory oath, the

---

[6] Ibid.
[7] Shach, *Choshen Mishpat* 24:1.
[8] See the previous two essays, "Oxen and Souls" and "The Four Guardians." Also see the introduction to vol. 1 (Genesis) of *The Inside Story*.

circumstances under which he is exempted of it—all have their counterpart in the spiritual dimension of Torah.[9]

Our life, our talents, our resources—these are a sacred trust that has been given us to safeguard and develop.[10] But what if, G-d forbid, we violate this trust? Spiritual "claims" against us may involve anything from an outright sin ("trespass"), to the failure to optimally realize our potential ("loss"). How do we defend ourselves against such claims?

But each and every one of us was created in the image of G-d.[11] Our soul is a spark of G-dliness, a glimmer of the goodness and perfection of the divine.[12] Our transgressions and failings are an aberration, a phenomenon that is inconsistent with our true self; in the words of the Talmud, "A person does not sin, unless a spirit of insanity has entered into him."[13] This is why, as the Talmud puts it, "sinners are full of regrets"[14]—our soul can never accept its deficiencies. Furthermore, "Even at the very moment that a person sins, the soul remains faithful to G-d."[15]

---

9   In fact, the spiritual dimension of these laws aids our understanding of their material aspect. For example, while the verse, "He who has a claim should approach them," seems to refer to all claims, the law derived from it (that we first deal with the plaintiff), as applied by *Shach*, is truly significant only in the case of the "partial conceder." On the spiritual level, however, we understand that *all* spiritual "claims" deal with a "partially culpable" defendant, as explained further in this essay.

10 See the previous essay, "The Four Guardians." Indeed, the verse quoted in the beginning of this essay, (Exodus 22:8), from which we derive the law of the "partial conceder," is speaking of the case of a guardian who has failed to take proper care of an object that has been entrusted to him (though the law applies to other cases of "partial conceders" as well).

11 Genesis 1:27.

12 See Job 31:2; *Tanya*, chapter 2.

13 Talmud, *Sotah* 3a.

14 Ibid., *Nedarim* 9b.

15 *Tanya*, chapter 24.

Furthermore, even on the behavioral level, the negative in us is never absolute. In the words of the sages, "Even the transgressors of Israel are as full of good deeds as a pomegranate [is full of seeds]."[16]

So when confronted with its misdeeds and failings, our soul responds: True, I have done wrong. True, I have failed to be equal to the resources and abilities that have been granted me. But this is not the real me. Only a most external aspect of my being was involved in these trespasses and losses.

In every life there come those occasions when a "claim" is leveled against us in the courtroom of the soul. Something happens to shake us out of our complacency, and confront us with our spiritual failings. At such times, every soul is a "partial conceder." We admit our trespass or lack, and commit ourselves to its rectification; but we also insist that our culpability is only partial, as it involved only a marginal aspect of our being.

The Oath

The "partial conceder" must take an oath to corroborate their rejection of the remainder of the claim. The same applies on the spiritual level. Although the quintessential core of our soul is indeed not a party to our misdeeds and imperfections, nevertheless, this denied aspect of the claim necessitates corroboration by "oath."

True, the Torah attests to the intrinsic goodness and perfection of the soul. But the function of the soul is to express this goodness and perfection in the person's character and conduct. Ultimately, then, the claim extends beyond the "partial" culpability of one's external self. How can we guarantee that, henceforth, our true, inner self will dominate our life? That it will not again fail to

---

16   Talmud, *Eruvin* 19a.

influence our behavior? So for the "remainder" of the claim, the Torah prescribes an oath.

What is the significance of this "oath"? Let us examine what our sages have said concerning another case of a spiritual oath-taking.

The Talmud relates that prior to the soul's descent into physical life, "it is made to swear: Be righteous, and do not be wicked."[17] But what, we might ask, is the purpose of this oath? The soul, a spark of G-dliness, obviously wants to do only good; it is only because of its enmeshment in a body and a physical identity that this quintessential desire may be suppressed or distorted. What is the point of making the soul swear to something to which it is already committed?

Chassidic teaching explains that the administration of an oath is an act of empowerment. Certainly, the soul wishes to fulfill the purpose of its creation. But the distortions and enticements of the physical world present a most difficult challenge. The oath, "Be righteous," fortifies the soul with the power and resolve to overcome this challenge and carry out its mission in life. Indeed, the Hebrew word for "oath," *shevuah*, is of the same root as *sova*, "fortitude." Thus, the above quoted saying from the Talmud that the soul "is made to swear" also translates as, "is fortified."[18]

And so it is when our soul, in the course of its sojourn on earth, suffers a "trespass" or "loss" in its spiritual life. The actual damage is minimal, for only the most external layer of self can be tainted by sin or deficiency. But even after this partial culpability has been admitted and rectified, there remains the need for an overall reinforcement of our soul's spiritual prowess. Especially in light of the fact that we have been lax in settling our spiritual accounts, and

---

17 Talmud, *Nidah* 30b.
18 Tzemach Tzedek's commentary on Chapter 1 of *Tanya*.

did not admit our "partial culpability" and make good on our shortfall until the "claim" being leveled against us.

This is the oath that the Torah mandates. An oath to deepen our soul's commitment to life, to supply it with even greater reserves of vigor and fortitude. An oath to bolster it in the challenge to realize its innate goodness and perfection in the arena of daily, physical life.

A Deathbed Reckoning

There is, however, a case of a "partial conceder" who is exempted from taking an oath (and assuming the greater responsibility it entails): the case of a defendant who did not attend to the plaintiff's claims out of the fear that "his property would depreciate."

The Talmud relates that when Rabbi Jochanan ben Zakai lay dying, his disciples came to visit him and found their master weeping. "Why do you weep?" they asked him. Rabbi Jochanan replied that he was weeping in trepidation. How will he be judged in the heavenly court? Perhaps he will be found wanting in the fulfillment of his mission in life?[19]

The impression one gets from the Talmud's account is that this was the first time that Rabbi Jochanan had confronted the issue of his personal worthiness. But why only now? Surely a person of Rabbi Jochanan's stature was not concerned over the rewards or punishments that may await him in the hereafter.[20] To him, the

---

19 Talmud, *Berachot* 28b.
20 In the words of Maimonides, "The person who serves G-d out of love occupies himself in the Torah and the *mitzvot* and walks in the paths of wisdom for no ulterior motive: not because of fear that evil will occur, nor in order to acquire benefit. Rather, he does what is true because it is the truth..." (*Mishneh Torah, Laws of Repentance* 10:2).

issue was a question of fulfillment or failure: Did he succeed in fully realizing his G-d-given potential?

But stocktaking of this sort is always a good idea. Why wait until one is lying on one's deathbed? Was this not a matter of concern for Rabbi Jochanan during his lifetime? Did he not once, in his long and fruitful years, pause to consider his spiritual state?

The answer is no. As far as Rabbi Jochanan was concerned, life was too precious a commodity to be squandered on such "selfish" matters. For him, every moment of time, every iota of energy granted to him, was a resource to be developed and utilized. In the words of the Talmud, "All these were created only to serve me, and I was created to serve my Creator."[21] To Rabbi Jochanan's way of thinking, what right had he to make use of these resources to contemplate his own existence? Are these not a sacred trust granted him, to be applied to the service of G-d in the manner that G-d commanded—to study the Torah and observe the *mitzvot*?[22] It was only as he lay dying, the productive phase of his life behind him, that he allowed himself the luxury of focusing his attention on his personal state.

The Vigilant Guardian

Now we can understand the spiritual meaning of the law that exempts from oath-taking a partial "conceder" who failed to settle

---

[21] Talmud, *Kidushin* 82a.

[22] It is true that many *mitzvot* involve the refinement and perfection of one's self and character, making this an integral part of one's service of the Almighty. And *teshuvah*, the duty to correct one's past misdeeds and lacks, is likewise a divine commandment in the Torah. But to Rabbi Jochanan ben Zakai, this is exactly what they were: a way of serving G-d. As he practiced them, these *mitzvot* were utterly devoid of of any concern over his own spiritual status and fate.

his accounts because of the fear that his "property would depreciate."

Ordinarily, we would tell the "partial conceder": You say that you admit your culpability regarding part of the claim, and are prepared to make good on the other part. So why haven't you dealt with the matter until now? Why do you wait for the eve of Yom Kippur, or for some earth-shaking event in your life, to search your soul? Because you delayed rectifying your personal deficiencies until you were "dragged to court," you will now have to deal with the entirety of the claim. True, you are only partly culpable, but also the unaffected part of you will have to be reinforced by the means of an oath.

All this, however, only applies to the individual to whom personal status is an issue. But those who wholly and selflessly devote their lives to the service of the Creator, without thought to their own spiritual affairs, are above such critique. Why didn't they deal with this earlier? Because they wished to preserve the value of their property! Because they wished to optimize the potential of their every minute and thought, and devote them entirely to their most "profitable" utility—the doing of another *mitzvah*. Why squander these invaluable resources on one's own insignificant self?

Such souls have no need for the spiritual booster of an "oath." Because they live not for themselves but for G-d, G-d takes responsibility for their life.[23] So while even the most righteous person will be called upon to correct the lacks or inadequacies that may mar the perfection of their soul,[24] they need not worry about the "remainder" of the claim. They have more important things on their mind.

---

23 See the previous essay, "The Four Guardians," pp. 183–183 above.
24 As King Solomon declares, "there is no perfectly righteous person on the earth who does only good and has not a failing" (Ecclesiastes 7:20).

THE THIRD CROWN

[Moses] took the book of the covenant, and read it in the ears of the people. And they said: "Everything that G-d has spoken, we will do, and we will hear."

Exodus 24:7

As the above-quoted verse attests, our covenant with G-d entails not only "doing" the divine will, but also "hearing" it—comprehending it and identifying with it. In other words, we serve G-d not only with our actions, but also with our minds and hearts, by studying His wisdom and gaining a love and awe of His truth.

Yet, as our sages point out, the people said, "We will do," before they said, "We will hear." This means that our observance of the divine commandments is not contingent on our understanding. First comes the unequivocal commitment to do what G-d commands. It was only after we made that commitment that we pledged to also "hear" and understand.

The Angels' Gifts

A beautiful Talmudic passage illustrates how G-d valued this declaration by the people:

> *At the moment that the people of Israel put "We will do" before "We will hear," six hundred thousand angels came, [one] for each Jew, and fixed two crowns upon his head: one for "We will do," and one for "We will hear."*[1]

A closer examination of the wording of this passage reveals an apparent inconsistency. Its opening words imply that the gifts borne by the angels were not for the declarations "We will do" and "We will hear" themselves, but for the fact that the people of Israel "put 'We will do' before 'We will hear.'" So why did they each get *two* crowns, "one for 'We will do,' and one for 'We will hear'"?

The chassidic masters explain: Giving precedence to "We will do" over "We will hear" is not just a virtue in its own right, signifying an unquestioning commitment to the divine will. It also has a profound effect upon the "doing" and "hearing" themselves, elevating them to a completely different level of achievement and comprehension.

When our fulfillment of a *mitzvah* is predicated on our understanding of its significance, the deed is bounded by the limitations of our mind and heart. Furthermore, each *mitzvah* has its own set of limits and conditions. Some *mitzvot* are more understandable; others, less so. Some are more emotionally stirring; others, less so. The *mitzvah* is thus reduced (at least in the experience of its observer) to a human deed, subject to the limitations and fluctuations of the human condition.

But when we put "we will do" before "we will hear," we are saying: "I will fulfill the divine will not on my terms, but on G-d's terms. I am doing this not because and to the extent to which I understand it, but because G-d commanded me." Our deed is thus

---

[1] Talmud, *Shabbat* 88a.

elevated from a finite and temporal human act to the infinity, eternity, and equivocality of the divine.

The same applies to the "we will hear" aspect of our service of G-d. In and of itself, the human effort to comprehend the divine remains just that: a human effort, delimited by the scope of human intellect and the particular prejudices of each individual mind. Certain aspects of the divine will are more comprehensible; others, less so. Certain *mitzvot* are more readily identified with, while others are more difficult to relate to. The only way to gain an uncircumscribed apprehension of the divine truth is to live that truth, fully and unequivocally, in our daily lives and everyday activities. It is only when we put "we will do" before "we will hear" that our "we will hear" achieves a true understanding of the divine.

G-d's Crown

According to this, however, the crown-bearing angels should have placed *three* crowns on each of the people. For the elevated doing and understanding that earned us our two crowns both derived from a third, underlying virtue: our unquestioning submission to the divine will, expressed by our placement of deed before understanding.

The answer to that can be found in a parable told by the Midrash:

> *There was once a king whose countrymen made him three crowns. What did the king do? He took one and placed it on his own head, and two he placed on the heads of his children.*[2]

---

2   *Midrash Rabbah, Vayikra* 24:8. The crown that G-d received at Sinai is also alluded to in the verse, "Go out, daughters of Zion, and behold

The two crowns delivered by the angels to each Jewish soul, one for "We will do" and the other for "We will hear," represent the magnificence of a deed done solely for G-d, and the depth of understanding gained by one who pursues wisdom to the sole aim of serving its divine author. There was, however, a third crown—a crown that is the source and root of the other two—which the angels did not bring: the crown of our unequivocal commitment to G-d.

This crown G-d entrusts to no angel, awards to no soul. Instead of placing it on the heads of His children, G-d does something that is an even greater demonstration of His regard for them: G-d wears it on His own head. This is My pride and glory, G-d's crown says. This is where My wearing it is tantamount to your wearing it, for this is where you and I are one.

King Solomon with the crown with which his mother crowned him on the day of his betrothal..." (Song of Songs 3:11). "King Solomon," say our sages, is a reference to "the Holy One, Blessed be He, the King to whom is peace"; "his mother" is the *Shechinah*, the collective soul of Israel, whose relationship with G-d takes the forms of "daughter," "sister," and "mother"; and "the day of his betrothal" is the day of the giving of the Torah at Mount Sinai (*Midrash Rabbah, Shemot* 52:5; Talmud, *Taanit* 26b).

PARASHAH
NINETEEN

TERUMAH

Exodus 25:1–27:19

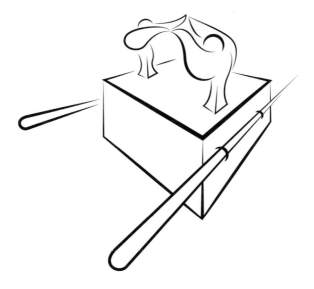

A dwelling for G-d

SON-IN-LAW

They shall make for Me a sanctuary, and I shall dwell amongst them.

Exodus 25:8

Following the giving of the Torah at Mount Sinai, G-d instructed the people of Israel to construct a "Tabernacle" (portable temple) that would travel with them in their journeys through the desert. The Tabernacle's innermost chamber, the "Holy of Holies," housed the Torah,[1] and served as the seat of the divine presence in the Israelite camp.

The Midrash offers the following parable to explain the connection between these two events—the giving of the Torah and the construction of the Tabernacle:

> *Once there was a king who had an only daughter. A prince came and married her. The prince wished to go back to his land and take his wife with him. Said [the king] to him: "The daughter I gave you is my only one, and I cannot separate myself from her. I cannot tell you not to take her— she is your wife. But do this one favor for me: Wherever you go, build me a small room so that I may live with you, for I cannot part from my daughter." In the same way, G-d says to Israel: "I have given you the Torah. I cannot part from her. I cannot tell you not to take her. But wherever you go, make a home for Me in which I may dwell."*[2]

---

[1] Inside the Holy of Holies was the ark, containing the two stone tablets on which the Ten Commandments were inscribed, and a Torah scroll.

[2] *Midrash Rabbah, Shemot* 33:1.

A Son by Choice

Our sages have said that "a son-in-law is like a son."[3] Indeed, a son-in-law can be said to be more of a son than a biological child, since a person does not choose his children, whereas a son-in-law is often chosen by the father-in-law[4] and thus, in a certain sense, reflects the self-vision he wishes to propagate more than does his natural child.

The Torah refers to the people of Israel as "G-d's children."[5] But it also speaks of a father-in-law/son-in-law relationship between G-d and Israel, as in the Midrashic parable quoted above.

Indeed we are both, as each of these two models describes an aspect of our relationship with G-d that the other does not. We are G-d's children by virtue of who we are, regardless of whether we exhibit the qualities our Father in Heaven imbued in us, regardless of whether our behavior befits that of a child of G-d. On the other hand, our status as divine "children-in-law" is via our relationship with G-d's daughter, the Torah. Through our commitment to and union with the Torah, we are not only G-d's "natural" children, but also G-d's children in the sense that we actualize the divine qualities imbued in us.[6]

---

3   Rashi on Talmud, *Shabbat* 23b. See *Yalkut Shimoni*, I Samuel, 24; *Shulchan Aruch, Yoreh De'ah*, 240:24; *Biurei HaGra* on *Shulchan Aruch*, ad loc.
4   Cf. Deuteronomy 22:16: "I gave my daughter to this man," pp. 232–237.
5   Exodus 4:22; Deuteronomy 14:1; et al.
6   See the essay, "The Face of a Child," pp. 232–237 below.

TRANSPLANTED CEDARS

You shall make the wall-panels of the Tabernacle of cedar wood, standing upright.

Exodus 26:15

One of the fifteen materials used in the construction of the Tabernacle was *shitim* wood, a type of cedar, which was used in the making of the wall panels, pillars, and many of the furnishings.

Rashi writes:

> How did the Children of Israel obtain [cedar wood] in the desert? Rabbi Tanchuma explained: Our father Jacob foresaw with his prophetic vision that the people of Israel were destined to build a Sanctuary in the desert. So he brought cedars to Egypt and planted them [there], and instructed his children to take them along when they left Egypt.[1]

Botanic Memories

At the time, Jacob's children might have wondered: Why carry trees from the Holy Land to plant in Egypt, for use in a building to be constructed centuries later? Surely, wood could always

---

[1] Rashi on Exodus 25:6.

be obtained, for a price, wherever their descendants might find themselves.[2]

But his grandchildren and great-grandchildren understood. As they watched the cedars grow, they were reminded that long before their enslavement by the Egyptians, these trees had grown in the soil of the Holy Land—the land promised them as their eternal heritage. They carried with them, and transmitted to their children, Jacob's instructions to take these trees along when they were to leave Egypt, to be fashioned into a Sanctuary for G-d.

Throughout their exile in Egypt, the cedars whispered to Jacob's descendants: This is not your home. You hail from a loftier, holier place. Soon you will leave this depraved land, to be reclaimed by G-d as His people. Soon you will uproot us from this foreign place and carry us triumphantly to Sinai, where you will construct of us an abode for the divine presence, which shall once again manifest itself in your midst.

Source of Comfort

Rashi cites a Midrashic account about the origin the Tabernacle's cedars in the name of "Rabbi Tanchuma." While many of Rashi's explanations have their source in the Talmudic and Midrashic teachings, as a rule, Rashi does not name the original author of the saying, unless this adds something to our understanding of his commentary on the verse.

In this case, the name *Tanchuma*, which means "condolence" and "comforting," illuminates Jacob's reason for transporting cedar trees from the Holy Land and transplanting them in Egypt.

---

2   See commentary by Taz of Rashi's commentary, ad loc. Also see Ibn Ezra, *Baalei HaTosafot*, and Chizkuni on Exodus 25:6.

In addition to providing the wood for the Tabernacle, these trees were a source of comfort for the Children of Israel in their long and bitter *galut* in Egypt.

Staves of Faith

"The *tzaddik* shall bloom as a palm," proclaims the Psalmist, "as a cedar of Lebanon, shall he flourish."[3] In our current *galut*, we too have trans-historic cedars transplanted by our father Jacob[4]—plantings that provide us with a link to the past and hope for the future.

The *tzaddik* is a soul that towers above the transience and turbulence of *galut*; a soul that is rooted in Israel's sacred beginnings and pointed toward its ultimate redemption. When our subjection to the temporal and the mundane threatens to overwhelm us, we need only look to the cedars planted in our midst. In these timeless staves of faith we find guidance and fortitude, comfort and encouragement.

---

[3] Psalms 92:13.

[4] The Hebrew word *nassi* ("leader") is an acronym of the phrase *nitzotzo shel Yaakov avinu*, "a spark of Jacob our father." The soul of every leader of Israel is an offshoot of the soul of Jacob, father of the people of Israel (*Megaleh Amukot*, section 84).

THE ALTAR
AND
THE ARK

Make an ark of cedar wood... and cover it with pure gold, within and without... and into the ark you shall put the [Tablets of the] Testimony, which I will give to you.

Exodus 25:10–16

Make the altar of cedar wood... and cover it in copper... As it was shown to you on the mountain, so they should make it.

Ibid., 27:1–8.

The Holy Temple in Jerusalem, as its forerunner, the "Tabernacle" constructed in the Sinai Desert, was the focal point of man's relationship with G-d, and of G-d's relationship with creation. On the one hand, the Temple was the prototype and the apex of our effort to bring the material world in harmony with its Creator; on the other hand, it was the place that G-d designated as the "tent of meeting"[1] where He would communicate with man and manifest His presence within the physical reality.

The Temple housed many "vessels" or furnishings, each minutely detailed in the Torah section of *Terumah* (Exodus 25:1–27:19),[2] each with a function of its own. The "ark" contained the

---

1. Exodus 29:42, et al.
2. *Terumah* includes G-d's instructions to Moses on how to make the

two "Tablets of the Testament" inscribed with the Ten Commandments, and a Torah scroll; the *menorah* had seven oil lamps which were lit every evening; the "table" held the twelve loaves of unleavened bread which were arranged on it every Shabbat; on the altar the *korbanot* (animal sacrifices) were offered; and so on.

Which of these "vessels" most represented the overall significance of the Holy Temple? In which of these various functions did the primary objective of the Temple lie? Two great Torah sages, Maimonides and Nachmanides, express differing views on the matter.

Maimonides, in his monumental codification of Torah law, *Mishneh Torah*, describes the Holy Temple thus: "It is an active *mitzvah* to construct a house for G-d to facilitate the offering of *korbanot*..."[3]

On the other hand, Nachmanides points out that the first item in G-d's instructions to Moses on the building of the Sanctuary is the ark. "The main object of the Sanctuary," explains Nachmanides, "is to serve as the resting place of the *Shechinah* (divine presence). This is realized in the ark, as G-d says to Moses (Exodus 25:22): 'I will commune with you there, and I will speak to you from above the ark's cover...'"[4]

The Halachic Perspective

One may view the Holy Temple in terms of what we do there to bring G-d's reality into the world; or, one can view the Temple in

---

ark, table, *menorah*, and the outer altar; in addition, the inner altar described in the *parashah* of *Tetzaveh*, and the laver in *Ki Tisa*.

3   *Mishneh Torah, Laws of the Holy Temple*, 1:1.
4   Nachmanides' commentary on Exodus 25:1.

terms of what it does for us, above and beyond what our efforts can achieve.

Maimonides' *Mishneh Torah* is a work of *halachah*, Torah law. *Halachah* is the actual application of Torah to daily living, the dos and don'ts of life. So the halachic perspective on the Holy Temple is defined by what we actually do there, and the role it plays in our life's work. Thus Maimonides focuses on the *korbanot*—the manner in which we serve G-d in the Holy Temple.

The word *korban* means "that which is brought near." The *korbanot* were animals that were sacrificed to G-d: the blood and fat were offered upon the altar, and the meat was eaten in conditions of ritual purity. An ordinary ox or sheep was uplifted from its mundane existence and brought close to G-d.

On a deeper level, the *korban* represents a person's efforts to elevate and sanctify the "animal" within him- or herself. The sages teach that we each posses both a "G-dly soul" and an "animal soul."[5] The G-dly in us is our spiritual essence, the transcendent self within us that perpetually seeks to escape the mundane and cleave to its divine source. But there is also an animal side to our psyche: a self that focuses on self-enhancement and self-gratification, and gives birth to our selfish drives and aspirations; a self that is driven and fulfilled by its physical needs and desires.

This is the animal in us that is to be offered as a *korban* to G-d. Its "blood"—its fervor and passion for material things—is to be sprinkled on the altar; its "fat"—its excessive indulgence and pleasure-seeking—is to be burned. But its "meat"—the gist of the animal soul—is not sacrificed, but reoriented. The physical drives

---

5 Rabbi Chaim Vital, *Shaar HaKedushah* 1:1–2; *Tanya*, chapters 1–12; also see Nachmanides' commentary to Genesis 2:7.

themselves are not to be disavowed and suppressed, but are to be refined and directed toward higher and loftier ends.

So the *korban* incorporates the very essence of *halachah*: our endeavor to orient our daily lives in a positive and holy manner. To "bring near" and sublimate every aspect of our material existence, by eliminating its negative and destructive elements, and developing the substance itself into something that serves a higher, more sanctified goal.

The Vision of the Mystic

Nachmanides, a famed kabbalist whose commentary on Torah includes its more sublime elements, describes a more "esoteric" function of the Holy Temple. In addition to facilitating the elevation of our lives through the service of *korbanot*, the Temple also served as the entry point for the infusion of a more spiritual reality *into* our world. While the altar enabled us to develop and refine our physical finite world, the ark represents a "higher" function of the Holy Temple: to manifest the infinite reality of G-d, expressed in the Torah.

In other words, the relationship between man and G-d involves both "parties." We reach upward to bring ourselves close to Him; but the sum of our efforts cannot transcend the inherent limits and definitions of our humanity. So G-d also reaches down to relate to us on His, infinite, terms.

The *korbanot* (and today, our "service of the heart" through prayer) represent our humanly finite endeavors to elevate our material nature and environment. Torah, G-d's communication of His wisdom and will, is G-d reaching down to inject of His infinite and all-transcendent reality into our existence. In the

Holy Temple, the ark containing the Torah served as a tangible expression of the divine infinity and transcendence.

Infinity: A Non-Definition

In truth, both the altar and the ark—both man's service and G-d's Torah—are necessary if G-d is to truly "dwell" within our world.

The human element represented by the *korbanot* can be seen simply as a way to allow our finite selves to also play a part in the creation of a "home for G-d in the physical world." In truth, however, it is far more than that: it is crucial to the very notion of a place that "houses" a truly infinite and transcendent divine reality.

For a reality to be confined to the infinite alone is itself a limitation of sorts. If it excludes the finite and the physical, then it, too, has parameters which define an area over which it extends, and an area from which it is excluded. A truly infinite reality is one that is not only transcendent, but also all-inclusive and all-pervading.

This idea is expressed by the fact that the Tablets and the Torah scroll were contained within an ark. While Torah expresses the divinely infinite aspect of the Holy Temple, this aspect is also "contained" by the parameters that define a purely infinite reality. What we call "infinity" is itself a definition of sorts.

This is why the Holy Temple cannot be described exclusively as the seat of the ark, nor can it be defined exclusively as the place of the altar. Rather, it is both. As the seat of the ark, it facilitates the drawing down of the infinite from above, through G-d's investment of His wisdom and will in the Torah and His continued communication to humanity via the ark. And as the place of the altar and the *korbanot*, it is the focus of man's service of G-d through our elevation of our finite self and world.

It was this integration of both the humanly finite and the divinely infinite that marked the divine presence in the Holy Temple as truly absolute: a presence not constrained by any boundaries and parameters, not even the boundaries and parameters of the infinite.[6]

Both Hands

This is the deeper meaning of the verse that describes the Holy Temple as, "The sanctuary of G-d, which Your hands have founded."[7] What do the "hands" of G-d represent?

In another verse, the prophet quotes: "My hand has laid the foundation of earth, and My right hand has spread out the heavens."[8] The Midrash expounds: "G-d extended His right hand and created the heavens; He extended His left, and created the earth."[9] In other words, the spiritual reality of the heavens are described

---

[6] This duality also found expression in the phenomenon that "the space of the ark was not part of the measurement" (Talmud *Yoma* 21a). The chamber that housed the ark—called the "Holy of Holies"—measured twenty cubits (approximately 32 feet) by twenty cubits. In its center stood the ark, also of a specified size—2.5 by 1.5 cubits. Nevertheless, the distance from each of the ark's outer walls to the interior walls of the Holy of Holies was ten cubits. In other words, the ark did not take up any of the space of the room, demonstrating how the divine infinity transcends the very definitions of the physical. At the same time, the ark itself did possess spatial dimensions. So it was neither finite nor infinite, but simultaneously both, both defying and possessing both "definitions."

[7] Exodus 15:17.
[8] Isaiah 48:13.
[9] *Pirkei D'Rabbi Eliezer*. In the words of the *Zohar* (2:20a): "He extended His right hand and created the supernal world; He extended His left, and created the lower world."

as possessing the strength and power of the divine "right hand," while the earth and physical reality embody the lesser, more finite element of G-d's creation.

This, however, is creation in its original, undeveloped state. The Holy Temple, however, represents a reality which "Your hands [plural] have founded"—a reality in which the all-pervading presence of G-d incorporates both "hands" equally. No longer is there a superiority in "right" over "left," in spirit over material, in infinite over definitive. Our involvements in the mundanities of physical life, as well as our spiritual aspirations and attainments, serve us equally in relating to our Creator.[10]

This is the eternal significance of the sanctuary that we are instructed, and empowered, to construct out of the material elements of our life. Often, we find that the bulk of our time and energy is consumed by the seemingly "petty" entanglements of daily living, and see this as an encumbrance on our freedom-striving spirit. In truth, however, our transcendent and spiritual activities are no less limiting, if we confine ourselves exclusively to them. But when we take the approach that everything in our lives, both the lofty and the lowly, can be utilized in a positive and holy way, we transcend all parameters and definitions, and relate to the ultimate Essence which knows no bounds.

---

10 See the essay, "One Horizontal Night," in Vol. I (Genesis) of *The Inside Story*.

WOOD AND STONE

Make the tabernacle out of ten curtains of fine-spun linen, and blue, purple, and crimson wool... Make curtains of goat hair... and a covering of ram skins dyed red, and a covering of tachash *skins, from above.*

Make the wall-panels for the tabernacle of cedar wood, standing upright... twenty panels for the southern side. And make forty silver foundation-sockets under the twenty panels...

Exodus 26:1–19

Which is greater: learning or doing? The Talmud records a debate between the sages on this question. The conclusion that was reached is that, "Learning is greater, as learning leads to action."[1]

"Learning" is the development and perfection of the self, while "doing" is the servitude of the self to the task at hand. So the issue of learning versus doing expresses one of the most fundamental questions of life: Which should a person strive for—personal growth, or commitment to a higher ideal? What should be the focus of our lives—to better ourselves, or to serve our Creator?

Characteristically, the Talmud does not settle the question by siding with one of the two opinions, but rather by showing us that

---

1 Talmud, *Kidushin* 40b.

both are correct. Learning is indeed "greater," but only because it leads to action. Personal growth is the "greater," more dominant aspect of our lives, occupying the bulk of our time and the greater concentration of our resources; but it is not an end in itself. The purpose of all this greatness is to better and more fully serve the purpose for which our Creator put us in this world.

Otherwise stated, there are two phases to our existence. In the first phase, which begins at birth and continues through our formative years, the emphasis is on growth and self-improvement. We know that the goal is to transcend the self and devote ourselves to a higher purpose, and this knowledge underlies our lives like a foundation underlies a building; still, it is the edifice of self-realization that constitutes the visible and dominant aspect of our existence. Ultimately, however, we reach a stage in which "doing" becomes the more dominant feature of our lives, with the "learning" aspect serving merely as an auxiliary and support for that goal.

The Model Home

Two structures, the first built mostly of wood and the second primarily of stone, embody these two phases of our mission in life.

Shortly after the giving of the Torah at Mount Sinai, G-d instructed Moses: "They shall make for Me a Sanctuary, and I shall dwell amongst them."[2] According to chassidic teaching, these words express the divine purpose in creation: G-d created the world because "He desired a dwelling for Himself in the lowly realms"—i.e., within the physical existence.[3]

---

2   Exodus 25:8.
3   *Tanya*, chapter 36, based on *Midrash Tanchuma, Naso* 16.

On the individual level, this is achieved when we perform the *mitzvot* of the Torah, utilizing the various elements of the physical world to serve G-d. Money is given to charity; grain is made into matzah for Passover, animal hide into *tefilin*, wool into *tzitzit*, and so on.

Furthermore, when a person devotes his or her life to the fulfillment of the *mitzvot*, everything which supports this life—the food they eat, the clothes they wear, the energy they consume—is involved in the realization of the supernal goal.

This is how the "lowly realms" of the physical world become a dwelling for G-d. Instead of the lowliness which previously defined its relationship to its Creator—for the physical world, with its apparent independence and concreteness of being, can be the greatest concealment of the divine truth—the physical world is now transformed into a home for G-d, an environment that serves G-d's will and expresses His all-pervading reality.

On the communal level, the people of Israel built a "home for G-d" in the form of the Sanctuary. By the command of G-d, various materials were used to construct an edifice to serve as the seat of G-d's manifest presence in the physical world. Although G-d is equally everywhere, this was the place where G-d chose to visibly permeate the material. This was a "dwelling" that represented the ultimate function of every physical thing.

Tabernacle and Temple

As there exist two phases in the life's work of man, so it is with the collective expression of humanity's mission, the Sanctuary.

First there was the "Tabernacle" (*Mishkan*)—the portable Sanctuary that the people of Israel carried with them for the forty years that they journeyed through the Sinai Desert. Then, after they settled and established themselves in the Holy Land, the permanent "Holy Temple" (*Beit Hamikdash*) was built on the Temple Mount in Jerusalem.[4]

The difference can be seen in the construction. The Tabernacle had an earthen floor, upon which were placed "foundation-sockets" made of silver. These sockets supported the wall panels, made of cedar wood. The roof consisted of three layers of tent-coverings: tapestries of wool and goat-hair, and a covering of animal hides.

The Holy Temple, on the other hand, was made almost entirely of earth and stone, from its marble floor, to its stone walls, to its mortar roof. The Holy Temple did include wood, in the form of support beams, but these were imbedded within the stone and cement. In fact, it was specifically forbidden for even the smallest part of these wooden beams to protrude and be visible.[5]

Thus, the Tabernacle included both lifeless minerals (earth, metal, etc.), and the products of plant and animal life. Indeed, the layering of these materials reflected the hierarchy of these materials in the physical universe. On the bottom were elements from the "mineral kingdom"; above these stood the walls of the structure, made of materials from the "vegetable kingdom"; and these, in turn, were topped by the roof coverings deriving from the

---

[4] The Holy Temple in Jerusalem was built by King Solomon four hundred and forty years after the people of Israel entered the Holy Land. During that 440-year period, the Tabernacle continued to serve as the Sanctuary, and was set up in a variety of places in the Land, most notably at Shiloh, where it stood for 369 years.

The Tabernacle at Shiloh was a semipermanent structure: it retained the cloth roof-coverings of the original Tabernacle, but the wooden walls were replaced with stone walls. Thus, it constituted an interim stage between the "organic" Tabernacle and the "mineral" Temple.

[5] See Talmud, *Rosh Hashanah* 4a; *Mishneh Torah, Laws of the Holy Temple*, 1:9; also see discussion in *Likutei Sichot*, vol. 28, p. 220.

"animal kingdom." In contrast, the Holy Temple was built almost entirely of materials of inanimate origin. The wood that it did contain was secondary and supportive in function, and was completely covered up by the stone.

In the "small world" that is the human being,[6] the inanimate element is our capacity for self-abnegation, as expressed by the verse, "May my soul be as dust to all."[7] This represents our capacity for devotion, service, and action. Plant and animal life are representative of the capacity for growth and development, of our emotional and intellectual life.

In the Tabernacle, which represents the initial stages of our mission in life, all these elements are visibly stressed. In fact, the emphasis is on our "higher" faculties of understanding and feeling. True, everything rests upon the foundation of servitude to the divine will; but the edifice that is built on this foundation is the development and realization of human potential.

Ultimately, however, we grow to visibly exemplify the purpose of it all—to serve our Creator. The Holy Temple, too, contains elements of growth, but growth of an utterly egoless nature. This is growth that is submerged within self-abnegation—growth that is solely a means to better fulfill G-d's will. In the entire edifice, from top to bottom, one sees only the "stone" and "earth" of deed.[8]

---

6   See *Midrash Tanchuma, Pekudei* 3.
7   *Siddur*, concluding verses of the *Amidah* prayer.
8   Also see the essay, "The Encounter," in Vol. I (Genesis) of *The Inside Story*.

MODEL HOME

They shall make for Me a Sanctuary, and I shall dwell amongst them...

You shall make a curtain of blue, purple, and scarlet [wool], and fine-spun linen ... and the curtain shall divide for you between the Holy and the Holy of Holies...

You shall make a courtyard for the Tabernacle ... one hundred cubits in length and fifty cubits in breadth...

Exodus 25:8, 26:31–33, and 27:9–18

Our sages tell us that the purpose of creation is that "G-d desired a dwelling for Himself in the lowly realms"—that the physical world should be made into a home for G-d, an environment that is receptive to and expressive of His truth.[1]

The building of the *Mishkan* ("Tabernacle") by the Children of Israel in the Sinai Desert marked the first such effort to construct a home for G-d. Fifteen physical substances, including gold, silver, copper, wood, wool, linen, animal skins, oil, spices, and gemstones[2]—representing a cross-section of the mineral, vegetable, and animal resources of the physical universe, and the human

---

1   *Midrash Tanchuma, Naso* 16. In the words of Rabbi Schneur Zalman of Liadi, "This is what man is all about; this is the purpose of his creation, and of the creation of all the worlds, higher and lower: that there be made for G-d a dwelling in the lowly realms" (*Tanya*, chapter 36).

2   The fifteen materials are listed in Exodus 25:3–7.

resources invested in their workmanship—were forged into an edifice dedicated to the service of G-d. When the divine presence came to rest in the Tabernacle, it became the prototype for the fulfillment of the divine purpose in creation: to transform our lives and our environment into "a dwelling for G-d."

Three Spaces of the Tabernacle

To better understand how the Tabernacle (and later, the Holy Temple in Jerusalem)[3] served as a prototype for the divine purpose of creation, we will first take a look at its structure and its primary components, as described in the Torah section of *Terumah* (Exodus 25:1–27:19).

The Tabernacle was comprised of three primary spaces: the courtyard (*chatzer*), the Holy (*kodesh*), and the Holy of Holies (*kodesh hakodashim*).

The "Holy" and the "Holy of Holies" occupied a structure whose inside area measured thirty cubits from east to west and ten cubits from north to south (approximately 48' x 16'), and was divided by a curtain into two chambers: an outer chamber measuring 20 x 10 cubits (the Holy), and an inner chamber measuring 10 x 10 cubits (the Holy of Holies).

The Holy contained the "indoor altar" (also called the "golden altar") upon which the incense (*ketoret*) was burned; the "table"

---

[3] The Tabernacle accompanied the people of Israel in their travels through the desert. Whenever the Israelites broke camp, the Tabernacle was dismantled, loaded onto ox-drawn carts, and erected anew at their next encampment. After entering the Holy Land, a more permanent version of the Tabernacle was erected (first at Gilgal, and later at Shiloh, Nob, and Gibeon) until it was replaced by the Holy Temple build by King Solomon in Jerusalem.

on which the "showbread" (*lechem hapanim*) was arranged; and the *menorah*, whose seven lamps were lit each afternoon to burn through the night. The Holy of Holies, into which no one ventured except for the *kohen gadol* (high priest) on Yom Kippur, contained only the ark holding the Tablets of the Covenant and topped by two *keruvim* (cherubs) of solid gold.

Surrounding the structure containing these two chambers was the "courtyard," an area 100 by 50 cubits in size enclosed by a partition of woven linen. Within the courtyard stood the "outdoor altar" upon which the *korbanot* and *menachot* (animal and meal offerings) were offered to G-d. Between the outdoor altar and the entrance to the Holy was the "laver" (*kiyor*), at which the priests washed their hands and feet before entering the Holy or performing any part of its service.[4]

As the prototype for the divine purpose of creation, the structure of Tabernacle mirrors the structure of creation on a variety of levels. The Tabernacle's three primary areas—the courtyard, the Holy, and the Holy of Holies—reflect three basic domains in the macro-universe, in time, in society, and in every individual life.

Three Strata of Creation

Maimonides writes that "all things that G-d created in His world are divided into three categories." The first category is the material world: "creations that are comprised of matter and form and are constantly deteriorating, such as the bodies of humans and

---

[4] The Holy Temple in Jerusalem was modeled after the Tabernacle, and included these three domains as well: the *azarah* (corresponding to the Tabernacle's *chatzer*), the *heichal* (corresponding to the "Holy"), and the "Holy of Holies."

animals, plants, and minerals." The second category includes physical entities of a more refined nature, such as the stars and other heavenly bodies; these, too, "possess matter and form, but they are not as ephemeral as the first category." The third and highest sphere of creation embraces the utterly spiritual creations, which are "forms alone, without matter. These are the angels, which are not physical bodies, but various forms" of divine energy.[5]

The human being is a universe in miniature, and the universe is a macrocosm of man.[6] The entirety of creation is reflected in our lives, and the structure of our lives is mirrored by the cosmos. Thus, our own lives are also divided into material, refined physical, and purely spiritual domains. As we shall see, this threefold structure can be discerned in all areas of life—in our activities, in our physiology, in time, and on the communal level.

Degrees of Matter

For most of our waking hours, our attention is focused on physical things and physical activities. Either we're eating, or preparing our meal, or earning the money to buy it; or else we are attending to another of the body's physical needs or wants, or to one of the numerous physical objects with which we furnish our lives.

But every so often, the physicality of life takes on a deeper significance, and we find ourselves looking at all of these physical things and activities in a different light. We realize that the person we're talking to is not just a body; that there is a soul within

---

[5] *Guide for the Perplexed*, 1:72; see also sources cited in the next footnote.
[6] *Midrash Tanchuma, Pekudei* 3; *Tikunei Zohar* 469. *Mishneh Torah, Laws of the Fundamentals of Torah* 2:3. See also *Avot d'Rabbi Natan*, 31; *Midrash Rabbah, Kohelet* 1:4; *Zohar* 1:134b.

that body that is striving for connection with our own soul. We realize that the food we're eating is not just food; it's the energy that drives the engine of our lives—energy that can be expended on useful, constructive, even spiritual things. We realize that our home, furniture, and bank account are not just objects and statements of material wealth; they are tools that can be utilized to achieve the deeper, more meaningful goals we've always dreamt of achieving. At such times, the physical things that surround us seem to shed the skin of corporeality that encases them at all other times. In our mind's eye, they becomes lighter, more porous, more refined, as if illuminated from within by a spiritual light. We have caught a glimpse into the soul of the physical world.

Finally, there is the rare moment in which the veil of materiality not only becomes more transparent, but falls away entirely: a moment in which we completely transcend the physical trappings of life to encounter its spiritual essence; a moment in which the physical body and its physical needs become utterly insignificant in the face of the infinity and eternity of the soul.

In the human being, these three domains are represented by the digestive system, which is the most materialistic component of our physiology; the higher senses of sight, smell, taste, etc.; and the intellect and speech, which are the loftiest and most transcendent of our faculties.

Domains in Time

These three visions of reality are also imbedded in the time-cycles that govern our lives. The Jewish calendar defines areas for material involvement; elevations from which the physical world is seen in a more refined state; and peaks of consummate spirituality.

"Six days you shall labor," decrees the Torah, "and do all your work."[7] The Midrash considers this statement as much of a *mitzvah* as the commandment contained in the next verse, "And the seventh day is a Sabbath-rest to G-d."[8] For six days of the week, we are commanded to develop the physical world, to engage with its material aspect. Although we foster an awareness of a more spiritual reality, and endeavor to infuse this awareness into our physical activities, on the whole, the world retains its mask of corporeality. The higher purpose of our activities resides in our own consciousness, but cannot be seen in the "real" world in which we are immersed.

But on the seventh day, the physical world shows us a holier, more refined face. It's not that our lives are less physical. On the contrary, we are commanded to honor the Shabbat with sumptuous food and drink, fine clothes, and the enjoyment of other physical pleasures.[9] But on Shabbat, these physical activities are aglow with spiritual content. We experience them not as material indulgences, but as a celebration of G-d's creation.

For fifty-plus weeks a year, we follow this cycle: six days of materiality, followed by a seventh day of refined physicality—physicality whose soul has been made visible. Then, once a year, comes Yom Kippur, the "Sabbath of Sabbaths."[10]

On the "Sabbath of Sabbaths," we forswear work, food, drink, and a host of other material needs and comforts, to focus exclusively on matters of the spirit. On this day, the bodily aspect of our existence recedes entirely, and our soul shines forth independently of its physical vessel.

---

7 Exodus 20:9.
8 *Mechilta d'Rashbi*, ad loc.
9 *Mishneh Torah, Laws of Shabbat* 30:3, 7 and 14; see also *Likutei Sichot*, vol. 12, p. 254, and sources cited there.
10 Leviticus 23:32.

The Nation

These three domains—material involvement, refined physicality, and total transcendence—also exist on the national level. The people of Israel are divided into three classes, each of whom is assigned another of these three areas as the focus of their lives.

Twelve of the thirteen tribes of Israel are designated as "Israelites." These are the farmers, merchants, and statesmen of Israel, whose lives, as a rule, are taken up with the business of material life.

One tribe, the tribe of Levi, was chosen by G-d for a more spiritual calling. The tribe of Levi includes the *kohanim* ("priests"), who conducted the service in the Tabernacle, and later in the Holy Temple, offering the *korbanot*, burning the incense, lighting the *menorah*, and performing a host of other rituals; and the Levites, who assisted the *kohanim* in their holy work.

The divine service performed by the *kohanim* and the Levites was not divorced from the physicality of human life. Animals were slaughtered; certain portions were offered to G-d, but the bulk of the meat was eaten by the *kohanim*, or by the person who brought the offering. The *menorah* shed physical light, and the incense filled the Temple with a physical aroma. The "showbread" which was displayed all week on the "table" was distributed every Shabbat to the *kohanim* for their consumption.

Yet these were sacred objects and activities: physical in substance and form, but with an aura of divinity about them. The meat was holy meat, the light was holy light, and the aroma was a sacred aroma. Even the most casual observer could see that the *kohanim* and Levites were not engaged in ordinary activities but in holy work, whose manifest purpose is the service of G-d (as with the visibly holy physicality of Shabbat).

Among the divine servants of Levi, a single individual was designated as a "holy of holies"[11]—as one whose holiness transcends even the sacred physicality practiced by his tribe. This was the *kohen gadol*, commanded to lead a life of total disassociation from material life. The *kohen gadol* "never leaves the Sanctuary,"[12] and does not partake in the social and civic activities that are integral to a person's life as an individual and a member of society.[13] His entire being is devoted to maintaining a state of perpetual, self-obliterating attachment to G-d.

In the Tabernacle

The Tabernacle—G-d's first home on earth—was a model of the universe, of time, of the nation of Israel, and of every individual life. Hence the "three domains" described above were represented in the three areas of the Tabernacle:

(a) The outermost domain of the Sanctuary, the courtyard, was also its most "material" part. Here the *korbanot*—which G-d refers to as "My food"[14]—were offered on the "outdoor altar." Many of the *korbanot* were cooked and eaten in the courtyard by the *kohanim*; some of the *korbanot* offered here were eaten by ordinary Israelites outside of the Holy Temple.

Not only was the courtyard the place for the "food" element of the service, it also contained elements of another signature feature

---

11 I Chronicles 23:13.
12 Leviticus 21:12. This is not an across-the-board prohibition for the *kohen gadol* to ever leave the Holy Temple, but the designation of the Temple as his permanent place (see *Mishneh Torah, Laws of the Sanctuary's Vessels and Those Who Serve in It* 5:7).
13 *Mishneh Torah*, ibid., 5:1–9.
14 Numbers 28:2. See the essay, "Bread for My Fire," in vol. 3 (Leviticus) of *The Inside Story,*

of materiality—waste.¹⁵ The ashes from the daily cleaning of the two altars and the *menorah's* lamps were deposited in a special place designated for them in the courtyard,¹⁶ as were the discarded "crop and feathers" from the bird offerings;¹⁷ in the courtyard were also deposited the shards of the broken earthen pots that had been used to cook the meat of sin-offerings.¹⁸ The courtyard also contained the "laver" at which the *kohanim* washed when they came in from the outside world, in order to cleanse themselves of the coarseness and materiality that clung to them from their stay outside the Tabernacle.

(b) In contrast, the outer chamber of the Tabernacle's structure, the "Holy," was the designated place for the more refined elements of the service—those involving sight (the lighting of the *menorah*) and smell (the incense offered on the indoor altar).¹⁹ There was one component of the "Holy" involving food and taste—the showbread—but this, too, emphasized the more subliminal nature of this chamber. The showbread had the special quality that it did not spoil or become stale even though it was arranged upon the "table" for a full week; thus it represented the higher order of physicality, described by Maimonides as the second stratum of creation, which is immune to dissolution. Furthermore, the showbread

---

15 In Maimonides' categorization of the three strata of creation cited above, the defining difference between the two types of physical creations is that the more material creations "are constantly deteriorating," while the loftier ones "are not as ephemeral as the first category." Also see Bechayei's commentary to Exodus 25:9.
16 Leviticus 6:3; *Mishneh Torah, Laws of the Daily and Additional Offerings* 2:12, 3:4, and 3:12.
17 Leviticus 1:16.
18 Talmud, *Zevachim* 93b (see Leviticus 6:21).
19 While smell is a physical phenomenon, it is devoid of the tactility of taste and the visibility of light; thus it is regarded as "nourishment for the soul" and as representative of spirituality (Talmud, *Berachot* 43b).

was distinctly a Shabbat food, and was eaten by the *kohanim* only, implying that its physicality is of the higher, more refined sort.

(c) The sole object in the Holy of Holies was the ark housing the Torah, which embodies the "intellect" and "speech" of G-d, so to speak, the loftiest and most transcendent component of the Creator's involvement in creation.

All Israelites were allowed entrance into the courtyard, while only the *kohanim* were admitted into the "Holy." But the "Holy of Holies" was off limits to all except the *kohen gadol*, who entered it only on Yom Kippur, the holiest day of the year.

The Holy of Holies was the "Sabbath of Sabbaths" of the Tabernacle: a space that epitomized the utter suspension of materiality and physicality. There was no "food" element in the Holy of Holies (just as there is no eating on Yom Kippur and no materiality in the *kohen gadol*'s life), not even the "Shabbat food" of the Tabernacle's "Holy" chamber. The only services performed in the Holy of Holies were the offering of the incense and the sprinkling of the blood of two "burnt offerings" (*korbanot* of which no part is eaten and which are wholly burnt on the altar), performed once a year on Yom Kippur.

Personal Home

When commanding us to construct the Tabernacle, G-d said to Moses: "They shall make for Me a sanctuary, and I shall dwell amongst them."[20] While the last word of this verse, *betocham*, is commonly translated "amongst them," its literal meaning is "within them." Rabbi Isaiah Horowitz, author of the classic

---

20 Exodus 25:8.

philosophical-kabbalistic work, *Shaloh*, explains that G-d is promising to dwell "within each and every one of them."[21]

Each and every one of us is a "Tabernacle," a virtual universe embodying the various strata of time, space, and humanity. And we are empowered to make our lives a sanctuary in whose every component G-d can be made to feel at home—be it the inner sanctum of unadulterated spirit, the more external chamber of sanctified physicality, or the outer courtyard of material life.

---

21 Shaloh, *Shaar HaOtiot, Lamed.*

THE FACE OF A CHILD

Make a kaporet *of pure gold... and two golden* keruvim... *at the two ends of the* kaporet.... *And you shall place the* kaporet *above, upon the ark; and into the ark you shall put the Testament, which I shall give you.*

I will meet with you there; and I will speak with you from above the kaporet, *from between the two* keruvim *that are upon the Ark of Testament, all that I will command you unto the Children of Israel.*

Exodus 25:17–22

Following the divine revelation at Sinai, G-d commanded that a Sanctuary be built to serve as a "tent of meeting"—a point of contact between G-d and His people. At the heart of the Sanctuary, in its innermost chamber, stood the ark that housed the "Testament"—the two stone tablets on which the Ten Commandments were inscribed by the hand of G-d. The ark, which had the form of a box open at the top, was covered by the *kaporet*—a cover made of solid gold, out of which rose the two winged *keruvim* ("cherubs") hammered out of the same piece of gold. When G-d spoke to Moses, Moses would hear the divine voice issuing from between the two *keruvim*.

The Testament housed by the ark was the essence of the divine communication to man, as the Ten Commandments encapsulate the entire Torah. Later, the ark also held the Torah scroll written by Moses, which embodies a more detailed rendition of the laws implicit in the Ten Commandments. So the ark was the container of the Torah, the vessel of the divine wisdom and will. Yet the divine voice did not emanate from the ark itself, but from a space "above the *kaporet*, between the two *keruvim*."

What was the significance of the *kaporet*? What were the *keruvim* and what do they represent? And why do they mark the point of contact between G-d and man?

Two Commentaries

Foremost among the commentaries compiled by our sages on the Torah are those by Rashi (Rabbi Shlomo Yitzchaki, 1040–1105) and Nachmanides (Rabbi Moshe ben Nachman, 1194–1270). Rashi defines his goal by stating: "I come only to explain the simple meaning of the verse";[1] indeed, Rashi's commentary has been universally accepted as the most basic tool for understanding the Torah, and serves as a first reference for schoolchild and scholar alike. On the other hand, Nachmanides, a noted mystic and kabbalist, often uncovers a "deeper" stratum of significance in the Torah's words, exposing its students to "delightful things, for those who know and understand the hidden wisdom [of the Torah]."[2]

Rashi and Nachmanides often differ in their interpretation of a particular word or verse. One example of this is their different conceptions of the *kaporet* and the *keruvim*.

Rashi sees the ark and the *kaporet* as two different objects. The Sanctuary contained various "vessels," each with a designated

---

[1] Rashi on Genesis 3:8; ibid., verse 24; et al.
[2] Nachmanides' introduction to his commentary on the book of Genesis.

function (the *menorah*, the "outer altar," etc.); according to Rashi the ark and the *kaporet* are two different vessels—it is only that the designated place of the *kaporet* is atop the ark.[3]

Nachmanides, on the other hand, sees the *kaporet* as the cover of the ark (indeed, the word *kaporet* means "cover")—as a component of the ark itself, rather than another of the Sanctuary's vessels.[4]

---

[3] Cf. *Tzafnat Paaneach* on Exodus 25:17 (based on the Talmud, *Sukkah* 5a, and *Torat Kohanim* 1:11): "It was not simply a cover (of the ark), but an entity of its own; it is only that it must be placed upon the ark."

[4] Thus, the very same verse implies different things to the two commentators. In Exodus 25:16, after instructing Moses on the design of the ark proper—before telling him how to make the *kaporet*—G-d commands: "You shall place the Testimony in the ark." Then, in verse 21, after the *kaporet* is described, we again read: "And into the ark you shall put the Testimony which I shall give you." Why does the Torah repeat itself? According to Rashi, the repetition comes to emphasize that the tablets are to be placed in the ark before it is covered by the *kaporet*. "Place it in the *ark*," the Torah is saying—in the ark as it stands alone, before the *kaporet* is placed upon it. According to Nachmanides, the repetition comes to make the very opposite point: that the Testament should be placed in the ark *after* it has been covered by the *kaporet*.

In other words, Rashi and Nachmanides both understand the verse's repetition as serving to emphasize that the tablets should be placed in the ark. But what exactly is the ark? According to Rashi, the *kaporet* is not part of the ark proper, but another, different component of the Sanctuary (though obviously related to the ark, as evidenced by the fact that it is to be placed atop the ark). So the verse is telling us that the tablets should be placed in the ark as it is unto itself, without the addition of the *kaporet*. Nachmanides, on the other hand, considers the *kaporet* to be an integral part of the ark; so the verse comes to tell us to place the tablets in the complete ark, not in an ark lacking its cover.

In addition to the question of when to place the tablets in the ark, there are a number of other halachic issues that relate to the question of whether the *kaporet* is part of the ark or a "vessel" on its own. See *Tzafnat Paaneach* on Exodus 37:6, and *Likutei Sichot*, vol. 26, p. 176.

Another difference between the interpretations of Rashi and Nachmanides concerns the form of the *keruvim*. According to Rashi, these were two winged figures, each with the face of a child (a boy and a girl).[5] Nachmanides is of the opinion that they were a representation of the celestial figures seen by the prophet Ezekiel in his vision of the divine "chariot."[6]

"There are seventy faces to the Torah,"[7] say our sages, for the divine truth reverberates on every level of reality and in every dimension of the mind. The differences between Rashi's and Nachmanides' visions of the *kaporet* and the *keruvim* reflect the different faces of Torah that their respective commentaries expound.

Revelation as Relationship

Speaking from the perspective of "those who know and understand the hidden wisdom," Nachmanides sees the Torah as the essence of the bond between G-d and His people. In the words of the *Zohar*, "There are three knots[8] that are bound with each other: G-d, the Torah, and Israel.... The people of Israel are bound with the Torah, and the Torah is bound with G-d."[9] G-d invested His wisdom in the Torah and His will in its commandments; the Jew studies Torah and implements its commandments in their daily life; thus the Jew is bound with G-d.

---

5   Rashi on Exodus 25:18.
6   Nachmanides' commentary on Exodus 25:21; see Ezekiel 10.
7   *Midrash Rabbah, Bamidbar* 13:15; *Zohar* 3:152a; et al. See also Talmud, *Sanhedrin* 34a.
8   *Kishrin*, in the Aramaic. So reads the version of this Zoharic passage that is quoted in the teachings of chassidism (the standard version reads "There are three levels..."). See note 12 below.
9   *Zohar* 3:73a.

According to Nachmanides, the divine presence in the "tent of meeting" radiated from the ark, the vessel of the Torah. The divine voice emerged "above the *kaporet*, between the two *keruvim*," all of which were components of the ark. The *keruvim* were in the form of the celestial beings described in Ezekiel's vision, which contains the most profound insights into the nature of the divine that can be perceived by man. For the stuff of the relationship between man and G-d is divine revelation: the revelation of His wisdom and will via the Torah, which attains its loftiest and most intense form in the mystic "hidden wisdom" represented by the *keruvim*.

The Child

Rashi, on the other hand, elucidates the "simple meaning of the verse."[10] Often, this is mistakenly perceived as the most literal and superficial stratum of meaning of the Torah. But simple is not superficial. On the contrary, the simple meaning of the verse is its most profound meaning, its most elemental significance. It is the root from which all other meanings and levels of understanding derive. It is the essence of the verse, of which the others are but particular facets and expressions.

Rashi's conception of the ark and *kaporet* reflects the truth that our relationship with G-d through the Torah is but the realization of a deeper, intrinsic bond that already exists between us. Thus, the *kaporet* is not part of the ark, but something else, something higher. For ultimately, the divine presence in the "tent of meeting" derives not from the Torah, but from the child-faced *keruvim* that hover above it.

---

[10] Rashi on Genesis 3:8, et al.

"For Israel is a youth, and I love him,"[11] proclaims the prophet. On the deepest, most basic level, G-d loves us not for our wisdom or piety, but for our childishness. He loves us because, as the Baal Shem Tov put it, "the simplicity of the simple Jew is of a piece with the simple essence of G-d." He loves us because we are the extension of His quintessential self, as a child is the extension of the quintessential self of its father.[12]

---

[11] Hosea 11:1; see *Baal HaTurim* on Exodus 25:18.
[12] See *Tanna D'vei Eliyahu Rabbah*, chapter 14: "Two things preceded G-d's creation of the world: Torah and Israel. Still, I do not know which preceded which. But when Torah states 'Speak to the Children of Israel...,' 'Command the Children of Israel...,' etc., I know that Israel preceded all."

This concept is also alluded to in the Zoharic passage cited above, which speaks of "three knots that are bound with each other." But if Torah is the link between G-d and Israel, then what we have are three entities (G-d, Torah, and Israel) linked via two bonds (Israel's connection to Torah, and the Torah's connection to G-d). What are the "*three knots*" of which the *Zohar* speaks?

Yet Israel's connection with G-d via the Torah derives from a deeper connection: the intrinsic connection between G-d and His people which the Torah comes to reveal. On this level, Israel's involvement in Torah is what connects the Torah to the Almighty—what causes Him to extend His infinite and wholly undefinable being via a medium of "divine wisdom" and "divine will." On this level, it is not the Jew who requires the Torah in order to be one with G-d, but the Torah which requires the Jew to evoke G-d's desire to project Himself via the Torah. Thus we have three interlinked "knots": G-d's connection with Israel, G-d's connection with the Torah, and Israel's connection with the Torah. On the experiential level, the Torah is the link between G-d and Israel; in essence, Israel is the link between G-d and the Torah.

HAVE WORD, WILL TRAVEL

Make two carrying poles... Insert the poles in the rings on the sides of the ark, to carry the ark with them. The poles should remain in the rings of the ark; they should not be removed from them.   Exodus 25:13–15

The ark, which housed the two tablets inscribed with the Ten Commandments, sat in the innermost chamber of the Holy Temple—a place so sacred that only the *kohen gadol* (high priest) was permitted entry, and only on Yom Kippur, the holiest day of the year.

When the people of Israel were in the Sinai Desert, they built a portable sanctuary—the "Tabernacle"—which they carried along with them on their journeys. At each of their encampments, the Tabernacle was assembled, and then dismantled when the time came to journey on. For this reason, all the vessels of the Tabernacle had specially-made carrying poles, which were inserted in rings affixed to the side of the vessel, in order to carry them from camp to camp.

Regarding the ark, there is a specific commandment (counted as one of the 613 *mitzvot* of the Torah) never to remove the carrying poles, despite the fact that the Tabernacle was often not moved for many months. Indeed, this law also remained in force for the 381 years that the ark stood in the Holy Temple in Jerusalem.[1] The

---

[1] The ark was installed in the Holy Temple upon its completion by King

prohibition to remove the carrying poles is unique to the ark—we do not find any such commandment regarding the other vessels of the Temple.

There is a lesson here to each and every individual, but particularly to the "arks" among us—those who devote their lives to the study of Torah. As the receptacle of the word of G-d, the ark is the holiest vessel in the Temple; its natural place is in the Temple's innermost chamber, in sacred seclusion from the cares and mundanities of the outside world. Nevertheless, the ark—particularly the ark—must be in a state of constant readiness to travel, perpetually poised to leave its inner sanctum for wherever it might be needed.

The Torah instructs that when the Shabbat must be violated in order to save a life, this should be done by the greatest and most venerated members of the community.[2] The same holds true when a fellow's spiritual life is in danger. If there is a soul thirsting for the word of G-d in the ends of earth, it is the "ark" who must leave his or her sacred chamber to carry the divine wisdom to that soul. And even when the "ark" is in its chamber, it must always have its carrying poles inserted in its rings—must always be aware of its responsibilities toward the outside world, always be ready to set out at a moment's notice.

Solomon in the year 2935 from creation (826 BCE), and was hidden away by King Josiah in 3316 (445 BCE).

2 Talmud, *Yoma* 84b; *Mishneh Torah, Laws of Shabbat*, 2:2.

SPIRITUAL SPACE

Make a menorah of pure gold... Make its lamps seven, and he shall kindle its lamps and illuminate toward its face.

Exodus 25:31–37

Our sages tell us that the physical universe is the last of a series of worlds generated by the Creator, the final link in a "chain of evolution" (*seder hishtalshelut*) from the abstract to the tactual and from the spiritual to the material. Thus, everything we see or experience in the physical world also exists in a higher, more spiritual form. If the physical world contains objects such as water and stones, these are but material incarnations of spiritual realities in the higher spheres of creation. If the physical world consists of four "kingdoms"—the mineral, vegetable, animal, and human—these four gradations of vitality likewise exist within the realm of the spirit. If our physical selves inhabit the physical phenomena of time and space, these are the product of a spiritual time and a spiritual space inhabited by our souls.

The ultimate physical representation of "spiritual space" was the Holy Temple in Jerusalem, the place and edifice chosen by G-d to serve as a meeting point of the supernal and the terrestrial. For while all of physical space mirrors its metaphysical prototype, a veil of concealment interposes between the material world and its spiritual source. A "holy" place, however, is a place where this veil is less opaque, where the spiritual soul of reality can be more readily glimpsed. The Holy Temple was the holiest place in the world, the place where the veil was most translucent and—in its innermost and holiest chamber—altogether dissolved.¹

So the physical dimensions of the Holy Temple are a model for the spiritual landscape of the soul. The Holy Temple consisted of numerous domains, chambers, and "vessels"; each of these correspond to another element of the inner life of man and illuminates its divine function and purpose.² In this essay, we will examine the spiritual significance of one of the significant components of the Holy Temple—the *menorah*—and its position within the space of the Temple.

Alignment of the Lights

The four walls of the Holy Temple were aligned with the four points of the compass, and the entire edifice described a progression from east to west. One entered the first of a series of courtyards—the "Women's Court"—from the east, and proceeded westward to the fifteen steps ascending to the "Israelite Court." At the western end of the Israelite Court were the steps leading to the "Priestly Court," where the outdoor altar stood and much of the Temple service was performed. West of the altar were the steps ascending to the Sanctuary. First one entered the "Hall" which extended across the eastern face of the Sanctuary; west of the

---

1. Thus the space of this chamber—called the "Holy of Holies"—was not physical or metaphysical, but neither and both in one. In the words of the Talmud, "The space of the ark was not part of the measurement" (Talmud, *Yoma* 21a; see footnote 6 on p. 214, for a discussion of this phenomenon).
2. See Bechayei on Exodus 25:9; Shaloh, *Parashat Terumah*, 324b; *Torat HaOlah* by Rabbi Moshe Isserlis. Also see the essay, "Model Home," pp. 221–231 above.

Hall was the Sanctuary itself, an oblong structure measuring sixty cubits from east to west and twenty cubits from north to south. The Sanctuary was divided into the "Holy" which occupied its eastern two-thirds, and the "Holy of Holies" which comprised the western third of the Sanctuary.

Each westward progression was an ascent to a higher level of holiness, requiring a greater degree of sanctity for admittance. The Holy of Holies, the most westerly and holiest part of the Sanctuary, was off limits to all except for the *kohen gadol* (high priest), and he, too, could enter there only on Yom Kippur, the holiest day of the year. In the words of our sages, "The divine presence is in the west."[3]

The greater sanctity of the west was also reflected in the "western lamp" (*ner hamaaravi*) of the *menorah*, the seven-lamp candelabra that stood in the Sanctuary and symbolized the Holy Temple's role as a source of light for the world. The *menorah* consisted of a central stem, from which six arms extended—three on each side—to the full height of the *menorah*. Each of these were topped by a lamp, forming a row of seven lamps that were lit each afternoon and burned through the night. The "western lamp" was unique in that though it contained the same amount of oil as the others, it burned longer than the rest. Often, it was still burning when the priest came to light the *menorah* the next day. The western lamp was also the source of light for the others: the other six lamps of the *menorah* were lit from the western lamp, while the western lamp was lit from the fire of the outdoor altar.[4]

---

3   Rashi on Talmud, *Sanhedrin* 91b. We face east in our prayers because the site of the Holy of Holies is east of those living in the lands that are west of Jerusalem (e.g., Europe, North Africa, and the Americas). Those who live east of Jerusalem face west in their prayers, those who live north of Jerusalem face south, and so on.

4   Leviticus 24:2, as per *Torat Kohanim*, ad loc.

Which lamp was the "western lamp"? The question is more complicated than it seems, since the Talmud records two opinions regarding the position of the *menorah* in the Sanctuary. According to Rabbi Judah HaNassi, the *menorah* was positioned along the length of the Sanctuary, so that the seven lamps were arrayed from east to west. Rabbi Elazar ben Rabbi Shimon is of the opinion that the *menorah* stood to the width of the Sanctuary, so that its lamps extended from north to south.[5]

But if the *menorah* was aligned north to south, which was the "western lamp"? Rabbi Elazar explains that the "western lamp" is in fact the middle lamp—the lamp atop the central stem of the *menorah*. The reason it is called the "western lamp" is that its wick faced westward, toward the Holy of Holies, while the other lamps were turned toward the "western lamp"—the three northern lamps facing southward and the three southern lamps facing northward. According to this opinion, this is the meaning of the Torah's stipulation that the lamps of the *menorah* should "illuminate toward its face"—the "face of the *menorah*" being the *menorah's* central stem.[6]

It would seem that according to Rabbi Judah, at least, identifying the "western lamp" is a simple matter: if the lamps ran from east to west, the "western lamp" would be the one at the *menorah's* western extremity—the lamp furthest from the entrance to the Sanctuary and closest to the Holy of Holies. Indeed, this is how Maimonides understands the opinion of Rabbi Judah.[7] Most of the other commentaries, however, are of the opinion that the "western lamp" according to Rabbi Judah is the second lamp from

---

5 Talmud, *Menachot* 98b.
6 Exodus 25:37 (quoted at the beginning of this essay) and Numbers 8:2.
7 Maimonides' commentary on the Mishnah, *Tamid* 3:9.

the east (sixth from the west), and derives its name from the fact that it is to the west of the most easterly lamp.⁸

The Axis

The Talmud relates how, on one occasion, a heavenly voice made itself heard regarding a difference of opinion among the sages in a matter of Torah law, proclaiming: "These and these are both the words of the living G-d."⁹ Since both opinions are based upon the divinely ordained methods of Torah interpretation, and both have been arrived at by individuals utterly committed to the divine truth, both are "the words of the living G-d." Both are Torah, G-d's articulation of His wisdom and will via the human mind.

In actual practice, only one viewpoint can be implemented. The *menorah* in the Holy Temple stood either to the length of the Sanctuary or its width—it could not have been aligned both ways

---

8   Rashi on Talmud, *Shabbat* 22b and *Menachot* 86b; Nachmanides, Ran, and Me'iri to *Shabbat*, ad loc.; Rabbeinu Gershon to *Menachot*, ad loc.; Raavad and Bartenura to *Tamid* 3:9; Rashba, *Responsa*, vol. I, section 309.

   The reason for this is the halachic rule that "one does not pass over a *mitzvah*" (Talmud, *Pesachim* 64b, from Exodus 12:17). If the *menorah* stood from east to west, then the priest coming to light the *menorah* first encountered the easternmost lamp, and thus ought to light it first. But the Torah also commands that the "western lamp" should be lit first, and all other lamps lit from it. If the "western lamp" were indeed the one closest to the Holy of Holies, this would mean that the priest would pass over six opportunities to perform the *mitzvah* of lighting the menorah. The "western lamp" is therefore determined to be the first one that can possibly be termed "western"—i.e., the second lamp from the east, which is west of the most easterly lamp.

9   Talmud, *Eruvin* 13b.

at the same time. The Torah itself instructs what to do when those who interpret its laws disagree: "follow the majority."[10] But if only one of two equally valid expressions of the divine wisdom can be realized in the definitive realm of physical action, this is not the case in the nebulous world of the soul. The heart can simultaneously be attracted and repelled; the mind can simultaneously be aware and forget. In the spiritual applications of Torah, the dictum, "These and these are both the words of the living G-d," can be fully implemented.

What is the spiritual significance of the debate on whether the *menorah* stood to the length or to the width of the Sanctuary? In spiritual space, a thing's "length" is its extent—how far it reaches, how low it descends. The concept of a "chain of evolution" described above is a typical example of spiritual length: a thing evolves from an abstract state to successively coarser and more mundane forms. The distance of its lowest incarnation from its initial state is the measure of its "length."

Spiritual "width" is a thing's manifestation in numerous parallel forms and expressions. As the term "width" implies, we are not speaking of greater and lesser forms or of closer and more distant expressions, but of parallel faces of a single truth, each as closely related to the original as the others.

These definitions of spiritual "length" and "width" are evident in the structure of the Holy Temple. The length of the Temple ran from west to east, so that an object or person's position in the longitude of the Holy Temple was also the measure of its proximity to the Holy of Holies. In the Holy Temple, more westerly is more holy. On the other hand, a thing's position in the width of the Temple—its southerliness or northerliness—did not imply its

---

10   Exodus 23:2.

greater or lesser holiness, but its particular place in the spectrum of expressions of a particular level of holiness.

"The soul of man is a lamp of G-d."[11] If all components and elements of the Holy Temple have their counterpart in the human soul, the *menorah* is the axis of the spiritual life of man.[12] What is this axis? What defines man? This is what lies at the heart of the debate between Rabbi Judah and Rabbi Elazar. For the position of the *menorah*—the question of whether its seven lamps were aligned with the length of the Holy Temple or with its width—turns on the question of what the *menorah* is: Is it the "long" element of our soul, or is it the "wide" component of the human psyche?

Intellectual Latitude

The human soul possesses many attributes and faculties, but there are two that stand out as the definers of its personality: the intellect and the emotions. Indeed, we commonly categorize people into two general types: "intellectual" people, or those who predicate their lives upon their reason and understanding; and "emotional" individuals, in whom the heart plays the decisive role, as they are primarily motivated by its feelings, intuitions, and commitments.

In other words, the soul has both an intellectual and an emotional "*menorah*," as both the mind and the heart can serve as the

---

[11] Proverbs 20:27.
[12] As opposed to the "table," which stood opposite the *menorah* in the Sanctuary, and which represents the needs and life of the body. (The ark, which was inside the Holy of Holies, represented a state of utter union with G-d—a state that is neither physical nor spiritual but transcends them both; see references in note 1 above).

"guiding light" of a person's life. In certain individuals, the intellectual *menorah* dominates, while in others the *menorah* of the heart is the focal point of their spiritual personality.

Intellect, by definition, is the capacity to apprehend a truth, hold it in one's mind, concentrate on it, and apply it to one's experience. In this sense, an "intellectual" is one who sets the objective truth as the basis for everything in his or her life, to the utter disregard of all personal prejudice. In terms of spiritual space, the intellect is a "wide" thing. Ultimately, there are no greater or lesser truths: something is either true or it is not. There are, of course, variant expressions of truth, as an objective reality is perceived in many and various contexts; but this is a projection to the width rather than to the length. No expression of a truth—if it is truly an expression of the truth—is "further" from the abstract axiom than any other. Rather, the many faces of truth are parallel to each other, being the same quality of truth as expressed in different areas of reality.

The soul's tool for the attainment of truth is the Torah, in which G-d revealed His wisdom and will to man. Thus, the *menorah* of the mind consists of seven lamps, corresponding to the "Written Torah" (the "Five Books of Moses"), which is the essence of the divine communication to man, and the six "orders" of the "Oral Torah"—the divinely empowered human endeavor to apply the Written Torah to the six primary areas of human life.[13]

---

13 The six "orders" are: 1) "Seeds" (*Zera'im*), which deals with the laws of agriculture and food consumption; 2) "Times" (*Moed*)—the laws of Shabbat, the festivals, and the Jewish calendar; 3) "Women" (*Nashim*)—marriage and divorce; 4) "Damages" (*Nezikin*)—torts, business, civil, and criminal law; 5) "Sacred Things" (*Kodashim*)—laws of the Temple service; 6) "Purities" (*Taharot*)—laws of ritual purity and impurity.

The "intellectual" *menorah* stands to the width of the Sanctuary. Its seven lamps are all the same distance from the Holy of Holies, for all of Torah law is in equal proximity to its divine source, regardless of which area of life it governs. The law regarding "an ox that gored a cow" is no "further" from the essence of the divine truth than "I am G-d your G-d."

The "western lamp" in this *menorah* is the center lamp, which represents the Written Torah—the "stem" from which the six branches of the Oral Torah derive. It alone faces the ark[14] and the divine presence in the west, for it is the sole source of divine truth—the other six lamps derive their luminescence from its light. Nevertheless, the six lamps are as westerly as the "western lamp," for every expression of truth is as true as its most sublime "original."

Emotional Longitude

The seven lamps of the emotional *menorah* are the seven attributes of the heart: *chesed, gevurah, tiferet, netzach, hod, yesod* and *malchut* (love, awe, harmony, ambition, devotion, connection, and receptiveness).[15]

---

14 The ark that stood in the Holy of Holies contained the two stone tablets upon which G-d inscribed the Ten Commandments—the essence of the Written Torah.

15 Each of the seven attributes (*midot*) is actually an entire field of human emotions. Only the original, Hebrew names of the seven attributes capture the full array of primary emotions and the many nuances of feeling and sensibility each includes. The English "translation" offered here is but a partial and arbitrary description of each attribute's general nature; alternate translations would be equally valid and equally inadequate. For a detailed discussion of the seven *midot* see *A Spiritual Guide to the Counting of the Omer* (MLC 1996), and *Ten Keys for Understanding Human Nature* (Zichron Press, 1994).

The emotional *menorah* stands to the *length* of the Sanctuary. Unlike the mind, the heart is subjective and equivocal; it includes lofty and coarser emotions, sophisticated and simple feelings, purer and more biased sentiments. Its seven lamps extend from west to east—from potent, altruistic "love," to pedestrian, malleable "receptiveness."

Yet the heart can yield a depth of commitment and a potency of drive that the most "intellectual" life cannot equal. This is achieved when the sixth lamp—the heart's capacity for connection and bonding—serves as the "western lamp" and kindles the other emotions. When a person negates all personal desires and aspirations[16] to bind their soul to G-d, the "subjective" heart will be illuminated with a divine light and guide their life toward its ultimate fulfillment.[17]

"These and these are both the words of the living G-d." Rabbi Elazar places the *menorah* from north to south, seeing the mind and its capacity to apprehend the divine truth revealed in the Torah as the gist of the spiritual endeavor of man. Rabbi Judah HaNassi places it from west to east, expressing a vision of the heart

---

16 Thus the "western lamp" is defined by its relationship with the most easterly lamp (as per note 8 above), which represents the attribute of *malchut* and the capacity for self-abnegation and receptiveness. Though *malchut* is the last and "lowest" of the seven attributes, it is what enables the sixth attribute to realize itself and predicate the person's entire life upon the foundation of their bond with G-d.

17 The sixth attribute is called *yesod*, which literally means "foundation," as it is the foundation for an emotional self aligned with the soul's mission and purpose in life.

Maimonides, however, has a different conception of the emotional *menorah*—that its first and most westerly lamp, corresponding with the attribute of love, is the "western lamp." This is based on Maimonides' vision of a life motivated by love of G-d as the ultimate realization of the soul's potential (see *Mishneh Torah, Laws of Repentance*, 10:2–3).

and its capacity for self-abnegating connection with G-d as the primary activity of the soul. Both are valid conceptions of our mission in life; both are to be realized in the life of every soul to the utmost of its capacity, in accordance with its nature and its G-d-given potentials.

PARASHAH
TWENTY

TETZAVEH

Exodus 27:20–30:10

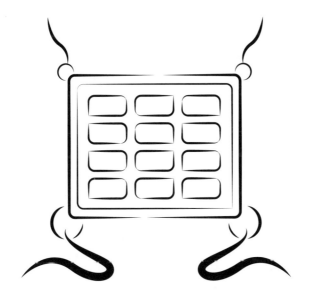

Garments and coatings

NOISE

Make the [priestly] robe.... And make on its hem pomegranates of blue, purple, and scarlet wool; and bells of gold between them all around.... It shall be upon Aaron when he serves; and its sound shall be heard when he enters into the holy before G-d...

Exodus 28:31–35

A great, strong wind rent the mountains and shattered the rocks... but G-d was not in the wind. After the wind came a storm, but G-d was not in the storm. After the storm came fire, but G-d was not in the fire. After the fire came a small, still voice.

I Kings 19:11–12

A rich man once invited a beggar to share his meal.

The host settled quietly into his seat and tucked his linen napkin beneath his chin. The guest, finding himself supported by silken cushions instead of the usual hard bench, sighed in surprised pleasure. With much creaking and squeaking he burrowed into the chair, determined to savor its opulence to the utmost.

The soup arrived and proceeded to make its casual way down the rich man's gullet. Across the table, a frontal attack was being launched against the delicate china bowl. The heavy silver spoon clanged and swooped, carrying every precious drop of steaming gold to an audibly eager mouth. The subsequent assault on the steak platter was no less enthused. As the wealthy man silently ingested bite-sized pieces of meat, his dinner partner, a maelstrom of clattering knives and chomping jaws, oohed and aahed his delighted way through the feast.

In the kitchen, the cook remarked to the butler: "At last, a man who appreciates fine cuisine! The master may be indifferent to the finer things in life, but his guest! What passion! How involved he is, how worshipful of quality. Now, here is a man with a sense of the sublime..."

"You are mistaken," countered the butler. "The very opposite is the case. The rich man's tranquility indicates the depth of his involvement with his dinner, while the pauper's noisy excitement only underscores how alien all this is to him. To the rich man, luxury is the very stuff of life; so he no more exclaims over it than you jump for joy upon finding yourself alive in the morning. But for the poor man, life is a boiled potato, and *this* is an otherworldly experience. All that noise you hear is the friction between his habitual self and the luxuriating self he is attempting to assume."

The Hem

Noise is the mark of resistance. Consider the sounds emitted by a log fire, a pile of burning straw, and an oil lamp. In each case, matter is succumbing to the energy locked within it. The log offers the most resistance, voicing its reluctance to part with its outer form with a noisy crackle and sudden explosions. The straw, not quite as physical as the log, protests with a whispering sizzle. And the oil in the lamp, the finest substance of the three, burns silently, freely yielding to the essence within.

Thus, Elijah the Prophet experienced G-d's immanence as "a small, still voice."[1] In his refined self, the material of the body did

---

[1] See citation from I Kings in the beginning of this essay.

not resist the spirituality of the soul.² Elijah perceived the divine reality not in a norm-shattering storm, but in the same tranquil manner in which a person is aware of the life within him- or herself.

Yet Aaron the *kohen gadol* (high priest), the epitome of refinement and spirituality, is commanded to wear a robe with bells sewn onto its hem, so that "its sound shall be heard when he enters into the Holy before G-d." For the *kohen gadol* represents the entirety of Israel in his service of the Almighty, including those for whom connection to G-d is still a noisy struggle—the struggle to transcend their external, earthbound selves and bring to light their true, inner identity.

Rabbi Israel Baal Shem Tov was once asked: Why do some of your disciples make such a ruckus while praying? They shout, they wave their arms, they virtually throw themselves around the room. Is this the appropriate way to commune with G-d?

The founder of chassidism replied: Have you ever seen a drowning man? He shouts, he thrashes his arms, he struggles with the waves that threaten to claim him. Throughout the day, a person is swamped by the demands of their material existence; prayer is the attempt to break free of the engulfing waters that threaten to extinguish our spiritual life.

True, a noisy service of G-d is an indication that we have not yet fully "arrived." Had we succeeded in transcending the mundane, our endeavor to draw close to the Almighty would be a tranquil one—our soul would strive upward with a silent, frictionless flame. Our tumultuous struggles reflect the fact that our spiritual self has not yet become the seat of our identity—that our "natural" self still lies with the material externalities of life. Nevertheless, this is a healthy sign: we have not succumbed. We are straining to

---

2   Elijah, who ascended to heaven with his physical body (II Kings 2:11), represents the ultimate in the refinement of the material.

free ourselves from the confining envelope of our material being, straining to rise above our presently defined self.

So the bells on the hem of the *kohen gadol*'s robe are an indispensable part of his divine service. "Its sound shall be heard when he enters into the holy before G-d," commands the Torah, "lest he die." Were the *kohen gadol* to disclaim the lowly "hem" of the nation he represents, he would be violating the very core of his mission. Were his service of G-d not to embody the struggles of his imperfect brethren, it would have no place in G-d's inner sanctum.

Apples and Pomegranates

In light of the above, we can understand the deeper significance of the debate between two of our sages regarding the bells and pomegranates on the *kohen gadol*'s robe.

The debate addresses the question of how to interpret the word *betocham*, which translates either as "between them" or "within them." Does the Torah (in Exodus 28:33) command to "make upon its hem pomegranates... and bells of gold *between* them" or to fix the "bells of gold *within* them"?

Rashi, in his commentary on the verse, maintains that,

> Between every two pomegranates, a bell was attached and hanging on the hem of the robe.

Nachmanides disagrees:

> I don't know why the master [Rashi] made the bells separate, a bell between two pomegranates. According to this, the pomegranates served no function. And if they were there for beauty, then why were they made as hollow

pomegranates? They should have been made as golden apples... Rather, [the bells] were literally within them, for the pomegranates were hollow—like small, unopened pomegranates—and the bells were contained within them.

The later commentaries enter into the debate. "Why does [Nachmanides] favor apples over pomegranates?" wonders Mizrachi.[3] Other commentaries explain that Nachmanides' difficulty with Rashi's interpretation is that the hollow form of the pomegranate (Rashi himself also says that they were "round and hollow"[4]) indicates that they served a functional rather than decorative purpose.[5] But what does Nachmanides mean when he says that "if they were there for beauty... they should have been made as golden apples"?

Indeed, the *menorah* was decorated with spheres resembling apples whose sole purpose was for beauty.[6] Perhaps Nachmanides derives from this that in the making of the Sanctuary and its furnishings, the decorative fruit of choice was the apple. But this itself requires explanation. Why apples? And why, according to Rashi, was the *menorah* beautified with apples and the *kohen gadol*'s robe with pomegranates?

Insulated Deeds

Both the apple and the pomegranate are representative of the Jewish people. The Torah likens the people of Israel to an "apple" ("Like an apple among the trees of the wood, so is my beloved")[7]

---

3   Rabbi Eliyahu Mizrachi, 1448–1526, wrote a super-commentary on Rashi's commentary.
4   Rashi to Exodus 24:33.
5   *Nimukei Shmuel*, ad loc.
6   Rashi on Exodus 25:31.
7   Song of Songs 2:3. See *Midrash Rabbah*, ad loc.; Talmud, *Shabbat* 88a; and *Zohar* 2:120b.

as well as to a "pomegranate" ("Your lips are like a thread of scarlet, and your mouth is comely; your temple is like a piece of pomegranate within your locks"). [8] But while the apple represents Israel in a virtuous state,[9] the pomegranate refers to the "hollow" or "empty ones amongst you." As interpreted by the Talmud, the verse "your temple is like a piece of pomegranate" comes to say that "even the empty ones amongst you are full of good deeds as a pomegranate [is full of seeds]."[10] (*Raka*, the Hebrew word used by the verse for "temple" is related to the word *reik*, "empty." Thus "your temple" is homiletically rendered "the empty ones amongst you.")

The pomegranate is more than a model of something that contains many particulars. On a deeper level, this metaphor also addresses the paradox of how an individual may be "empty" and, at the same time, be "full of good deeds as a pomegranate."

The pomegranate is a highly "compartmentalized" fruit: each of its hundreds of seeds is encased in its own sac of flesh and is separated from its fellows by a tough membrane. In the same way, it is possible for a person to do good deeds—many good deeds—and yet, they remain isolated acts, with little or no effect on the person's nature and character. So unlike the "apple," whose deliciousness is from core to skin, the "pomegranate" *contains* many virtues, but they do not become him or her. The person may be full of good deeds, yet they remain morally and spiritually hollow.

This explains the connection between the pomegranates and the bells on the hem of the priestly robe. As explained above, the noisy bells represent a point in our spiritual development where we are striving to transcend our deficient state. Although we are still spiritual paupers, we refuse to act as such—hence the noisy friction that characterizes our lives.

---

8   Song of Songs 4:3.
9   See *Likutei Torah, Bechukotai* 49d; *Ohr HaTorah, Noach* 58a-b.
10 Talmud, *Berachot* 57a.

Beautiful Noise

To become an apple we must first be a pomegranate. We must act unlike ourselves, like a poor man feasting at a rich man's table; a clumsy spectacle, perhaps, but a necessary one if we are to transcend the animalistic, egocentric self into which we are all born.[11] The first step to becoming perfect is to behave as if perfect. Indeed, before Elijah experienced G-d in a "small, still voice," he first beheld the wind, the storm, and the fire.

Nachmanides therefore sees the pomegranate-encased bells on Aaron's hem as a preliminary phase of one's divine service, rather than as the service itself.[12] Beauty, however, is to be found in the apple-perfection of the *menorah*—seven lamps of pure olive oil, representing the soul's silent, tranquil flame. If the pomegranates on the priestly robe were for beauty, argues Nachmanides, they would not be pomegranates, but apples. These hollow fruits are purely functional, a preparatory stage in the soul's quest for perfection and union with its source in G-d.

According to Rashi, however, the beauty of Israel lies also in its pomegranates. In fact, in a certain sense, the struggle of the imperfect soul is even more beautiful than the serene perfection of its more virtuous fellow. For the perfectly righteous individual serves G-d by being what he or she is, while every positive deed of the "empty ones amongst you" is an act of sacrifice and self-transcendence. So even before we attain perfection—even if our entire life is spent in the quest for perfection—the clamor of our efforts is music to G-d's ear.

---

[11] See Job 11:12: "Man is born a wild ass."
[12] See Nachmanides' commentary on Exodus 28:43, where he compares the ringing of the robe's bells to the requesting of permission before entering into the presence of a king.

A Contemporary Application

There are those who claim that the Torah and its *mitzvot* are a private matter between the Jew and G-d, not something to be paraded in the streets. *Tefilin*, Shabbat, the sanctity of family life, esoteric concepts such as "divine reality" or "Moshiach," are not to be hawked on a downtown sidewalk or catch-phrased on a slick billboard. Never in our history as a nation has anything like this been done, they say. You are vulgarizing the soul of Judaism, they accuse.

But our generation is the hem of history, the lowliest and most superficial generation yet. To this generation, the small, still voice of G-d sounds like alien noise. Should this voice be hushed, to be whispered only among the apples? Or should its call be sounded, noisy though it may be, until it is heard above the din?

Speaking to this generation in its own language—the language of the sound-bite, of incessant compartmentalization and hollow packaging—ever further raises the noise level. But fighting fire with fire is not only effective; it also brings to light facets of one's own potential that would otherwise remain unrealized. The bells and pomegranates that broadcast the divine truth are more than the means toward a tranquil end—they are themselves things of beauty.

PRINCESSES ON HORSEBACK

They shall make the ephod of gold, and blue and purple and scarlet-dyed [wool], and fine-spun linen, artfully woven.

Exodus 28:6

One of the eight priestly garments worn by the *kohen gadol* (high priest) was the *ephod*, or "apron." Many of the commentaries struggle to arrive at a conclusive determination of its form, as the verses describing it (Exodus 28:6–14) are somewhat ambiguous. Rashi writes:

> *I haven't heard, nor have I found in the mishnaic writings, an explanation of [the ephod's] form. My heart tells me that it is tied on the back, its width the width of a person's back, its form like the apron called* pourceint[1] *worn by princesses when they ride horses.*[2]

"My heart tells me" is an uncharacteristic phrase for Rashi, who usually explains the meaning of the verse without citing sources or telling us how he arrived at a particular meaning. When he does cite a source for his explanation, it is because this imparts an additional insight or lesson.[3]

---

1 In Old French.
2 Rashi on Exodus 28:4.
3 See, for example, the essay, "Transplanted Cedars," pp. 206–208 above.

Rabbi Israel Baal Shem Tov, the founder of chassidism, famously taught that, "From everything that a person sees or hears, they should derive a lesson in the service of the Almighty." Based on this teaching, we might envision Rashi walking to the study hall one day and encountering a party of noblewomen on horseback. For a long time after that, Rashi wonders to himself why, and to what purpose, divine providence has shown him this sight—a scene seemingly devoid of any usefulness or meaning. Then, one day, Rashi is laboring to describe the construction of the *ephod*. He analyzes every word of the several verses the Torah devotes to the *ephod* and searches for hints in the Talmudic and post-Talmudic writings. Still, Rashi can form no clear picture in his mind. Then he recalls the scene of royal maidens on horseback, and understands to what purpose his path crossed theirs that morning…

JOINED AT THE WAIST

They shall bind the choshen *by its rings to the rings of the* ephod ... *so that the* choshen *shall not budge from the ephod.*

Exodus 28:28

The *choshen* ("breastplate") and the *ephod* ("apron") were two of the eight special garments worn by the *kohen gadol* (high priest). The *choshen* was a square cloth set with twelve precious stones, each inscribed with the name of one of the twelve tribes of Israel. It was worn on the breast, over the heart. The *ephod* was an "apron-like garment... worn in the back from opposite the heart below the elbows, down to the ankles, with a belt that tied in the front."[1]

Two gold rings sewn on the *ephod*'s belt lined up with two gold rings sewn to the bottom corners of the *choshen*. The rings of the *choshen* and the rings of the *ephod* were bound together with ribbons of blue wool. It is of utmost importance, the Torah stresses, that the two should remain securely fastened at all times that the priestly garments are worn. In fact, the imperative that "the *choshen* shall not budge from the *ephod*" is counted as one of the six hundred and thirteen *mitzvot* of the Torah!

Therein lies a lesson applicable to each and every one of us. There should be no disconnect between the "upper" and "lower"

---

1 Rashi on Exodus 28:6.

aspects of life, or between its "inner" and "back" elements. True, the human being consists of both the sensitive heart, and the crass, functional foot. True, life is composed of sublimely spiritual moments, as well as the banal tending to one's material needs. But the two must be securely joined at the waist. The upper must permeate the lower, and the external must never lose sight of its inner soul and essence.

THE SUPERFICIAL COAT

Make an altar for the burning of incense; make it of cedar wood… and cover it with gold…
Exodus 30:1–3

All the vessels in the Sanctuary required immersion, except for the Golden Altar and the Copper Altar … because they were coated.
Talmud, Chagigah 26b

During the three annual pilgrimage festivals of Passover, Shavuot, and Sukkot, when the entire community of Israel would come to the Holy Temple in Jerusalem, the vessels of the Temple were exposed to contact with many individuals, including some who might not be well-versed in the complex laws of ritual purity. So following each festival, all the Temple's vessels were immersed in a *mikveh,* to cleanse them of any possible contamination by a visitor who might have been ritually impure.

The law is that "wooden vessels that are used only in a fixed place are not susceptible to contamination."[1] The two altars of the Tabernacle—the indoor "Golden Altar" and the outdoor "Copper Altar"[2]—which were used only in their fixed places, were made

---

1 See discussion in Talmud and commentaries, *Chagigah* 26b–27a.
2 The Copper Altar existed only in the "Tabernacle," the portable sanctuary built in the desert that was the forerunner of the Temple in Jerusalem. In the Holy Temple, the outdoor altar was built of stone.

of wood and covered with gold or copper. This is the meaning of the above-quoted law that the altars did not require immersion after the festivals "because they were coated": although a metal vessel could become impure under such circumstances, since the metal of these altars was only a coating, it was "nullified" (*batel*) in relation to their wooden bodies, and they were thus immune to contamination.

Body and Soul

The laws of the Torah always have more than one meaning. The Torah, as the human being it comes to instruct and enlighten, consists of both a "body" and a "soul." Every law, story, or saying in Torah also has a deeper, spiritual import; every legal technicality also addresses the inner world of the human soul.

The Tabernacle is more than a physical edifice dedicated to the service of G-d; it is also the model after which we are to build our own lives as "sanctuaries" that house and express the divine. In commanding the Children of Israel to build the Tabernacle, G-d says to Moses, "They shall make for Me a Sanctuary and I shall dwell amongst them."[3] Our sages point out that the Hebrew word *betochom* ("amongst them") literally means "within them"; in effect, G-d is saying that He desires a dwelling "within each and every one of them."[4] This is why the Torah describes the various components and vessels of the Sanctuary in such detail,[5] as they

---

3   Exodus 25:8.
4   *Reishith Chochmah, Shaar HaAhavah*, chapter 6; Shaloh, *Shaar HaOtiot, Lamed*.
5   Thirteen chapters in the book of Exodus—more than one-third of the book—are taken up with the details of the Sanctuary's construction.

each represent another of the faculties and attributes that comprise the human being.⁶

Incorruptible Sacrifice

Therein lies the deeper significance of the law regarding the altars' immunity from impurity.

The other vessels of the human "sanctuary," representing a person's various intellectual and emotional faculties, may, at times, become tainted by negative influences. But the "altars" of the soul, the soul's capacity for selfless devotion and sacrifice for its Creator, are not susceptible to contamination.

In the words of Rabbi Schneur Zalman of Liadi in his *Tanya*:

> *In the majority of cases, even the most deficient and sinful Jew will sacrifice their life and suffer the harshest tortures rather than deny the one G-d ... as if it were utterly impossible for them to deny Him... This is because of the divine essence that is embedded in each soul's faculty of* chochmah, *which is beyond any graspable or understood knowledge...*⁷

This inner core of purity is not always visible or readily accessible. The glitter of material life, or, conversely, the despair of poverty and hardship, may obscure the soul's intrinsic commitment to G-d. But these encumbrances, be they of "copper" or "gold," are mere coatings on the soul's altar—coatings that are "nullified" before the incorruptible well of sacrifice within.

---

6   See the essay, "Model Home," pp. 221–231 above. Also see *Derech Mitzvotecha*, pp. 172–174.
7   *Tanya*, chapter 18.

PARASHAH TWENTY-ONE

KI TISA

Exodus 30:11–34:35

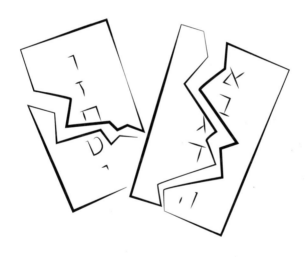

The second tablets

PARTNER

This they shall give: ... a half-shekel of the sacred shekel; twenty gerah is the shekel...

Exodus 30:13

When the Holy Temple stood in Jerusalem, each Jew would contribute an annual half-shekel to the Temple. The money was used to purchase the daily offerings brought in the Holy Temple on behalf of the entire community of Israel.

The Torah is insistent that the contribution should consist of exactly half a shekel, repeating this requirement no less than three times in as many verses:

> *This they shall give: ... a half-shekel of the sacred shekel. Twenty gerah is the shekel; half a shekel, a contribution to G-d...*
>
> *The rich man should not give more, and the pauper should not give less, than the half-shekel; to give a contribution for G-d, to atone for your souls.*[1]

Why *half* a shekel? We know that, as a rule, "Everything that is for the sake of G-d should be of the best and most beautiful. When one builds a house of prayer, it should be more beautiful than one's own dwelling. When one feeds the hungry, one should feed them of the best and sweetest of one's table.... Whenever one designates something for a holy purpose, one should sanctify the finest of one's possessions; as it is written,[2] 'The choicest to G-d.'"[3]

---

1 Exodus 30:13–15.
2 Leviticus 3:16.
3 *Mishneh Torah, Laws of Things Forbidden to Be Brought on the Altar* 7:11.

KI TISA (1)

For this reason, Torah law mandates, in many cases, that the object of a *mitzvah* (divine commandment) must be *tamim*, "whole." A blemished animal cannot be brought as an offering to G-d, nor can a blemished *etrog* be included in the "four kinds" taken on the festival of Sukkot. Even when this is not an absolute requirement, Torah law states that, whenever possible, one should strive to fulfill a *mitzvah* with a whole object. For example, it is preferable to recite a blessing on a whole fruit or a whole loaf of bread, rather than on a slice (hence our use of two whole loaves at all Shabbat and festival meals).[4]

Why, then, does the Torah instruct that each Jew contribute *half* a shekel toward the Temple service?

Half of Twenty

The Torah's repeated reference to this contribution as a "half-shekel" is all the more puzzling in light of the fact that, in these very same verses, the Torah clarifies that a shekel consists of twenty *gerah*. In other words, the amount contributed by each individual to "atone for your souls" was ten *gerah*.

Ten is a number that denotes completeness and perfection. The entire Torah is encapsulated within the Ten Commandments; the world was created with ten divine utterances;[5] G-d relates to His creation via ten *sefirot* (divine attributes); and the soul of man, formed in the "image of G-d," is likewise comprised of ten "powers."[6] But instead of instructing to give ten *gerah*, the Torah says to give half of a twenty-*gerah* shekel, deliberately avoiding

---

4   See Talmud, *Berachot* 39b.
5   *Ethics of the Fathers*, 5:1.
6   *Sefer Yetzirah*; *Tanya*, chapter 3; et al.

mention of the number ten and emphasizing the "half" element of our "contribution for G-d."

The Marriage Partnership

The prophets compare the bond between G-d and Israel to the union of man and woman in marriage. Indeed, the symbolism of the half-shekel contribution reflects the very essence of marriage.

If each partner approaches the marriage with a sense of him- or herself as a complete entity, they will, at best, achieve only a "relationship" between two distinct, self-contained lives. Marriage, however, is much more than that. The kabbalists explain that husband and wife are the male and female aspects of a single soul, born into two different bodies. For many years, these two half-souls live distinct and separate lives, often at a great distance from each other and wholly unaware of the other's existence. But divine providence contrives to bring them together again under the wedding canopy, and accord them the opportunity to become one again: not only one in essence, but also one on all levels—in their conscious thoughts and feelings and in their physical lives.[7]

Marriage is thus more than the union of two individuals. It is the reunion of a halved soul, the fusion of two lives that are originally and intrinsically one.

To experience this reunion, each must approach his or her life together not as a "ten," but as a "half." This half-shekel consists of ten *gerah*—each must give their all to the marriage, devoting to it the full array of resources and potentials they possess. But each must regard themselves not as a complete being, but as a *partner*—a part seeking its other part to make itself whole again.

---

7   *Zohar* 1:91b, 2:7b, 2:109b and 2:296a; Ari's *Likutei Torah, Bereishith* 15a.

The Divine Marriage

The same applies to our marriage-bond with G-d.

The human soul is "a part of G-d above"[8]—a part that descended to a world whose mundanity and materiality conspire to distance it from its supernal source. So even a soul who is in full possession of her ten powers is still but a part. And even when G-d fully manifests the ten attributes of His involvement with creation, He is still only partly present in our world. It is only when these two parts unite in marriage that their original wholeness and integrity is restored.

To truly connect with G-d we must contribute half of a twenty-*gerah* shekel. We must give ourselves fully to Him, devoting the full spectrum of our ten powers and potentials to our marriage with Him. But even as we achieve the utmost in self-realization in our relationship with G-d, we must be permeated with a sense of our halfness—with the recognition that we, as He, are incomplete without each other.[9]

---

8 Job 31:2; *Tanya*, chapter 2.

9 The connection between the half-shekel and the marriage bond is alluded to in the story of the first marriage described in detail by the Torah—the marriage of Isaac and Rebecca.

The twenty-fourth chapter of Genesis relates how Eliezer, sent by Abraham to find a wife for Isaac, meets Rebecca at the well, and bestows on her the following gifts: "a golden ring, a half-shekel in weight; and two bracelets of ten shekels' weight of gold for her hands" (Genesis 24:22). Rashi explains that these gifts were representative of the half-shekels that Isaac and Rebecca's descendants were destined to contribute to the Sanctuary and the Temple service, and the two tablets on which were inscribed the Ten Commandments.

FOUNDATION

The rich man should not give more, and the pauper should not give less, than the half of a shekel.

Exodus 30:15

The silver from the counting of the community... a half-shekel per head... was to cast the foundation sockets of the Sanctuary.

Exodus 38:25–27

To build the Tabernacle in the Sinai Desert, the people of Israel were called upon to donate the fifteen materials used in its construction: gold, silver, copper, dyed wool, wood, etc. Each was to donate according to how "their heart impels them to give."[1]

One exception, however, was the silver used to cast the blocks which served as the foundation for the Tabernacle. This silver was obtained by levying a half-shekel tax on each individual, regardless of their means or desire. "The rich man should not give more, nor should the pauper give less, than the half of a shekel."[2]

Our own lives also include these two elements—the edifice and its foundation.

---

[1] Exodus 25:2.
[2] Exodus 30:15. The half-shekel-per-head tax was levied annually, and in subsequent years was used to purchase the daily offerings brought in the Holy Temple on behalf of the community—see previous essay, "Partner," on pp. 268–271.

The Edifice

As the Midrash points out, no two human beings are alike: "Just as their faces are different, so too are their minds and characters different."[3] So when it comes to the myriads of deeds, insights, and experiences which make up our lives, we each must strive for the optimum that our spiritual and material resources allow. In the words of our sages, "A wealthy person who brings a pauper's offering has not fulfilled his duty."[4]

The same is true also within the "miniature universe" that is the human being. We each have our strengths and weaknesses. We each have rich, inspired moments, as well as the more impoverished periods of our life. In every area and in every period of our life, we are called upon to utilize our potentials to the utmost, never sufficing with less than what we are truly capable of.

The Foundation

There is, however, a common denominator in all this diversity, a single truth which underlies the life of each and every one of us, and each and every area and moment of our own life: our basic commitment to our Creator.

This is the foundation of all: the fact that our lives are purposeful, and we are duty-bound to the Almighty to fulfill His will and implement His purpose in Creation.

We each may understand G-d's Torah on our individual level. We each may relate to G-d with the specific degree and variety of love and awe determined by the nature of our soul and its present

---

3 *Midrash Rabbah, Bamidbar* 21:2.
4 Talmud, *Nega'im* 14:12.

spiritual condition. But we are all equal in our commitment to serve Him.

In this, the foundation of our personal "Tabernacle," no individual can claim that he or she is unique—neither for the better nor for the worse. The simplest individual, in their lowest moment, is capable of submitting to G-d's will no less than is the spiritual giant in their finest hour.

WASHSTAND

Make a basin of copper, and its stand of copper, for washing; and place it between the Tent of Meeting and the altar.... Aaron and his sons should wash their hands and feet from it, when they enter into the Tent of Meeting ... or when they approach the altar to serve...

Exodus 30:17–20

Every morning, a person should wash his face, hands, and feet before praying.

Mishneh Torah, Laws of Prayer, 4:1

Since the destruction of the Holy Temple in Jerusalem more than nineteen centuries ago, G-d does not commune with us in a "Tent of Meeting," nor do priests offer sacrifices to G-d upon its altar. Yet the Holy Temple and the service performed in it remain, to this day, the vehicle for our relationship with G-d; it is only that today they assume the form of rituals and practices in our daily lives.

This truth is expressed in many sayings of our sages. "The daily prayers were instituted in place of the daily offerings."[1] "A person's table is comparable to the altar."[2] "From the day that the Holy Temple was destroyed, G-d has only the four cubits of *halachah* (Torah law) in His world."[3] Accordingly, many of the laws that govern our lives as Jews today derive from the laws of the Temple

---

1 Talmud, *Berachot* 26a and b.
2 Ibid., *Chagigah* 27a.
3 Ibid., *Berachot* 8a.

and its service. The designated times for prayer are the times in which the daily offerings were brought in the Holy Temple; when sitting down to a meal we dip our bread in salt, because salt was part of every offering placed upon the altar; and so on.

The Cleansing

The *kiyor* ("laver") was a copper basin that stood in the Temple courtyard. The priests who performed the Temple service were commanded to wash their hands and feet with its waters before entering into the Sanctuary or performing any act of service. The Temple's washbasin thus symbolized the transition from worldly to sacred endeavors, and the cleansing that such transition requires.

The Torah instructs us to "know G-d in all your ways"[4] and that "all your deeds should be for the sake of Heaven."[5] This means that all areas of life, including our ordinary, everyday activities, form an integral part of our relationship with G-d. Nevertheless, we still need to distinguish between the sacred environment of the Holy Temple, where the divine presence is palpable and everything is exclusively devoted to serving G-d, and the material world outside the Temple walls, where everything carries the taint of self-interest and materialism. So when entering the sanctuary of G-d, the priests are instructed to "wash their hands" of the mundanity of everyday life.

In its post-Temple incarnation, this law takes the form of the obligation to wash one's face, hands, and feet prior to the morning prayers. In this way, we cleanse and purify ourselves before making the transition from a material being living in a material world, to a soul communing with its Creator.[6]

---

4   Proverbs 3:6.
5   *Ethics of the Fathers* 2:12.
6   Talmud, *Shabbat* 50a; *Mishneh Torah, Laws of Prayer*, 4:1.

Upon closer examination, however, there seems to be a small but significant difference between the original Temple law and its present-day application. In the Holy Temple, the priests would wash "their hands and their feet" at the basin; the laws of prayer, on the other hand, enjoin us to wash our "face, hands, and feet." Why this difference?

Manual Labor

"If you eat of the toil of your hands," proclaims the Psalmist, "fortunate are you, and good is to you."[7] Chassidic teaching explains that this verse is telling us to invest only our more external faculties ("the toil of your hands") in the pursuit of material livelihood, leaving our higher talents free to devote themselves exclusively to our spiritual goals.

Our ancestors sustained themselves exclusively with the toil of their hands. The Patriarchs were shepherds, and the Israelites who settled in the Holy Land were tillers of the soil. Many of the greatest Talmudic sages, whose teachings are a source of wisdom and guidance to us to this very day, were manual laborers: Rabbi Jochanan HaSandlar was a cobbler, Rabbi Joshua a blacksmith, Shammai was a bricklayer. There were also merchants and shopkeepers, but business was free of the craftiness and obsessive preoccupation that characterize it today. Scholarship and teaching were not professions but sacred callings, not to be sullied by the remuneration of material reward. Earning one's daily bread was a matter for the hands and feet and the most rudimentary of mental exercises, not something upon which to expend the mind's ingenuity or the heart's devotion, which were reserved only for life's higher aims.

---

[7] Psalms 128:2.

That world is no longer. Today, we not only invest time and energy in the endeavor to procure our material needs, we give it our "all"—our keenest mental capabilities, our strongest passions, our most forceful will. Our "careers" consume our days and nights, our minds and hearts, indeed, our very identities (we don't ask each other, "What do you do to make money?"—we say, "What do you do?").[8]

This explains the difference between the two laws. In the time of the Holy Temple, only the "hands and feet"—externalities of human life—were involved in material pursuits; so only they required purification before being devoted to the service of G-d. The "face"—our higher prowess and inner self[9]—required no such cleansing, for it was not sullied in the first place.

But in later generations, the mundanity of life has encroached on our inner selves. Today, the effort to commune with G-d also requires the cleansing of our "faces" of the taint of the material. Our minds and hearts must be purged of the prejudices and affinities that adhere to it in the course of their involvement in earthly affairs, so that we can truly relate to the essence and purpose of life.

---

8   The story is told of a chassid who opened a factory for the manufacture of galoshes, and was soon completely consumed by his flourishing business. Said Rabbi Shalom DovBer of Lubavitch to him: "I have heard of people who insert their *feet* in galoshes; but to put one's head in galoshes?"

9   In the English language, the word "face" often refers to the external aspect of things (as in "surface," "superficial," "façade," "on the face of it," "put a face on things," etc.). But the Hebrew word for "face," *panim*, actually means "innerness," expressing the idea that the face is the part of a person's body in which their higher faculties reside and which most reflects the person's nature and personality.

SIN AND SANCTUARY

The people divested themselves of the gold earrings in their ears, and they brought [the gold] to Aaron ... and he made of it a cast calf.

Exodus 32:3–4

They came, every person whose heart roused him, and whose spirit moved him to donate; they brought [their] contribution to G-d for the work of the Tent of Meeting... a bracelet, an earring, a ring, a buckle, every object of gold.

Exodus 35:21–22

"I have built You a home," proclaimed King Solomon at the dedication of the Holy Temple in Jerusalem, "a base for Your eternal dwelling... But can G-d reside on earth? Behold, the heavens and the heaven of heavens cannot contain You; how, then, can this house that I have built You?"[1] G-d, who cannot be defined by the most spiritual of abstractions, how can He be said to "dwell" in a physical edifice?

And yet, such is G-d's express desire and command: "They shall make for Me a sanctuary, and I will dwell amongst them."[2] Indeed, a significant part of the book of Exodus,[3] the book that describes

---

1   I Kings 8:13 and 27.
2   Exodus 25:8.
3   Chapters 25–31 and 35–40, or about 35 percent of the book.

our birth as a nation and the formation of our covenant with G-d, is devoted to recounting G-d's detailed instructions on how to build this sanctuary—i.e., the "Tabernacle" that served the people of Israel during their journeys in the desert, and was forerunner of Solomon's Temple.

G-d, who transcends *and* pervades both the spiritual and the physical, wished for "a dwelling in the lowly realms."[4] G-d desired that we should sanctify the elements of our material existence by dedicating them to serve Him, thereby divesting them of their mundanity and bringing to light their divine essence. "This," writes Rabbi Schneur Zalman of Liadi, "is what man is all about, this is the purpose of his creation and the creation of all the worlds… that G-d should have a dwelling in the lowly realms."[5]

The Tabernacle and the Calf

The divine command to build the Tabernacle came in the first year following Israel's liberation from Egypt, soon after the revelation at Mount Sinai where G-d chose Israel as His people and gave them the Torah. Another event that transpired during that same period was the sin of the Golden Calf. When Moses failed to return from the mountaintop on the day that the Israelites were expecting him,[6] they abandoned their covenant with G-d. Revert-

---

4 *Midrash Tanchuma, Nasso* 16.
5 *Tanya*, chapter 37.
6 Moses ascended Mount Sinai on the 7th of *Sivan*, the day following the revelation, to receive the detailed communication of Torah from G-d, telling the people of Israel that he would return in forty days. Because of a miscalculation, they expected him a day earlier than he was to actually return. When he failed to come down from the mountain, "Satan came and filled the world with darkness and confusion… and

ing to the paganism of Egypt, they made and worshipped an idol of gold in the form of a calf.

Indeed, the Golden Calf is the ultimate perversion of the Tabernacle: ostensibly analogous to it, but in truth its very antithesis. Both are physical objects—particularly, objects of gold,[7] the ultimate symbol of materiality—that are consecrated and attributed a divine function. But while the Golden Calf exemplifies the worship of the material per se, the Sanctuary represents the subjugation of the material to serve and express the divine. Thus, Israel's construction of the Tabernacle was the ultimate rectification of their lapse with the Golden Calf, and when G-d manifested His presence within the Tabernacle, this was the ultimate sign that He had forgiven their transgression.[8]

Which came first—the Golden Calf or the Tabernacle? We know that the Torah was given seven weeks after the Exodus, on the 6th of *Sivan*.[9] We also know that the Golden Calf was made forty days later, on the 16th of *Tammuz*, and that on the next day, Moses, upon returning from the mountain and finding the Israelites worshipping it, smashed the two tablets on which G-d had inscribed the Ten Commandments.[10] Israel then repented of their transgression, and Moses returned to the mountaintop to

---

showed them a mirage of his coffin." Convinced that Moses had died, they turned to the Golden Calf as the new focus of their religious lives (Talmud, *Shabbat* 89a; Rashi on Exodus 32:1).

7   Fifteen materials were used in the Tabernacle's construction, but gold was by far its most dominant element. Most of the Tabernacle's vessels (the ark, the menorah, the table, the inner altar) as well as its wall sections and fittings were gold or gold-plated.

8   *Midrash Rabbah, Shemot* 51:3; *Midrash Tanchuma, Terumah* 8; et al.

9   See Talmud, *Shabbat* 86b–88a.

10 Talmud, *Taanit* 28b. This is one of the five tragic events remembered each year on the fast day of the 17th of *Tammuz*.

beseech G-d to forgive them. On Yom Kippur—the tenth day of *Tishrei*, or eighty days after the breaking of the first tablets—G-d expressed His complete forgiveness of the people and gave them a second set of tablets.[11] As for the Tabernacle, we are told that it was completed and erected almost six months later, on the first of the month of *Nissan*.[12]

But when, exactly, did G-d give the command to build the Tabernacle? Was it before or after the Golden Calf affair? And when did the people actually begin the implementation of this command? There are no less than three different opinions among the *Midrashim* and commentaries as to the chronology of events following the revelation at Sinai.

The Three Opinions

In the Torah, the events appear in the following order.

a) The giving of the Torah (Exodus 19–24).

b) G-d's command to donate the gold and the other materials for the Tabernacle's construction, and the detailed instructions on how to build it (chapters 25–31).

c) Israel's worship of the Golden Calf, Moses' breaking of the first tablets, Israel's repentance, and the granting of the second tablets and G-d's final forgiveness on Yom Kippur (chapters 32–34).

d) The Torah returns to the subject of the Tabernacle, describing the Jewish people's donation of its materials, its actual construction, its completion, and its erection and dedication on the first of *Nissan* (chapters 35–40).

---

11 Rashi on Exodus 33:11, based on Deuteronomy 9:9, 9:18 and 10:10.
12 Exodus 40:17. Our sages tell us that all the components of the Tabernacle were completed by the 25th of *Kislev* (Chanukah), but that G-d commanded that it be erected only on the first of *Nissan*.

Nachmanides[13] is of the opinion that the order in which the Torah relates these events is the order in which they transpired. Thus, G-d commanded the building of the Tabernacle *before* Israel's worship of the Golden Calf, but the actual implementation of this command began on the 11th of *Tishrei*, the day after Yom Kippur, when the people donated the materials for its construction (as recounted in Exodus 35).

Rashi disagrees. Citing the rule, "The Torah does not necessarily follow a chronological order,"[14] he maintains that G-d's instructions to Moses concerning the Tabernacle came only after Israel's repentance for the sin of the Golden Calf and G-d's complete forgiveness of their sin.[15] Rashi follows the opinion of *Midrash Tanchuma*, which states:

> *On Yom Kippur they were forgiven, and on that day G-d said to [Moses], "They shall make for Me a sanctuary, and I shall dwell amongst them," in order that all the nations should know that they have been forgiven for the making of the Calf.... Said G-d: May the gold of the Tabernacle atone for the gold of which the Calf was made.*[16]

A third opinion, that of the *Zohar*, is that both the divine command concerning the Tabernacle and Israel's contribution of its materials occurred before the making of the Golden Calf. According to the *Zohar*,

> *G-d preempted the Golden Calf with the gold of the Tabernacle.... Thus it is written, "They divested themselves of*

---

13 In his commentary of Exodus 35:1. See also Rabbi Chiya's opinion, cited in *Zohar* 2:195a.
14 Talmud, *Pesachim* 6a, et al.
15 Rashi on Exodus 31:18 and 33:11. See note 27 below.
16 *Midrash Tanchuma, Terumah* 8.

the golden earrings in their ears" [in order to make the Golden Calf].[17] *Would they have needed to divest their ears of gold if they had had other gold? But all their gold was already donated to the Tabernacle....*[18]

These three opinions represent more than three scenarios of the order in which the above events occurred. They also reflect three different interpretations of the place that the Tabernacle holds in our lives—three different approaches to the question of when, and under what conditions, a person can sanctify the material as an abode for G-d.

The Tzaddik and the Baal Teshuvah

Our sages tell us that when the people of Israel stood at Mount Sinai, they were like newly-born children, having been cleansed of all vestiges of their deficient past.[19] There, at the foot of the mountain, we were all *tzaddikim*, perfectly righteous individuals.

Then came the fall. With the sin of the Golden Calf, we lost the purity and perfection that characterized our first forty days as a nation. Indeed, the sin of the Golden Calf is the prototype of all subsequent corruptions and failings. In all of our history, states the Talmud, "there is no misfortune that does not have in it something of the sin of the Golden Calf."[20]

---

17 Exodus 32:3.
18 *Zohar* 2:224a.
19 Talmud, *Shabbat* 146a. At Sinai, we all had the status of *gerim* ("converts") who are like newly-born infants, free of all blemishes of the past (see Talmud, *Yevamot* 22a and 46a–b).
20 Talmud, *Sanhedrin* 102a, based on Exodus 32:34; Rashi on Exodus, ibid.

Then, on Yom Kippur, we attained the status of *baalei teshuvah*. A *baal teshuvah* ("returnee") is a person who rebounds from his or her past failings, exploiting the momentum of their descent to propel themselves to even greater heights; a person who learns to channel the frustration and pain over their deficiencies to deepen their relationship with their Creator, and their commitment to their life's purpose.[21]

On Yom Kippur, the Golden Calf breakdown was sublimated as the essence of a renewed, intensified bond between G-d and His people—the unique connection achieved by the *baal teshuvah*.[22]

Who Can Make a Sanctuary?

The *tzaddik* and the *baal teshuvah* are two very different individuals: the achievements of the one are anathema to the other, the strengths of one are the weaknesses of the other, where one is immune, the other is vulnerable.

The *tzaddik*'s course is straight and true, whereas the *baal teshuvah* is haunted by the past and uncertain of the future.[23] The *tzaddik*'s life is a pure expanse of unblemished virtue, whereas the *baal teshuvah* has turned blemish into virtue and failing into the impetus for achievement. The *tzaddik*'s life "is not a fleshly life but a spiritual life, consisting wholly of faith, awe, and love of

---

21 See *Tanya*, chapter 7.
22 See the next two essays, "The Anonymous Essence," pp. 290–299 below, and "Intellectual Waste," pp. 300–303, and the citations from the Midrash and Talmud on pages 301 and 302. See also the essay, "G-d's Business," in vol. I (Genesis) of *The Inside Story*.
23 See Psalms 51:5: "My sin is before me always."

G-d,"[24] whereas the *baal teshuvah*'s is an unceasing struggle with the material.[25]

Who is qualified to build a Sanctuary to G-d out of earthly matter? The *tzaddik*, who stands above the entanglements of the material, and has the purest vision of its spiritual potential? Or the *baal teshuvah*, who, having been there and back, has intimate knowledge of the material world, and is best equipped to exploit it to a G-dly end?

And what about the individual who is neither *tzaddik* nor *baal teshuvah*—the individual who is still plagued by his failings and deficiencies, still imprisoned by the trappings of a mundane self and world? Does such an individual have any role in the refinement and development of the material existence as a home for G-d?

This is the deeper significance of the three opinions cited above. According to the *Zohar*, the construction of a sanctuary for the divine dwelling is an endeavor for the perfectly righteous; only the *tzaddik* is truly capable of sublimating the material. Thus, the command to build the Tabernacle was addressed to a nation of *tzaddikim*, and its materials were consecrated by a nation of *tzaddikim*. Indeed, it was only because the gold of the Tabernacle preempted the gold of the Calf, that the Tabernacle was able to rectify the descent into material corruption that the Golden Calf entailed. Had not the Tabernacle's materials been contributed by

---

24 *Tanya, Igeret HaKodesh*, 27.
25 Thus our sages state that "On the level that *baalei teshuvah* stand, even perfect *tzaddikim* cannot stand" (Talmud, *Berachot* 34b). On the other hand, it is the *tzaddik* who is "the foundation of the world," the embodiment of G-d's conception of life on earth and His initial motive for creating the universe (Proverbs 10:25; see *Midrash Rabbah*, Ruth 2:3).

those untouched by sin, a nation of *baalei teshuvah* could not have consecrated them, after having shown themselves to be vulnerable to the pitfalls of involvement with the material.[26]

On the other hand, the approach of *Midrash Tanchuma* and Rashi is that, on the contrary, the command and empowerment to build the sanctuary is G-d's response to the people's *teshuvah* over their worship of the Golden Calf. Precisely because they had descended to the nadir of materiality only to reclaim, and surpass, their prior perfection, were they deemed capable of constructing a material edifice to house and express G-d's presence in the world. Precisely because they had demonstrated their ability to sublimate failing into achievement, could they now transform physical gold, wood, and animal hides into a vessel and vehicle for G-dliness.

Nachmanides goes even further. According to him, G-d's commandment to Moses concerning the Tabernacle came before Israel's sin, but its implementation began only after the incident with the Golden Calf. In the interim, the Tablets of the Covenant were smashed because the covenant between G-d and Israel had been violated, and a new set of tablets had to be issued on Yom Kippur. But no new franchise to make a home for G-d was necessary.[27]

---

26 See *Likutei Torah*, *Va'etchanan* 9d: "The *baal teshuvah* requires greater vigilance in distancing himself from anything that may entice him to sin. Thus, Rabbi Dov Ber of Mezheritch taught that although our sages have said, 'A person should not say, "I am repelled by the taste of meat mixed with milk," rather, he should say, "It is attractive to me, but what can I do if my Father in Heaven has forbidden it to me"'—this applies only to one who hasn't already sinned. A *baal teshuvah*, however, must make all evils and transgressions abhorrent to himself, lest he fall, G-d forbid."

27 Indeed, according to some of the commentaries, this is the very point of contention between Rashi and Nachmanides. As the commentators on Rashi explain, the reason Rashi insists that the command to contribute to the Sanctuary came after the divine forgiveness on Yom

In other words, the divine command to consecrate materials for the Sanctuary remained in effect even as the Children of Israel were worshipping a calf of gold! For no matter to what depths a person has fallen, it is still within their ability to transcend their circumstances and make their life receptive to the goodness and perfection of their Creator.

Three Homes in One

"These and these are both the words of the living G-d,"[28] says the Talmud of variant opinions among Torah sages. Historically, only one of the three scenarios of the sequence of events surrounding the Tabernacle's construction can represent how they occurred in physical time thirty-three centuries ago at the foot of Mount Sinai. But on the conceptual level, all three are valid and correct interpretations of the Torah's account.

On the conceptual level, the sanctification of the material follows all three courses. It is divinely ordained and implemented "before" the corruption of the Golden Calf. It is born out of the *teshuvah* that "follows" the Golden Calf. And it also "coincides" with the worship of the Golden Calf, for it embodies a potential that the most terrible betrayal cannot efface.

Indeed, the Tabernacle itself (and later, Solomon's Temple) incorporated all three elements. At the heart of the Tabernacle, in its innermost and most sacred chamber, was the ark, which, as

---

Kippur—contrary to the order in which the events are related by the Torah—is that otherwise the original command would have had to have been reiterated, just as a second set of tablets had to be issued (see Mizrachi, *Siftei Chachamim*, et al).

[28] Talmud, *Eruvin* 13b.

the container of Torah, embodied the Tabernacle's function as the facilitator of G-d's manifest bond with His people.[29] And "both the [second] tablets and the broken tablets were placed in the ark."[30] In other words, the divine sanctuary houses the Torah as it reflects all three states of the people of Israel. It holds the second tablets, which embody the relationship with G-d attained through *teshuvah*. It also contains the first tablets, given to a nation in a state of perfection. But these are broken, representing also the breakdown of this perfection.

The sanctuary is three divine dwellings in one. It is the home for G-d created by those who rise from the depths of depravation to redeem and sublimate their material-worshipping past. It is the sanctification of the material incumbent on even the most spiritual and saintly individual. And it is the abode of a G-d "who dwells among them in the midst of their impurities"[31]—who treasures and manifests Himself in the positive efforts of every individual, regardless of their present moral and spiritual condition.

---

29   "The main object of the Sanctuary is the Ark, the resting place of the divine presence"—Nachmanides' introduction to Exodus 25.
30   Talmud, *Bava Batra* 14b.
31   Leviticus 16:16. See Rabbi Schneur Zalman of Liadi's *Laws of Torah Study*, 4:3, and *Kuntres Acharon*, ad loc.

THE ANONYMOUS ESSENCE

Moses returned to G-d, and he said: "I beseech You: this nation has sinned a great sin and have made themselves a god of gold. Now, if You will forgive their sin; and if You will not, please erase me from the book that You have written."

And G-d said to Moses: "Whoever has sinned against Me, him will I erase from My book." Exodus 32:31–33

No human being is as deeply identified with the Torah as Moses. The prophet Malachi goes so far as to refer to the revealed word of G-d as "the Torah of My servant Moses."[1] As the Midrash explains, "Because he gave his life for it, it is called by his name."[2]

Yet there was one thing that was even more important to Moses than his connection with the Torah: his connection with the people of Israel. In order to secure G-d's forgiveness of Israel for their sin in worshipping the Golden Calf, Moses was prepared to forgo his place in the Torah. Following Israel's transgression, Moses gave G-d an "ultimatum": if You cannot forgive them, erase me from the book that You have written.

---

1   Malachi 3:22. Indeed, the core text of the Torah is commonly referred to as "The Five Books of Moses."
2   *Mechilta* on Exodus 15:1.

The Two Precedents

Our sages tell us that "the righteous emulate their Creator."[3] The same is true in this case: in giving precedence to Israel over the Torah, Moses was following the divine example. As the Midrash states:

> *Two things preceded G-d's creation of the world: Torah and Israel. Still, I do not know which preceded which. But when the Torah states, "Speak to the Children of Israel," "Command the Children of Israel"—I know that Israel preceded all.*[4]

In other words, because G-d's purpose in creating the world is that the people of Israel should implement His will as outlined in the Torah,[5] the concepts of "Torah" and "Israel" both precede the concept of a "world" in the Creator's "mind." Yet, which is the more deeply rooted idea within the divine consciousness, Torah or Israel? Does Israel exist in order for the Torah to be implemented, or does the Torah exist in order to serve the people of Israel in the realization of their relationship with G-d? Says the Midrash: If the Torah describes itself as a communication to the people of Israel, this presumes the concept of Israel as primary to that of Torah. The very idea of a Torah was conceived by the divine mind as a tool to enhance the bond between G-d and His people—a bond that "predates" it and which it comes to serve.

Thus our sages have said: "A Jew, although he has sinned, is a Jew."[6] Even if the Jew sins, thereby violating his or her relationship with G-d as defined by the Torah, they are still a Jew. For

---

3   *Midrash Rabbah, Bereishith* 67:8.
4   *Tana D'vei Eliyahu Rabbah*, chapter 14.
5   See Rashi on Genesis 1:1.
6   Talmud, *Sanhedrin* 44a.

the essence of our relationship with G-d runs deeper than those aspects of the relationship that are realized through our fulfillment of the divine will as formulated in the Torah.

Beyond the Word

Therein lies the deeper significance of Moses' declaration to G-d, "...if You will not [forgive them], please erase me from the book that You have written," and of G-d's response, "Whoever has sinned against Me, him will I erase from My book."

At first glance, Moses' words, dramatic and moving as they are, are very puzzling. Other than its dubious value as some sort of "threat" to G-d (?!), how would Moses' eradication from the Torah help the people of Israel attain atonement for their sin?[7]

G-d's reply also requires explanation. G-d seems to be rejecting Moses' plea, saying, in effect, "I will do what I see fit with My Torah. You are in; they go out." But that is not what G-d does. He forgives the people of Israel, and gives them a second set of tablets engraved by G-d's own hand with the Ten Commandments to replace those broken as a result of their sin. Moses' words have their desired effect: the people of Israel are rehabilitated, and their place in Torah is preserved, even enhanced.[8] So what does G-d

---

[7] Rashi explains that Moses was saying to G-d, "If You won't forgive them, erase me from Your Torah, so that it should not be said that I was not worthy to arouse Your mercy on them" (Rashi on Exodus 32:32). But this, too, is puzzling: Could it be that Moses was more concerned over what would be said of him in future generations than with his connection to Torah? (See note 16 below for the deeper meaning of Rashi's explanation.)

[8] See the essay, "Intellectual Waste," on pp. 300–303 below, and the passages from *Midrash Rabbah, Shemot* 46:1, and Talmud, *Nedarim* 22b, quoted there.

mean when he says, "Whoever has sinned against Me, him will I erase from My book"?

But according to what we have explained, we can understand the deeper meaning implicit in this exchange. Moses is saying to G-d: It is true that Your people have sinned a great sin. A sin so great, a sin that so acutely violates Your relationship with them, that in terms of how Torah defines that relationship, their betrayal is unpardonable. But Your bond with them runs deeper than Torah, deeper than anything that can be expressed or destroyed by their deeds. If You cannot forgive them, it is because You are relating to them on Torah's terms, defining Your bond with them on a level on which their sin cannot be tolerated.

Well, said Moses, I, for myself, will not accept such a state of affairs. If the Torah does not allow for their forgiveness, then erase me from the Torah, as I do not wish to be part of a framework that severs me from the people of Israel. Cut me out of the very thing that has consumed my mind, heart, and life so completely that the book that You have written has come to be called "the Torah of Moses." Divest me of my identity as conveyer of Torah, so that I shall stand denuded of everything but my very essence—my relationship with my people.

Now it was the Creator who emulated the righteous. "Whoever has sinned against Me, him will I erase from My book," G-d promised. Those whom Torah cannot forgive, those with whom I can no longer sustain the relationship delineated by My book, I will exempt from My book. I will transcend My Torah to revert to the quintessential bond between Me and Israel, which precedes and supersedes My word, wisdom, and will. I will follow your example, Moses, your preparedness to relinquish everything you have and are, should it interfere with your most quintessential priority—your oneness with your people.

The Book Is Broadened

Ultimately, Israel's "erasure" from the Torah resulted not in a diminution, G-d forbid, of their Torah-defined relationship with the Almighty, but in its reinforcement and intensification.

For once the quintessential bond between G-d and Israel had been reiterated, this selfsame bond could now be manifested via the vehicle of Torah, which would now be broadened to accommodate that which was previously beyond its realm. The Torah would now incorporate the highest level of *teshuvah* ("return")—the level on which "sins are transformed into virtues"[9] and the greatest failing and the most terrible betrayal can be sublimated into even greater achievement and even deeper connection.

The same is true regarding Moses: His readiness to divest himself of his identity as the vehicle through whom G-d communicated His Torah to man actually resulted in a deepening of his identification with Torah. This can be discerned in the phenomenon of Moses' "disappearance" from the Torah section of *Tetzaveh* (Exodus 27:20–30:10), as will be discussed below.

The You of Moses

Given the centrality of Moses' role to the transmission of Torah to humanity, it comes as no surprise that his name is mentioned, often as much as several dozen times, in every single section (*parashah*) of the books of Exodus, Leviticus, and Numbers.[10]

---

9 Talmud, *Yoma* 86b.
10 The first of the Five Books of the Torah, Genesis, relates events that occurred before Moses' birth. The fifth book, Deuteronomy, consists wholly of Moses' own words to the people of Israel before his passing.

Every section, that is, but one. The single exception is the section of *Tetzaveh*, in which the word "Moses" does not appear. Most amazingly, *Tetzaveh* is the section that, by rights, should be most saturated with Moses' name. In the annual Torah-reading cycle, *Tetzaveh* is almost always read either on the Shabbat preceding the 7th of *Adar* or on the Shabbat that follows it. *Adar* 7 is the day most closely related to the life of Moses, as it is both the date of his birth and the date of his passing.[11]

The *Baal HaTurim* commentary on the Torah explains this omission as the result of Moses' words, "erase me from the book that You have written." Our sages have said that the words of a *tzaddik*, even when expressed conditionally, always have an effect.[12] So once Moses uttered those fateful words, they were destined to somehow be realized. Thus, concludes the *Baal HaTurim*, even after G-d forgave the people of Israel and the conditions for Moses' proclamation no longer applied, there remains one section of the Torah devoid of his name.[13]

Upon closer examination, however, Moses is hardly absent from the section of *Tetzaveh*—indeed, he is more profoundly present there than any mention of his name could possibly express. *Tetzaveh* consists entirely of G-d's ongoing communication to Moses, instructing him with the details of the *menorah*-lighting in the Tabernacle, the construction of the priestly garments, and the Tabernacle's inauguration. All that is missing is the customary

---

11 Cf. Shaloh, introduction to *Parashat Vayeishev*: " 'To everything there is its season, the appointed time for each purpose' (Ecclesisates 3:1). Certainly, the arrangements of the festivals and days of commemoration of the year, both the [biblical] 'seasons of G-d' and those rabbinically ordained... all have a connection to the [weekly] *parashah* in which they fall, for all is arranged by the hand of G-d."
12 Talmud, *Makot* 11a.
13 *Baal HaTurim* on Exodus 27:20.

"G-d spoke to Moses, saying..." that precedes the divine directives in the rest of the Torah. Thus, *Tetzaveh* begins almost in mid-sentence: "And you [i.e., Moses] shall command the Children of Israel to bring to you pure olive oil, crushed for illumination, to light up a perpetual lamp...."

On the surface, there is a diminution of Moses' presence—his name does not appear in the entire section. But Moses is the subject of its first word, *ve'atah*, "and you"—a word that is a truer and deeper reference to Moses than his name.

A name, after all, is something that is *given* to a person, something appended to an already existent being (in Moses' case, the name "Moses" was given to him by Pharaoh's daughter more than three months after his birth). "You," on the other hand, is a reference to the person himself. Thus, a person's "name" represents his or her manifest self—their intellect and character, their communicable thoughts and feelings; whereas the abstract "you" refers to the person's anonymous essence—anonymous because it is too sublime and ethereal to be articulated.[14] *Tetzaveh* is thus the section of Torah that embodies the "you" of Moses, his transcendent essence.

This is fully in keeping with the *Baal HaTurim*'s explanation that Moses' anonymity in *Tetzaveh* is the result of his expressing the possibility that he be erased from G-d's book. Moses was prepared to forgo his place in Torah because his bond with his people was on the level of his "you," his truest, most quintessential self—a self even deeper than his connection to the Torah. In effect,

---

14 Our sages have said that a person's name is the conduit of his life, the channel that carries the flow of vitality from his soul to his body (*Shaar HaGilgulim, Hakdamah* 23, et al). But this itself indicates that it is secondary to the person's very essence, as "the soul, prior to its entry into the body, has no name whatsoever" (*Likutei Torah, Behar* 41c).

Moses actually *did* obliterate his "name"—his identification with Torah—in order to be one with his people. As a result, G-d, too, was moved to forgo His "name." Our sages have said, "The entire Torah is names of G-d"[15]—i.e., the expressed aspect of G-d's relationship with us. Inspired by Moses' example, G-d withdrew from relating to us on Torah's terms, and reaffirmed His quintessential bond with us. This was followed by a renewed giving of the Torah, in which this deeper bond could also be "named" and expressed.

Nevertheless, even after Moses' and Israel's identity were reestablished in Torah, there remains one section—the section most intimately related to Moses—in which Moses' anonymous essence reigns supreme, unencumbered by name and name-defined identity. The section of *Tetzaveh* stands as an eternal tribute to Moses, as the Torah's own testimony to his greatness in relinquishing everything, including his bond with Torah, in order to preserve his bond with his people and restore them to their G-d.[16]

Moses Today

The Torah section in which Moses is rendered "nameless" serves as a lesson for every leader of Israel as to the true nature of G-d's bond with His people, and the lengths to which they must go to affirm it. It is also of eternal relevance to each and every one of us.

We all sense that beyond our expressed self lies a deeper, more intimate self—thoughts, feelings, convictions, and potentials that

---

[15] Nachmanides' introduction to his commentary on Torah.

[16] Therein lies the deeper meaning in Rashi's words, cited in note 7 above. You must erase me from Your Torah, Moses is saying to G-d, so that future generations should know to what lengths a leader of his people must go to preserve his bond with them and reunite them with their G-d.

are too sublime to articulate to others, or even to our own conscious self. But what effect does this deeper self have on our actual behavior? Does it remain in a "seventh heaven" of abstraction, or can it somehow be made to impact our daily lives?

We know that Moses, in his greatest moment, touched this purest core of self. But Moses was the most perfect human being ever to walk the face of the earth;[17] of what relevance are his achievements to us?

The Talmud cites the verse, "And now, Israel, what does G-d want of you? Only that you be in awe of G-d...,"[18] and asks: "Is awe of G-d a minor thing?" The answer given is: "Yes, for Moses it is a minor thing."[19] But the above-quoted verse is addressed to all of Israel. How does Moses' capacity for the awe of G-d answer the question?

In his *Tanya*, Rabbi Schneur Zalman of Liadi explains: "Each and every soul of the house of Israel contains within it something of the quality of our teacher Moses. For [Moses] is one of the 'seven shepherds' who feed vitality and G-dliness to the community of the souls of Israel.... Moses is the sum of them all, called the 'shepherd of faith'[20] in the sense that he nourishes the community of Israel with the knowledge and recognition of G-d."[21]

Indeed, it was Moses' uncompromising identification with his people, no matter to what depths they had fallen, that ensured that

---

17   Maimonides' introduction to *Perek Chelek*, Principle 7.
18   Deuteronomy 10:12.
19   Talmud, *Berachot* 33b.
20   *Raaya mehemna*, usually translated as "faithful shepherd"; here Rabbi Schneur Zalman renders it "shepherd of faith," in the sense that Moses is Israel's conduit of faith, the one who inculcates them with their quintessential recognition of G-d, like a shepherd who feeds his flocks their vital needs.
21   *Tanya*, chapter 42.

each and every one of us, regardless of our spiritual station and moral circumstances, possesses, and can readily access, the "Moses" within him or herself—our quintessential source of faith and oneness with G-d.

INTELLECTUAL WASTE

G-d said to Moses: "Hew for yourself two tablets of stone like the first; and I will inscribe on these tablets the words that were on the first tablets, which you broke."

Exodus 34:1

"Hew for yourself"—[G-d] showed him a quarry of sapphire under his tent, and said to him: "The waste shall be yours." From this Moses became very rich.

Rashi, ad loc.

The first tablets, on which the Ten Commandments were initially inscribed, were "the handiwork of G-d."[1] These were broken by Moses when the people of Israel worshipped a golden calf, violating the covenant with G-d to which the tablets attested. The nation repented, and G-d agreed to reissue the Torah to Israel. This time, however, G-d instructed Moses to fashion the tablets. The inscription would again be by the divine hand, but the tablets were to be of human manufacture, hewn by Moses.

In its "first edition," the Torah was wholly divine. Not only its content, but also the vehicle of its delivery to us was of divine origin. Accordingly, the Torah as contained in the first tablets

---

1   Exodus 32:16.

was a clear, concise communication of the divine wisdom; had we not sinned by worshipping the Golden Calf, our study of Torah would have been free of the struggles, debates, and equivocations it knows today. In the second tablets, G-d inscribed His wisdom upon a medium of human creation, with the result that the divine word is now accessible to us only via the finite and deficient tool that is the human mind.

The Divine and the Human in Torah

Otherwise stated, the first tablets incorporated only the "Written Torah," the divine revelation to man; whereas the second tablets necessitated the addition of the "Oral Torah"—the system of interpretation, handed down through the generations, without which the Written Torah would be a closed book to us. Because of the breaking of the first tablets, our present-day pursuit of the divine wisdom twists and twines through the labyrinth of Talmudic logic, retarded by the false starts, refuted propositions, ambiguous nuances, and circuitous reasoning that characterize human learning.

And yet, with the second tablets we gained a dimension of Torah which the first tablets could not have given us. In the words of the Midrash:

> Said G-d to Moses: *Do not be distressed over the first tablets, which contained only the Ten Commandments. In the second tablets I am giving you also* halachah, Midrash, *and* aggadah.[2]

---

[2] *Midrash Rabbah, Shemot* 46:1.

Similarly, the Talmud states:

> Had Israel not sinned with the Golden Calf, they would have only received the five books of Moses and the book of Joshua. Why? Because, as the verse says (Ecclesiastes 1:18): "Much wisdom comes through much grief."[3]

For there is a depth to the knowledge that has been gained through toil that tranquil learning cannot impart; there is a keenness to a truth that emerges from refuted falsehoods that the most lucid revelation will not reveal. The regression caused by Israel's sin and the breaking of the first tablets imparted to us the potential to achieve a more profound appreciation of the divine wisdom than could be derived from a suprahuman Torah.

The Profit in the Waste

Therein lies the deeper significance of Moses' enrichment by the "waste" of the second tablets, as related in the Talmud and cited in Rashi's commentary on the Torah. The Torah tells us that G-d commanded Moses, "Hew for yourself two tablets of stone," to replace the ones that were broken because of Israel's sin. The words, "hew for yourself"—*pesal lecha* in the Hebrew—can also be interpreted as "the waste (*pesolet*) will be yours." As the tablets were hewn of solid sapphire, this "waste" became a source of great wealth for Moses.

When, as students of Torah, we spend many hours pursuing a line of reasoning only to reject it; or when we expend energy and acumen in a debate in which we are bested by our fellows; this might seem an unfortunate waste. How much better would it be

---

[3] Talmud, *Nedarim* 22b.

if we were just shown the light, if we had the capacity to imbibe the divine truth directly, without resorting to the convoluted pathways of human reason! But the "waste" of the second tablets, said G-d to Moses, is My gift to you. It is the dividend of the painful process of repentance, of rebounding from sin and failure, to a deeper commitment to Me. Treasure it, as it will prove a source of great spiritual riches to you.

MOSES' MASK

The people of Israel saw Moses, and behold, the skin of his face was radiant; and they were afraid to approach him.

Moses called to them... and he instructed them all that G-d spoke to him on Mount Sinai. When Moses finished speaking with them, he placed a mask upon his face....

Whenever Moses came before G-d to speak with Him, he would remove the mask... he would go out and speak to the people of Israel all that he had been instructed... Moses would then replace the mask upon his face, until he would [once again] come to speak [with G-d].

Exodus 34:30–35

In the closing verses of the Torah section of *Ki Tisa*, there appears the enigmatic account of the veil or "mask" (as the Torah calls it) that Moses wore. The Torah relates that when Moses descended from Mount Sinai, his face shone with a G-dly light—a result of the fact that "G-d would speak to Moses face to face, as a man would speak to his fellow."[1] So brilliant was this light that the people were afraid to be in Moses' presence. Moses, however, summoned them to him, and taught them "all that he had been instructed" by G-d. After he concluded teaching them, Moses donned a veil to conceal the divine brilliance emanating from his face.

---

[1] Exodus 33:11.

This process would repeat itself throughout the forty years that the people of Israel traveled through the wilderness and received G-d's communication of His wisdom and will—i.e., the Torah—through the agency of Moses. Every time that Moses was called to the "Tent of Meeting"[2] to hear more of G-d's instructions to the people, he would remove his mask. Still maskless, Moses would teach the people what he had been taught, replacing the mask only when he finished delivering G-d's teachings to them.

It would seem, however, that at the very times when the "mask" was most needed, Moses declined to use it. He insisted on teaching the people without covering his face, despite the fact that they were intimidated by the rays of divine light radiating from it. Also in his meetings with G-d, he eschewed the veil that would have mitigated the intensity of the encounter. At all other times, however, he did wear his mask.

When to Filter

A mask conceals. A mask also protects: when we need to come in contact with something that is alien and threatening to us (for example, a hazardous chemical substance) we make use of a mask to filter our involvement. The mask allows us to exploit the constructive potential of the substance while shielding us from the undesirable aspects of the encounter.

Therein lies the lesson of Moses' mask. Moses received and communicated the Torah without any barriers or "filters" to dim the intensity of the encounter; but at all other times, he made use of the screening detachment of his mask. This sums up how we are to approach the various involvements of life.

---

[2] The Tabernacle, where G-d would summon Moses to communicate with him.

Everything that concerns our relationship with G-d—the study of Torah, the observance of its *mitzvot*, our spiritual development—should be approached without inhibition or constraint. For no matter how lofty and intimidating our endeavor may seem, here we are in *our* element, for G-dliness is the natural habitat of our soul.

But when it comes to our material, everyday pursuits, we need to maintain a distance. Here we don an intellectual and emotional mask: we get involved, but not too involved. We realize that we are treading on alien, if fertile, ground. True, we are enjoined to make optimum use of the material elements of G-d's creation, developing them creatively and constructively; but at the same time, we must filter our involvement, exploiting its resources without allowing its surface mundanity to overwhelm us.

Future Scenario

The alien and dangerous nature of the material world is itself a result of another mask: the mask of the Creator, who shrouds His involvement in our lives with the guise of a "natural order," allowing a world seemingly ruled by chance and caprice to obscure the divine truth.

But there will come a time, promises the prophet, when "No longer shall your Master be cloaked."[3] G-d will cast aside His mask and expose the material world for what it is: merely another expression of G-d's all-pervading reality. We, too, shall then be mask-free—no longer will there be the need for screens and constraints to shield us from a potentially corrupting world. The era of the mask will come to its end.

---

3   Isaiah 30:20.

PARASHAH TWENTY-TWO

VAYAK'HEL

Exodus 35:1–38:20

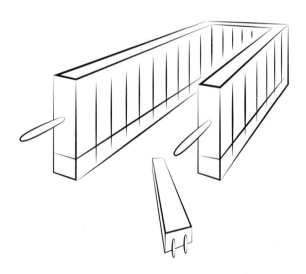

Home and hearth

HEAVEN AND EARTH

According to all that I show you, the form of the Tabernacle and the form of all its vessels; and so shall you make [them].

Exodus 25:9

The *Chumash* (the "Five Books of Moses") is a very concise document. Consisting of less than 80,000 words (about the size of a short novel), it encapsulates the entirety of Torah. Everything is here: all of *halachah* (Torah law); the stories of the Midrash; the vast homiletic sea of the *aggadah*; the innumerable insights of the mystical, philosophical, and ethical Torah works of all generations. Indeed, there is nary a superfluous word or letter in the *Chumash*: If a verse is lyrically repetitive, if two words are used where one would suffice or a longer word when a shorter word would do, there is a message here—a new concept, another law. Rabbi Akiva, the Talmud tells us, would derive "mounds upon mounds of laws from the serif of a letter" in Torah.[1]

Yet there are two sections in the *Chumash*—*Vayak'hel* (Exodus 35:1–38:20) and *Pekudei* (Exodus 38:21–40:38)—that consist, almost in their entirety, of a seemingly needless repetition. In the previous sections of *Terumah* and *Tetzaveh* (Exodus 25–30), the Torah gives a detailed account of G-d's instructions to Moses

---

[1] Talmud, *Menachot* 29b. Cf. Jerusalem Talmud, *Pe'ah* 2:4: "Scripture, Mishnah, Talmud and *aggadah*, and anything a qualified student is destined to state before his teacher, all was already said to Moses at Sinai."

regarding the construction of the Sanctuary (the "Tabernacle"), its furnishings, and the priestly garments worn by those who would perform the service in it. Then, in *Vayak'hel* and *Pekudei*, it relates how the people of Israel carried out these instructions. Again we are informed of the construction of the Sanctuary in exacting detail, down to the dimensions of every pillar, wall-panel, and tapestry, the materials in every garment, and the decorative forms sculpted in the gold of the *menorah* (twenty-two goblets, eleven spheres, and nine flowers). A single sentence, on the order of "The Children of Israel made the Sanctuary exactly as G-d had commanded Moses," would have "saved" the Torah more than a thousand words!

The Translation

Actually, there were two Sanctuaries: a heavenly model and a terrestrial edifice. In His instructions to Moses, G-d refers to "the form that you are being shown on the mountain."[2] On the summit of Mount Sinai, Moses was shown an image of the home in which G-d desired to dwell; at the foot of Mount Sinai, the people of Israel translated this spiritual vision into a physical structure of cedar and gold.

Never in history had a translator been challenged by two more diverse "languages." Spirit is nebulous, matter is concrete. Spirit is infinite, matter is defined by time and space. Most importantly, spirit is naturally subservient, readily bespeaking a higher truth, while matter recognizes nothing save its own immanence. Yet it was a *physical* abode that G-d desired. It was in the earthly

---

2   Exodus 25:40, 26:30, and 27:8.

Sanctuary that the divine presence came to reside, not in the spiritual Sanctuary atop Mount Sinai.

Yes, the material universe is the lowliest of G-d's creations—lowliest in the sense that it is least aware of its innate nullity before G-d, least expressive of its divine source and purpose. But it is precisely because of their "lowliness" that G-d desired that physical substances should be made into a Sanctuary to house Him. G-d desired that the material world, with all its limitations and imperfections, should be sanctified and elevated by being made to serve a G-dly end.[3]

Therein lies the lesson of the two Sanctuaries: Do not be discouraged by the tremendous gap between spirit and matter, between theory and practice, between the ideal and the real. True, it is virtually impossible to duplicate the perfection of the spirit on mundane earth, but it is not a duplication that G-d desires. G-d desires an earthly sanctuary, a sanctuary constructed of the finite materials of physical life.

To emphasize this point, the Torah expends close to two hundred "extra" verses in its account of the earthly construction of the Sanctuary. Every wall panel, every tent peg, and every tassel made by the Children of Israel mirrored, in every detail, the spiritual model described several chapters earlier; but it was a different item, a different Sanctuary.

Yes, earth must be made to mirror the heavens, to reflect, in every detail, the divine blueprint for life. But it remains earthly in nature and substance—a physical home for G-d, employing the unique characteristics of the physical to express the divine truth.

---

3   See *Midrash Tanchuma, Naso* 16, and *Tanya*, chapter 36.

THE VESSEL

And all the wise-hearted people, the artisans, made the Tabernacle…
Exodus 36:8

Why are we here?

This, the mother of all questions, is addressed in turn by the various streams of Torah thought, each after its own style.

The Talmud states, simply and succinctly, "I was created to serve my Creator."[1] The moralistic-oriented works of *Mussar* describe the purpose of life as the refinement of one's character traits. The *Zohar* says that G-d created us "in order that His creations should know Him."[2] Master kabbalist Rabbi Isaac Luria offered the following reason for creation: G-d is the essence of good, and the nature of good is to bestow goodness. But goodness cannot be bestowed when there is no one to receive it. To this end, G-d created our world—that there should be recipients of His goodness.[3]

Chassidic teaching explains that these reasons, as well as the reasons given by other kabbalistic and philosophical works, are but the various faces of a singular divine desire for creation as expressed in the various "worlds" or realms of G-d's creation. Chassidism also offers its own formulation of this divine desire: that we "make a home for G-d in the material world."[4]

---

1 Talmud, *Kidushin* 82b.
2 *Zohar* 3:42b.
3 *Eitz Chaim, Shaar HaKelalim*, ch. 1.
4 *Tanya*, chapter 36, based on after *Midrash Tanchuma, Naso* 16; *Yom Tov*

A Home for G-d

What does it mean to make our world a home for G-d?

A basic tenet of our faith is that "the entire world is filled with His presence"[5] and "there is no place void of Him."[6] So it's not that we have to bring G-d into the material world—G-d is already there. But G-d can be in the world without being at home in it.

Being "at home" means being in a place that is receptive to your presence, a place devoted to serving your needs and desires. It means being in a place where you are your true, private self, as opposed to the public self you assume in other environments.

The material world, in its natural state, is not an environment hospitable to G-d. If there is one common feature to all things material, it is their intrinsic egocentrism, their placement of the self as the foundation and purpose of existence. With every iota of its mass, the stone proclaims: "I am." In the tree and in the animal, the preservation and propagation of the self is the focus of every instinct and the aim of every action. And who more than the human being has elevated ambition to an art, and self-advancement to an all-consuming ideal?

The only thing wrong with all this selfishness is that it blurs the truth of what lies behind it: the truth that creation is not an end in itself, but a product of and vehicle for its Creator. And this selfishness is not an incidental or secondary characteristic of our world, but its most basic feature. So to make our world a "home" for G-d, we need to transform its very nature. We need to recast the very foundations of its identity, from a self-oriented entity into something that exists for a purpose that is greater than itself.

Shel Rosh Hashanah 5666, p. 7; Ibid., p. 446; see *Likutei Sichot*, vol. 6, p. 21, notes 69 and 70.

5   Isaiah 6:3.
6   *Tikunei Zohar*, 57.

Every time we take a material object or resource and enlist it in the service of G-d, we are effecting such a transformation. When we take a piece of leather and make a pair of *tefilin*; when we take a coin and give it to charity; when we employ our minds to study a chapter of Torah—we are effecting such a transformation. In its initial state, the piece of leather proclaimed, "I exist"; now it proclaims, "I exist to serve my Creator." A coin in one's pocket says, "Greed is good"; in the charity box it says, "The purpose of life is not to receive, but to give." The human brain says, "Enrich thyself"; the brain studying Torah says, "Know thy G-d."

The Frontier of Self

There are two basic steps to the endeavor of making our world a home for G-d. The first step involves priming the material resource as a "vessel for G-dliness": shaping the leather into *tefilin*, donating the money to charity, scheduling time for Torah study. The second step is the actual employment of these "vessels" to serve the divine will: binding the *tefilin* on the arm and head, using the donated money to feed the hungry, studying Torah, etc.

At first glance, it would seem that the second step is the more significant one, while the first step is merely an enabler of the second, a means to its end. But the Torah's account of the first home for G-d built in our world places the greater emphasis on the construction of the "home," rather than its actual employment as a divine dwelling.

A sizable portion of the book of Exodus is devoted to the construction of the Tabernacle built by the Children of Israel in the desert. The Torah, which is usually so sparing with words that many of its laws are contained within a single word or letter, is uncharacteristically elaborate. The fifteen materials used in the

Tabernacle's construction are listed no less than three times;[7] the components and furnishings of the Tabernacle are listed eight times;[8] and every minute detail of the Tabernacle's construction, down to the dimensions of every wall-panel and the colors in every tapestry, is spelled out not once, but twice—in the account of G-d's instructions to Moses, and again in the account of the Tabernacle's construction.

All in all, thirteen chapters are devoted to describing how certain physical materials were fashioned into an edifice dedicated to the service of G-d, and the training of the priests who were to officiate there—significantly more than is devoted to describing the actual service conducted in it.

The Tabernacle is the model and prototype for all subsequent homes for G-d constructed on physical earth. So the overwhelming emphasis on its "construction" stage (as opposed to the "implementation" stage) implies that in our lives, too, there is something

---

7 "Gold, silver and copper; blue-, purple-, and red-dyed wool; linen and goat hair; red-dyed rams' skins, *tachash* skins, and acacia wood; oil for lighting, and spices for the anointing oil and the incense; *shoham* stones and gemstones for setting in the *ephod* and in the breastplate." The above verses are from Exodus 25:3–7, in G-d's initial instructions to Moses; the list again appears in full in Moses' repetition of these instructions to the people of Israel (ibid., 35:5–9), and a third time in the Torah's account of the people's donation of these materials and G-d's appointment of Betzalel to head the construction of the Sanctuary (ibid., verses 22–35).

8 In G-d's instructions to Moses (ibid., chapters 25–27); in G-d's instructions to anoint the Tabernacle's parts and "vessels" (30:26–28); in G-d's appointment of Betzalel (31:7–11); in Moses' instruction to the people (35:11–19); in the Torah's account of the making of the parts and vessels of the Sanctuary (36:8–39:32); in the Torah's account of how the finished parts and vessels were brought to Moses (39:33–41); in G-d's instructions to Moses to erect and anoint the Sanctuary (40:3–11); and in the account of the erection of the Sanctuary (40:18–33).

very special about forging our personal resources into things that have the potential to serve G-d. Making ourselves "vessels" for G-dliness is, in a certain sense, a greater feat than actually bringing G-dliness into our lives.

For this is where the true point of transformation lies—the transformation from a self-oriented object to a thing committed to something greater than itself. If G-d had merely desired a hospitable environment, He need not have bothered with a material world; a spiritual world could just as easily have been enlisted to serve Him. What G-d desired was the transformation itself: the challenge and achievement of selfhood transcended and materiality redefined. This transformation and redefinition occurs in the first stage, when something material is forged into an instrument of the divine. The second stage is only a matter of actualizing an already established potential, of putting a thing to its now natural use.

Good Morning

You meet a person who has yet to invite G-d into his or her life. A person whose endeavors and accomplishments—no matter how successful and laudable—have yet to transcend the self and self-oriented goals.

You wish to expand their horizons; to show them a life beyond the strictures of self. You wish to put on *tefilin* with him, to share with her the divine wisdom of Torah.

But they're not ready yet. You know that the concept of serving G-d is still alien to a life trained and conditioned to view everything through the lens of self. You know that before you can introduce them to the world of Torah and *mitzvot*, you must first make them receptive to G-dliness, receptive to a life of intimacy with the divine.

So when you meet him on the street, you simply smile and say, "Good morning!" You invite her to your home for a cup of coffee or a Shabbat dinner. You make small talk. You don't, at this point, suggest any changes in his lifestyle. You just want them to become open to you and what you represent.

Ostensibly, you haven't "done" anything. But in essence, a most profound and radical transformation has taken place. The person has become a vessel for G-dliness.

Of course, the purpose of a vessel is that it be filled with content; the purpose of a home is that it be inhabited. The Tabernacle was built to house the presence of G-d. But it is the *making of vessels for G-dliness* that is life's greatest challenge and its most revolutionary achievement.

CASUAL LABOR

Six days work shall be done; and the seventh day shall be holy to you, a Sabbath of rest to G-d.   Exodus 35:2

In the above-quoted verse, Moses delivers to the assembled people of Israel the divine commandment to cease work on the seventh day of the week. According to the Midrash, however, the first half of the verse—"Six days work shall be done"—is also a divine command. Just as we are instructed to rest on Shabbat, so too is it a *mitzvah* to work on the six days that precede it.[1]

In truth, the very notion of a human being devoting time and energy for the advancement and betterment of his or her self is not something that can be taken for granted. The Talmud observes that "one who makes a gesture in the presence of a king forfeits his life."[2] If such is the case with a mortal king, how much more so when it concerns the supreme sovereign of the universe. As we are constantly in the presence of G-d,[3] to preoccupy ourselves with our personal needs would constitute a blatant affront to the divine sovereignty. It is only because G-d Himself instructs that "for six days work shall be done," that we are permitted, indeed obligated, to concern ourselves with earning a living, and to develop the talents and resources that have been placed at our disposal.

---

1 *Mechilta d'Rashbi*, ad loc.
2 Talmud, *Chagigah* 5b.
3 "I fill the heavens and the earth, says G-d" (Jeremiah 23:24).

To Do or to Have Done

In this context it is significant that the Torah chooses to express the instruction to work during the first six days on the week in the passive voice, "work shall be done," rather than the active, "do work." The selfsame words with which we are given license to work and produce, also express the attitude we are to employ when approaching our workday pursuits.

The sages of the Talmud encourage us to believe that "everything was created to serve me"—but only because "I was created to serve my Creator."[4] Our six-day involvement with the physical world is not an end in itself, but the means to attain the spiritual state represented by Shabbat—a state in which the whole of creation is in harmony with its Creator.

Thus, the Torah states, "Six days work shall be done." Do your work, but regard it not as something you actively do, but as something that is passively done. Do not get so caught up in the fervor of creative talent or the excitement of the marketplace that you come to regard them as ends unto themselves. Rather, reserve your passion and zeal for the purpose of the work—the perfection and tranquility of Shabbat.

---

4   Talmud, *Kidushin* 82a.

THE FIRE

> *Moses assembled the whole community of the Children of Israel, and he said to them: "These are the things that G-d commanded, to make them. Six days work shall be done; and the seventh day shall be holy to you, a Sabbath of rest to G-d… Do not burn a fire in all your habitations on the Shabbat day…"*
>
> Exodus 35:1–3

What kind of work is forbidden on Shabbat? Why, for example, is writing a single word regarded as "work," while carrying a heavy load of stones inside an enclosed courtyard is not? The answer can be found in the context in which the commandment to cease work on Shabbat is communicated in the Torah.

The first three verses of the Torah section of *Vayak'hel* (Exodus 35:1–38:20) describe how Moses assembled the entire people of Israel and relayed to them the divine commandment to cease work on the seventh day of the week. Immediately following comes the account—which takes up the remainder of *Vayak'hel*—of the construction of the "Tabernacle," the portable sanctuary built by the Israelites in the Sinai Desert at G-d's behest that "they shall make for Me a sanctuary, and I will dwell amongst them."[1] The Talmud explains that the Torah is using its method of "juxtaposition" (*hekesh*) to teach us what constitutes "work" on Shabbat: any productive activity that was part of the Tabernacle's construction. The

---

[1] Exodus 25:8.

Talmud identifies thirty-nine such activities, from "ploughing" to "transferring from domain to domain."[2]

The Other Six Days

The endeavor of constructing the Tabernacle not only establishes what work is forbidden on Shabbat; it also defines the nature of the work incumbent on us for the other six days of the week.

Our sages teach that the first part of the verse, "six days work shall be done," is no less a *mitzvah* than its conclusion, "the seventh day shall be... a Sabbath of rest."[3] Indeed, the essence of Shabbat is that we should emulate our Creator, reenacting, with our weekly cycle of work and rest, the divine cycle of creation. As G-d created the world in six days and rested on the seventh, so do we, G-d's "partners in creation."[4] Six days a week, we apply our creative energies to the world He charged us to develop; on the seventh, we withdraw to a more spiritual plane of being, as G-d withdraws from the more tangible aspect of His work as "Creator" on Shabbat.[5]

Thus, the laws of Shabbat are also the laws of life. In telling us what we should not do on Shabbat, the Torah is also telling us what we should do in the materially creative workdays that comprise the bulk of our lives. This is why the "works" (*melachot*) of Shabbat are also the works of the Tabernacle: The endeavor of life is to build a "dwelling" for G-d out of the materials of our existence, by developing them into an environment that is receptive to and expressive of His truth. So every aspect and detail of the work

---

2   Talmud, *Shabbat* 49b; Rashi, ad loc.; Talmud, ibid., 73a.
3   *Mechilta d'Rashbi*, Exodus 20:9.
4   See Talmud, *Shabbat* 10a and 119b.
5   See the essay, "The World of Thought," in *Inside Time* (MLC 2015), vol. 1, pp. 89–94.

that went into the making of the prototypical dwelling for G-d in the Sinai Desert, has its corresponding lesson and significance for our working lives.[6]

Always Constructive

A general rule that applies to the "thirty-nine works" of Shabbat is that for an action to be considered "work," it must accomplish something constructive. A case in point is the one example of Shabbat work cited in the opening verses of *Vayak'hel*: "Do not burn a fire... on the Shabbat day."[7] The law is:

> *One who burns something on Shabbat is liable, but only if he did so because he needed the ashes.*[8]

In other words, burning something—as opposed to lighting a fire for light or for warmth—is a destructive act. So while "burning" is one of the thirty-nine categories of work forbidden on Shabbat, it is only considered "work" in the case that the fire achieves something useful, as when a person burns something because they have use for its ashes.

As applied to the work we accomplish during the six-day week, this law teaches us that also when the challenges posed by a material world compel us to respond with "fire"—i.e., in a combative manner—it must always be to a fruitful end. The negative things in life are never there merely to be defeated; something positive and useful should result from our every action.

---

6   See the essays, "A Private World," in *Inside Time*, vol. 1, pp. 95–105, and "The King in the Field," ibid., vol. 3, pp. 304–313.
7   See Talmud, *Shabbat* 70a, and commentaries there, for the reasons why this particular "work" is singled out by the Torah as an example.
8   *Mishneh Torah, Laws of Shabbat*, 12:1; based on Talmud, *Shabbat* 106a.

Burning and Being

More specifically, the above-cited law regarding the usefulness of "burning" has a particular application to the spiritual life of the soul.

Chassidic teaching describes the phenomenon of life as the tension between a soul's two basic drives: *ratzo* ("escape") and *shuv* ("return"). *Ratzo* is the soul's quest to escape definition and confinement by the body and the ego; to transcend the trappings of physicality and self, and reunite with its divine source. Countering this quest is *shuv*, the drive for being and achievement. For even as it yearns to be free of all that personifies it and concretizes it, the soul is attracted to the physical state, for only as a physical being can it realize its role as G-d's partner in creation.

Ultimately, however, the soul's *ratzo* is no less crucial to its purpose in life than its *shuv*. For were the human psyche to consist solely of the drives and desires that feed our involvement with the material, we would be in no position to transform the physical reality into a dwelling for G-d. We would be as corporeal as the world we are seeking to elevate, as self-engrossed and as spiritually obtuse as the most brute block of matter. It is only because our soul is ever reaching for the heavens, only because we are constantly struggling to escape our material self, that we can develop it, and the material environment it inhabits, into a receptacle for a higher truth.

This is the deeper significance of the work of "burning." Fire is the release of energy from the material that embodied it, the unleashing of the forces that held an object together and gave it function and form. Indispensable to our life's work of building a dwelling for G-d is that we should burn with the desire to escape our physical embodiment.

Of course, were this desire to be fully realized, were the spirit to actually break free of the body, physical life would cease. But the *ratzo* of the soul is frustrated by its *shuv*, which binds it to the body and physical life. The *shuv*, in turn, is checked by the *ratzo*, whose perpetual striving for transcendence prevents the soul's over-immersion in the material. Life, then, is the constant vacillation between the soul's polar pulls, from *shuv* to *ratzo* and back again; a dancing flame that pulls ever upward, only to be held down by its material tether.[9]

Useful Ashes

Death is the ultimate *ratzo*: the soul ascending to merge with its supernal source, leaving but ashes behind—matter out of which all function and potential appears to have been drained. On the physical level, this happens when the body, compromised by illness, trauma, or the aging process, can no longer hold the soul. On the spiritual level (of which the physical dynamics of death are but an outcome and expression), death occurs when the soul's mission in physical life—the source of its attraction to the material—is completed. The *shuv* has run its course, freeing the *ratzo*-flame to ascend on high.

But even the ultimate *ratzo* has its *shuv*. This is the lesson of the law that for "burning" to be a proper work, its purpose must be to produce "useful ashes." Although it might seem that the departure of soul from body has no physically constructive function, the purpose of a soul's "burning" is always a *shuv*, a "return" to involvement with the material world. Even the conflagration of death

---

9 Rabbi Israel Baal Shem Tov is said to have remarked, "It is a miracle that one remains alive after prayer"—i.e., that the *shuv* of the soul can counteract its tremendous striving to unite with its Source during prayer.

leaves behind "useful ashes," a material residue of the incinerated life to which we are to impart a function and utility.

This is the basis for the Jewish custom that after a person's passing, those close to the departed—relatives, friends, disciples, etc.—do things "in memory" and "for the merit" of his or her soul: the recital of *Kaddish*, the study of Mishnah, the giving of charity, the establishment of foundations and institutions on his or her name, and so on. The purpose of all this is commonly understood to be "for the ascension of the soul" (*le'ilu nishmat*): the *mitzvot*, Torah study, and prayer on the departed soul's behalf contribute to the elevation of the soul as it rises from material life to ever-increasing heights of spirituality and closeness to G-d. For this reason, these activities take on a greater intensity at the time of the departed one's *yahrzeit* (anniversary of the passing), for the *yahrzeit*, as the date of the soul's initial rise to spirituality, is especially suited to effecting its further elevation.

There is, however, another function to these activities, one that is different from—indeed, it can be said to be the very opposite of—the endeavor to aid the soul's "ascension": to perpetuate its connection to earth. When we, the living, respond to a death by giving charity, studying Torah, praying, and by founding institutions that will be the source of such *mitzvot* in the years and generations to come, the *ratzo* of death becomes an instrument of *shuv*, of constructive involvement in the material world. The ashes of death are revitalized as fuel for the endeavor of life—fuel to drive the creation of the dwelling on earth that G-d desires.¹⁰

---

10   This essay is based on a talk delivered by the Rebbe on *Shevat* 22, 5749 (January 28, 1989), the first *yahrzeit* of his wife, Rebbetzin Chayah Mushka Schneerson.

PARASHAH TWENTY-THREE

PEKUDEI

Exodus 38:21–40:38

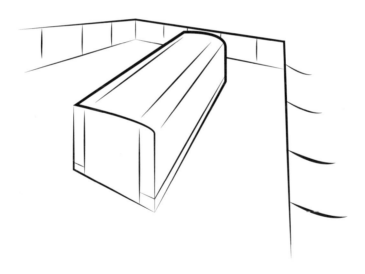

The edifice

WEIGHT

These are the accounts of the Tabernacle… All the gold that was used in the work … twenty-nine talents and seven hundred and thirty shekels… The silver contributed by the community: one hundred talents, and one thousand, seven hundred and seventy-five shekels… And the contributed copper: seventy talents, and two thousand and four hundred shekels…

Exodus 38:21–29

A significant part of the book of Exodus (thirteen of its forty chapters) is devoted to a detailed description of the Tabernacle build by the Children of Israel in the Sinai desert. The materials used—fifteen substances, from gold to copper, and from cedar wood to goat hair—are specified, as well as the dimensions of every wall panel and the colors in every tapestry. For the Tabernacle was more than a "house of worship" or "spiritual center"; it was the realization of the divine purpose in creation that G-d should have "a dwelling place in the physical world."[1] The Tabernacle (and its subsequent incarnation as the Holy Temple in Jerusalem) represented the height of man's efforts to build a home for G-d out of the materials of physical life.

The Tabernacle was a prototype—a people's collective implementation of the divine desire for a home on earth. On the individual level, we construct a sanctuary for G-d each time we perform a *mitzvah*.

---

[1] *Midrash Tanchuma, Nasso* 16; *Tanya*, ch. 36.

A *mitzvah* is a physical deed employing physical substances in the fulfillment of a divine command: animal hides are fashioned into *tefilin*, wool into *tzitzit*, and flour and water into matzah for Passover, to be bound, worn, or eaten by our physical selves.[2] A *mitzvah* also has a spiritual side—the awareness that accompanies the deed, the love and awe of G-d that motivate it, the commitment and joy that permeate it; but by focusing on the physical description of the Tabernacle, the Torah emphasizes that it is our physical deeds that house the divine presence. The *mitzvah*'s spiritual accoutrements are the "interior decorating" that impart beauty, warmth, and light to the edifice constructed by our deeds. But the deed itself is the essence of the divine home; it is the physical act that realizes G-d's objective in creation.[3]

The Accounts of the Tabernacle

The primacy of the actual is also underscored by the Torah's description of the "accounts" taken of the three precious metals—gold, silver, and copper—contributed by the Children of Israel toward the making of the Tabernacle. Usually, accountings of this sort are calculated by currency sums—so many dollars' worth (or whatever the prevalent currency) of gold, so many of silver, etc.

---

[2] Even the more "spiritual" of the *mitzvot*, such as Torah study and prayer, are ultimately physical actions performed by our physical brain, heart, and lips.

[3] As Rabbi Schneur Zalman of Liadi put it, no reality is more spiritual than the incandescent nothingness that preceded creation. So if G-d had wanted "spirituality," He would have done nothing. The fact that He did create a world implies that His objective lies in that aspect of creation that is most contrary to the pre-creation reality—the physical world (*Tanya*, chapter 36.).

But the accounts of the contributions to the Tabernacle were calculated by weight—so many talents and shekels of gold, so many of silver, and so many of copper. (The biblical "shekel" was a unit of weight equivalent to 320 barley grains, or approximately 16 grams; the biblical "talent"—*kikar* in the Hebrew—weighed 3,000 shekels, or about 48 kilograms.)[4]

Deeds, too, can be measured by weight or by value. For example, two people may each give a dollar to a pauper. One gives willingly, with a smile, and out of the recognition that they are privileged to be able to help a fellow human being. The second person gives grudgingly, annoyed at having been browbeaten into parting with a dollar. In terms of the "weight" of the deed—its physical mass and impact—both deeds are equal. Both dollars will buy the same loaf of bread and will equally satisfy their recipients' physical need. But the two deeds differ greatly in terms of "value"—in terms of the more abstract criteria (beauty, rarity, etc.) that make an ounce of gold that much more precious than an ounce of copper.

Certainly, "value" is significant in our construction of a dwelling for G-d. The Torah tells us which items of the Tabernacle are to be made of copper, which of silver, and which require the purest gold. But in summing up the peoples' contributions for the divine dwelling, the Torah calculates their physical weight rather than their qualitative value. For the bottom line in our efforts to bring G-d into our lives is what we do; everything else is of secondary significance.

---

4   The "shekel" is actually both a unit of currency and a unit of weight; here it is used to denote the weight of the contributed metals rather than their value—see Rashi, Exodus 38:21. In fact, the Hebrew word *shekel* literally means "weight."

ASSEMBLED PARTS

They brought the Tabernacle to Moses: The tent and all its implements, its hooks, panels, connecting bars, pillars, and foundation sockets...

Exodus 39:33

To the casual reader, the names by which the fifty-four *parashiot* (sections) of the annual Torah-reading cycle are called seem quite incidental: a *parashah* is almost always named after the first distinctive word or phrase to appear in its text. Chassidic teaching, however, which sees every event and phenomenon as determined by divine providence, rejects the very concept of "incidence." Furthermore, the name of an object in the Holy Tongue constitutes its soul and essence; so there certainly cannot be anything incidental about the name of a section of Torah.

The same is true of the two concluding *parashiot* of the book of Exodus: *Vayak'hel* (Exodus 35:1–38:20) and *Pekudei* (Exodus 38:21–40:38). The interesting thing, however, is that the names of these two *parashiot*, which follow each other in the Torah, and in certain years are even joined together to form a single reading,[1] express two opposite ideas. The name *Vayak'hel*, which is related to the Hebrew word for "community," evokes the concept

---

1 Due to the varying lengths and configurations of the Jewish year, there are often less than 54 Shabbat readings in the course of the year. Thus, the annual reading cycle includes 14 *parashiot* that form seven "paired readings" which may, in certain years, be combined as a single reading. One of these pairs is the *parashiot* of *Vayak'hel* and *Pekudei*.

of collectivity; whereas *Pekudei*, "to be counted," brings to mind the significance of the individual as a unit. So these two *parashiot* express the conflict, interaction, and paradox of two features of the human soul: a) our need and desire to bond together in a communal identity; and b) our need and desire for an individual identity distinct and unique from our fellows.

Even more interestingly, if we look beyond the names *Vayak'hel* and *Pekudei* to their actual content, we discover that the two *parashiot* seem to have switched names. The content of the *parashah* that carries the name *Vayak'hel* would seem to be more appropriately named *Pekudei*, while the content of the *parashah* of *Pekudei* begs the name *Vayak'hel*!

Vayak'hel begins by relating how Moses assembled the people of Israel to instruct them on the observance of Shabbat and the making of the Tabernacle; this act of assembly gives the *parashah* its name (*vayak'hel* means "and he assembled" and is a form of the word *kahal*, "congregation"). But the remainder of the *parashah* is filled with the particulars of the Tabernacle's construction. Each of the Tabernacle's dozens of components is individually listed and described: the roof coverings, wall panels, foundation sockets, pillars, braces, brackets, and curtains; the ark, the table, the *menorah*, the two altars, and even the washbasin and its pedestal. We are given the exact dimensions of each of these components, the materials out of which they were made, and the details of their design.

Pekudei means "accounts," and the *parashah* begins with the statement, "These are the accounts of the Tabernacle…" The etymological root *pakod* means to count, to remember, and to appoint—expressing the idea of itemization, of particular attention to detail. But while *Pekudei* also includes details of the Tabernacle's construction (specifically, those of the priestly garments), a major part of the *parashah* is devoted to the Tabernacle's assembly.

In *Pekudei*, the Torah relates how the components listed and described in *Vayak'hel* were fitted together to form the Tabernacle, and how the divine presence came to dwell in the completed structure.

In other words, the *parashah* of *Vayak'hel* is taken up with the individual natures of the Tabernacle's parts, while the *parashah* of *Pekudei* describes how these are combined to form the greater structure—the very opposite of what each *parashah*'s name means!

Five Lessons

To summarize:

1) The Torah includes a *parashah* called *Vayak'hel*, and a *parashah* called *Pekudei*.

2) In certain years they are joined as a single reading, called *Vayak'hel-Pekudei*.

3) In other years, these two *parashiot* form two separate Torah readings, read on separate weeks.

4) *Vayak'hel* means "community," but the content of this *parashah* is the value of individuality. *Pekudei* implies "individuality," but its content is the advantage in union and integration.

5) *Vayak'hel* comes first in the Torah, followed by *Pekudei*.

Each of these nuances is significant. Each illuminates the relationship between our individual and communal identities.

Lesson #1: We have and need them both. The fact that the Torah contains two *parashiot*, one called *Vayak'hel* and the other called *Pekudei*, teaches us that our need for communality and our striving for individual distinction are both important and desirable components of the human soul.

Lesson #2: We can achieve a synthesis of the two. If *Vayak'hel* and *Pekudei* were only to appear in the Torah as two separate *parashiot*, this would imply that while both are necessary, each has its time and place: that there are times when our communality must be emphasized (to the negation of our individuality), and there are times when an assertion of individuality is called for (albeit disruptive to our communality). We would not know that the two could be integrated.

The fact that, on certain years, *Vayak'hel* and *Pekudei* are joined to form a single reading, teaches us that we can, and should, achieve a synthesis of the two: a community that is not a faceless mass but a community of individuals, each contributing his or her distinct personality and capabilities toward the communal goal, with the community, in turn, providing the framework within which each can strive for his or her personal best.

Lesson #3: We must also nurture each of the two as a thing of value in and of itself. On the other hand, if *Vayak'hel* and *Pekudei* were to appear *only* in their joint form, this would imply that the only desirable objective is the achievement of some sort of balance between these contrasting drives—a balance that may well entail a compromise of one or the other (or of both). Perhaps our individuality has value only in that it contributes in some way to the community; or perhaps the sole function of the community is to provide a framework for the development of the individual. We would not know that each is also an end unto itself.

The fact that *Vayak'hel* and *Pekudei* also appear as two *separate* Torah readings teaches us that—in addition to the objective of integrating the two—individuality and community are viable objectives in their own right as well. Individual perfection has value independent of how it contributes to the communal good; and the creation of a community is likewise an end unto itself, for it represents a state that is greater than the sum of its individual parts.

Lesson #4: Each consists of the other. We have seen how community (*Vayak'hel*) and individuality (*Pekudei*) each represent a desirable goal, and how they can be integrated to form a third model, a community of individuals (*Vayak'hel-Pekudei*). But the Torah goes even further. It tells us that even when each is considered as an end unto itself, the two are inexorably bound with each other.

This lesson is derived from the fact that the content of *Vayak'hel* is the nature of individual things, while *Pekudei* describes diverse parts being joined into a greater whole. The Torah is telling us that even when the objective is solely the creation of a perfect community, the most perfect community is a community of individuals who are fully exercising their individuality (as *Vayak'hel*, even as a *parashah* on its own, is comprised of manifestly individual parts). The Torah is also telling us that also when the sole objective is the realization of individual potential, an individual can optimally actualize their uniqueness only as a member of a community (as the *parashah* of *Pekudei* includes the creation of community).

Lesson #5: Imperfect individuals make a perfect community. The question remaining is: Which should come first?

Logic would seem to dictate that individual development (*Pekudei*) should come before community building (*Vayak'hel*). First one needs the parts, and then one can assemble these parts into the greater organism. So the initial emphasis, it would seem, should be on the perfection of the individual, after which these perfected individuals could be knit into the ideal community.

The Torah, however, places *Vayak'hel* before *Pekudei*, teaching us that the very opposite is the case. Our very first objective must be to bring people together, regardless of their individual state. Personal perfection will follow, fostered by the love and fellowship we show toward each other.

SOURCES

Note: The sixty-two essays in this volume are adaptations, rather than direct translations, of the teachings of the Lubavitcher Rebbe, Rabbi Menachem M. Schneerson, and of his predecessors, the rebbes of Chabad-Lubavitch. The listing below provides the primary sources which served as the basis and the inspiration for each essay. All works listed are from the Rebbe, unless otherwise attributed.

THIRTEEN: SHEMOT
(1) **Name and Number** • Likutei Sichot, vol. 6, pp. 6–12.
(2) **The Brick Factory** • Likutei Sichot, vol. 6, pp. 13–25.
(3) **The Cult of the River** • Likutei Sichot, vol. 1, pp. 111–113.
(4) **The Infant Shepherd** • Likutei Sichot, vol. 16, pp. 13–19.
(5) **The Runaway Kid** • Torat Menachem Hitvaaduyot 5743, vol. 3, pp. 1561–1563; et al.
(6) **A Heart of Flame** • Rabbi Yosef Yitzchak Schneersohn of Lubavitch, Sefer HaSichot 5702, pp. 46–47.
(7) **The Essence of Existence** • Likutei Sichot, vol. 26, pp. 10–25.
(8) **The Numerology of Redemption** • Likutei Sichot, vol. 11, pp. 8–13.
(9) **Moshiach's Donkey** • Likutei Sichot, vol. 1, pp. 70–72.

FOURTEEN: VA'EIRA
(1) **Have a Heart** • Likutei Sichot, vol. 3, pp. 854–862; vol. 16, pp. 47–57; et al.
(2) **On Freedom and Authority** • Sefer HaSichot 5752, pp. 174–186; et al.
(3) **Of Snakes and Sticks** • Likutei Sichot, vol. 26, pp. 57–58.
(4) **The Red Nile** • Likutei Sichot, vol. 1, pp. 120–125.
(5) **The Frog in the Oven** • Likutei Sichot, vol. 1, p. 123.
(6) **Crime, Punishment, and Suspended Precipitation** • Likutei Sichot, vol. 6, pp. 46–56.

FIFTEEN: BO
(1) **The Soul of Evil** • Sefer HaSichot 5752, vol. 1, pp. 280ff.
(2) **The Fifth Element** • Likutei Sichot, vol. 16, pp. 87–93.
(3) **The Freedom to Passover** • Likutei Sichot, vol. 21, pp. 68–76; Igrot Kodesh, vol. 2, pp. 39–40.
(4) **Great Wealth** • Likutei Sichot, vol. 3, pp. 823–827.
(5) **Ambition** • Reshimot #37.

- (6) **Speed in Three Dimensions** • Based on a public letter by the Rebbe, Nissan 11, 5746 (April 20, 1986). Published in the Rebbe's *Haggadah* (5751 ed.), p. 781.
- (7) **Dialogue** • Igrot Kodesh, vol. 28, pp. 212–26 and 219–224.
- (8) **Tomorrow's Child** • Likutei Sichot, vol. 6, pp. 268–270.

SIXTEEN: BESHALACH

- (1) **The Mountain and the Sea** • Likutei Sichot, vol. 3, pp. 876–887.
- (2) **The Amphibian Soul** • Likutei Sichot, vol. 20, p. 172; vol. 11, p. 76. Also see Likutei Torah, Tzav 14bff.
- (3) **On the Essence of Leadership** • Likutei Sichot, vol. 31, pp. 69–76.
- (4) **Bringing G-d Home** • Likutei Sichot, vol. 16, p. 245; based on Shaloh, Asarah Maamarot, 1 (40a).
- (5) **The Manna Eaters** • Likutei Sichot, vol. 3, p. 1035.
- (6) **Reason, Doubt, Faith, and Memory** • Likutei Sichot, vol. 26, p. 227; et al.

SEVENTEEN: YITRO

- (1) **Captains of Thousand** • Likutei Sichot, vol. 16, pp. 203–210; et al.
- (2) **Shards or Sparks?** • Likutei Sichot, vol. 11, pp. 35–37.
- (3) **Sighting the Sounds** • Likutei Sichot, vol. 6, pp. 119–129.
- (4) **A Gift and a Test** • Tzemach Tzedek, Derech Mitzvotecha, 186a.

EIGHTEEN: MISHPATIM

- (1) **Oxen and Souls** • Reshimot #31, pp. 5–8; Sefer HaSichot 5752, vol. 2, pp. 369–371. Also see Rabbi Yosef Yitzchak Schneersohn of Lubavitch, Sefer HaSichot 5701, p. 64.
- (2) **The Four Guardians** • Likutei Sichot, vol. 31, pp. 112–118.
- (3) **The Resourceful Oath** • Likutei Sichot, vol. 16, pp. 269–274.
- (4) **The Third Crown** • Torat Menachem Hitvaaduyot 5712, vol. 2, p. 226ff.

NINETEEN: TERUMAH

- (1) **Son-in-Law** • Igrot Kodesh, vol. 1, pp. 262–263.
- (2) **Transplanted Cedars** • Likutei Sichot, vol. 31, pp. 142–148.
- (3) **The Altar and the Ark** • Sefer HaSichot 5751, vol. 1, pp. 324–326; Likutei Sichot, vol. 7, pp. 201–202; et al.
- (4) **Wood and Stone** • Torat Menachem Hitvaaduyot 5746, vol. 2, pp. 249ff.; Rabbi Schneur Zalman of Liadi, Torah Ohr, Vayigash 43c.
- (5) **Model Home** • Reshimot #81–85.
- (6) **The Face of a Child** • Likutei Sichot, vol. 26, pp. 175–182.
- (7) **Have Word, Will Travel** • Likutei Sichot, vol. 15, pp. 334–335.
- (8) **Spiritual Space** • Based on Reshimat HaMenorah, the Rebbe's notes for a treatise on the *menorah*, dated "Paris, 5699" (1938–1939).

TWENTY: TETZAVEH

(1) **Noise** • Likutei Sichot, vol. 16, pp. 336–341.
(2) **Princesses on Horseback** • Likutei Sichot, vol. 26, pp. 198–199.
(3) **Joined at the Waist** • Sefer HaSichot 5748, vol. 1, p. 314.
(4) **The Superficial Coat** • Likutei Sichot, vol. 3, pp. 910–912.

TWENTY-ONE: KI TISA

(1) **Partner** • Likutei Sichot, vol. 3, pp. 926–930; Maamar *Zeh Yitnu 5715*. Also see Rabbi Dov Ber of Mezheritch, Ohr Torah, Behaalotecha; Rabbi Schneur Zalman of Liadi, Likutei Torah, Shir HaShirim 34d.
(2) **Foundation** • Likutei Sichot, vol. 1, pp. 181–182.
(3) **Washstand** • Likutei Sichot, vol. 26, pp. 188–189.
(4) **Sin and Sanctuary** • Likutei Sichot, vol. 6, pp. 153–157.
(5) **The Anonymous Essence** • Likutei Sichot, vol. 11, pp. 173–180; Sefer HaSichot 5751, pp. 352–358.
(6) **Intellectual Waste** • Likutei Sichot, vol. 19, p. 114. Also see Rabbi Shalom DovBer of Lubavitch, Yom Tov Shel Rosh Hashanah 5666, pp. 86–93.
(7) **Moses' Mask** • Based on an address by the Rebbe, Shabbat Ki Tisa 5752 (1992).

TWENTY-TWO: VAYAK'HEL

(1) **Heaven and Earth** • Likutei Sichot, vol. 1, pp. 195–198.
(2) **The Vessel** • Likutei Sichot, vol. 25, pp. 424–435.
(3) **Casual Labor** • Likutei Sichot, vol. 1, pp. 187 ff.
(4) **The Fire** • Sefer HaSichot 5749, vol. 1, p. 225–237.

TWENTY-THREE: PEKUDEI

(1) **Weight** • Likutei Sichot, vol. 26, pp. 278–279.
(2) **Assembled Parts** • Likutei Sichot, vol. 21, pp. 250–259; Sefer HaSichot 5752, vol. 2, p. 440; et al.

GLOSSARY

Italicized terms are Hebrew unless otherwise indicated. Names (e.g., Rashi), or words that have entered common English usage (e.g., kabbalah), are not italicized.

Terms appearing in the text with a dotted underline are themselves entries in this glossary.

Terms that are translated and/or explained inside the essays in which they appear are not included in this glossary.

A

Aaron Elder brother of Moses. Served as *kohen gadol* (high priest) during the Israelites' travels in the desert following the Exodus from Egypt.

Abarbanel Don Isaac Abarbanel (or Abravanel), 1437–1508. Lived in Portugal, Spain, and Italy. A scholar, philosopher, statesman, and financier, Abarbanel served as treasurer to several monarchs, including Alfonso V of Portugal. He had extensive dealings with Ferdinand and Isabella of Spain, whom he attempted to persuade to rescind their infamous edict of expulsion of the Jews from their lands in 1492. When his efforts failed, he spurned their offer to allow him to remain and took up the wanderer's staff with his exiled brethren.

Abraham The first Jew, and the first of the three Patriarchs of the Jewish people —Abraham, Isaac, and Jacob. Born into pagan Mesopotamia in the 18th century BCE, Abraham discovered the truth of a one G-d and devoted his life to spreading the teachings and ethos of monotheism. By divine instruction, he traveled to the Holy Land, where G-d promised to make his descendants into a great people and bequeath the Land to them as their eternal inheritance.

Abram The original name of Abraham, before G-d changed his name (see Genesis 17:3–5).

Aggadah; aggadic Nonlegal Torah teachings, including ethics, homilies, narratives, etc. Sometimes contrasted with *halachah* (teachings pertaining to Torah law). The Talmud, for example, is seen as consisting of both halachic and *aggadic* portions.

Akiva, Rabbi 1st and 2nd century; Benei Berak, Israel. One of the most important personalities in the history of the transmission of Torah through the ages. Rabbi Akiva was a descendant of converts to Judaism and was an illiterate shepherd until the age of 40, when he was "discovered" by his employer's daughter Rachel, who promised to marry him on the condition that he devote his life to the study of Torah. Soon after his marriage he left home to study under the leading sages of his day; after twenty-four years of study he returned with thousands of students of his own. His disciples became seminal figures in Torah's chain of tradition, and much of the material in the Talmud and the Midrashim is based on the teachings they received from him. Toward the end of his life Rabbi Akiva defied a Roman ban on teaching Torah publicly, and was arrested and cruelly executed.

Altar, The One of the main features of the Tabernacle and the Holy Temple, upon which offerings to G-d were brought. There were two altars: 1) The "outer altar," which stood in the Temple courtyard, on which the korbanot (animal and meal offerings) were brought; in the Tabernacle, it was also called the "copper altar," as its outer coating was of copper. 2) The "inner altar," which was inside the Sanctuary, upon which the ketoret (incense) was burned; also called the "golden altar" (as it was covered with gold), and the "incense altar."

Amalek The first nation to attack the people of Israel after the Exodus. Regarded as the archenemy of Israel and the nemesis of divinity and holiness.

Amidah Lit., "standing." The central portion of each of the daily prayers, so called because it is recited while standing, as at an audience with a king. It is also known as Shemoneh Esreh ("Eighteen"), after the number of blessings in its original composition (a nineteenth blessing was added in the late 1st century under the direction of Rabban Gamliel). The first three blessings of the *Amidah* offer praise to G-d; the middle thirteen blessings are requests from G-d for various personal and communal needs (health, sustenance, redemption, etc.); and the three concluding blessings are expressions of thanks to G-d. The versions of the *Amidah* for Shabbat and most Jewish holidays contain seven blessings, with the thirteen middle blessings of the weekday version replaced with a single blessing on the theme of the day.

Animal soul In chassidic teaching, one of the two souls that comprise the human psyche. The animal soul is the engine of physical life, and the source of the drives and instincts that are oriented toward self-preservation and self-gratification.

Annual Torah reading cycle In keeping with a tradition dating back to the days of Moses to hold public readings of the Torah each Shabbat, the Five Books of Moses are divided into 54 portions or *parashiot* (singular, *parashah*), each of which serves as the weekly reading in an annual cycle. Due to the varying lengths of the Jewish year, and the coincidence of certain holidays with Shabbat (in which case the regular weekly *parashah* is superseded by a reading relating to the holiday), there are usually less than 54 Shabbat readings in the course of the year; in most years, therefore, two *parashiot* are combined into one reading on certain weeks.

Ari Rabbi Isaac Luria (1534–1572) of Safed, Israel. Preeminent master of kabbalah whose interpretations of the Zohar and other kabbalistic texts are widely considered the most authoritative basis of all subsequent study in this area.

Ark, The Heb. *aron*. The receptacle containing the Tablets of the Testament which G-d gave to Moses at Mount Sinai. It stood in the innermost chamber of the Tabernacle, and later, of the first Holy Temple. The ark was absent in the second Temple, and according to most opinions it was hidden underground in advance of the first Temple's destruction. The structure that houses the Torah scrolls in a synagogue is also referred to as the "ark" or "holy ark."

Ark of Testament See Ark, The.

Avot d'Rabbi Natan One of the "minor tractates" of the Talmud. It expands on the teachings quoted in Ethics of the Fathers, providing biblical sources for them and illustrating them with examples.

B

Baal HaTurim Commentary on the Five Books of Moses focusing on allusions to Talmudic and Midrashic teachings derived from the biblical text by means of *gematria* (numerical values of letters), juxtaposition of topics, and the use of similar words or phrases elsewhere in the Bible. Extracted from a larger work of biblical commentary by Rabbi Yaakov ben Asher, c. 1270–1345, who lived in Germany and Spain.

Baal Shem Tov Rabbi Israel Baal Shem Tov, 1698–1760, Mezhibuzh, Ukraine. Founder of the chassidic movement.

Baal teshuvah; baalei teshuvah (pl.) Literally, "returnee" or "master of return." A person who returns to G-d in *teshuvah* (repentance) after willful or unknowing transgression of the Torah's commandments.

Baalei HaTosafot Commentaries by the sages of the Tosafot.

Bartenura Rabbi Ovadiah of Bartenura, late 15th to early 16th centuries, Italy and Jerusalem. Author of a lucid commentary to the Mishnah which became a primary point of reference for the study of that work.

Bechayei Rabbi Bechayei (or Bachya) ben Asher ibn Chalawah, c. 1255–1340, Zaragoza, Spain. Author of an extensive commentary on the Bible.

Bittul literally, "nullification." A commitment to G-d and divine service that transcends self-concern. The term is also used in various halachic contexts to mean "renouncement," or a legal "cessation of existence."

Biurei HaGra Halachic work containing the elucidations of Rabbi Elijah, the Gaon of Vilna ("Gra") on the Shulchan Aruch.

C

Chabad; Chabad-Lubavitch Branch of chassidism, founded in 1772 by Rabbi Schneur Zalman of Liadi, emphasizing the role of the mind in assimilating divine truths and developing and guiding a person's emotions and behavior. The name "Chabad" is an acronym for the three intellectual faculties chochmah, binah, and daat. The movement is also called "Chabad-Lubavitch," or simply "Lubavitch," after the Russian town, Lyubavichi, which served as its headquarters from 1813 to 1915. (The two terms are not completely synonymous, however, as there also existed other branches of Chabad, headquartered in other towns.)

Chanukah An eight-day festival beginning on the 25th of the Jewish month of Kislev, celebrating the Hasmoneans' recapture of the Holy Temple from the Syrian-Greeks and its rededication to the service of G-d in the 2nd century BCE. The holiday is marked by the kindling of lights, in commemoration of a miracle where a single day's supply of oil sufficed to keep the Temple menorah lit for eight days.

Chariot, The divine A mystical vision by the prophet Ezekiel that the describes the angels and spiritual forces that emanate from G-d, and which serves as the source for many kabbalistic concepts..

Chassidism; chassidic; chassid Jewish revivalist movement founded in 1726 by Rabbi Israel Baal Shem Tov, stressing the mystical dimension of Torah, joyfulness in serving G-d, love of all Jews regardless of material or spiritual station, intellectual and emotional involvement in prayer, finding G-dliness in every aspect of one's existence, the elevation of the material universe, and the role of the tzaddik (righteous leader) in guiding and facilitating a person's relationship with G-d. Many of the ideas of chassidism are based on the Zohar and the teachings of Ari, and of later mystics such as Maharal and Shaloh. Its in-depth exploration of the esoteric soul of Torah attracted many of the great minds of European Jewry, and at the same time it enfranchised the unlettered masses by teaching that sincere faith and good deeds are no less precious in the eyes of G-d than the Torah learning of the most accomplished scholar. By the time of the passing of its second leader, Rabbi Dov Ber of Mezheritch, in 1772, the movement had spread throughout Eastern Europe, with many of Rabbi Dov Ber's disciples establishing followings in different towns and regions. Thus were born the various branches or schools within chassidism, each with its own leader or rebbe.

Chesed "Benevolence" and "kindness." Can refer to these qualities in interpersonal relationships, or to the parallel divine attribute (*sefirah*), associated with the diffusion of G-dly energy to lower levels of existence.

Chiya, Rabbi Late 2nd century, Babylonia and Israel. A member of the transitional generation between the sages of the Mishnah and the sages of the Talmud.

Chizkuni Commentary on the Bible by Rabbi Hezekiah ben Manoah, of mid-13th-century France.

Chochmah "Wisdom." In kabbalistic and chassidic terminology, this refers to the first of the ten sefirot (divine attributes), and the first of the three intellectual faculties of the human soul.

Choshen Mishpat "Breastplate of Judgment." The fourth of the four sections of Shulchan Aruch (code of Jewish law). *Choshen Mishpat* codifies civil and criminal law.

Chumash Literally, "fifth." Properly speaking, one of the Five Books of Moses. In common parlance *Chumash* also means the Five Books as a whole.

Cubit Heb. amah, lit. "arm." A measure of length used in the biblical and Talmudic eras, and for assorted halachic purposes. It is defined as the distance from the average person's elbow to the tip of the middle finger. Various halachic authorities put the length of the standard cubit at between approximately 48 and 63 centimeters.

D

Daat Zekeinim MiBaalei HaTosafot An anthology of commentaries on the Torah by 12th- and 13th-century sages known as "Tosafists" (see entry for Tosafot).

Daniel Leader of Babylonian Jewry in the 5th and 4th centuries BCE, and the name of a biblical book describing his life and prophesies.

Daughters of Zelophehad The five sisters who approached Moses with the claim that they should inherit their father's portion in the Land of Israel, and were instrumental in establishing the Torah's laws of inheritance for female heirs (as related in the 27th chapter of the biblical book of Numbers).

David, King 907–837 BCE, Bethlehem and Jerusalem. First Judean king and composer of the biblical book of Psalms.

Derashot HaRan A collection of eight essays by 14th-century sage Rabbi Nissim Gerondi. See entry for Ran.

Derech Chaim Commentary by Maharal (c. 1520–1609) on *Ethics of the Fathers*.

Derech Mitzvotecha A work by Tzemach Tzedek (Rabbi Menachem Mendel of Lubavitch, 1789–1866).

Deuteronomy Fifth of the biblical Five Books of Moses.

Dikdukei Sofrim Compilation of variances in the talmudic text from numerous manuscripts and editions of the Talmud, compiled by Rabbi Raphael Nathan Rabinovitch (1835–1888).

Divrei Dovid Commentary on Rashi by Rabbi David Segal, 1586–1667 (see entry for Taz).

Dov Ber of Mezheritch, Rabbi Also known as "Maggid of Mezheritch." Successor of the Baal Shem Tov as the leader of the chassidic movement. Passed away in 1772.

E

Ecclesiastes Biblical book authored by King Solomon, in which he distills messages from his own life experience about the futility of material pursuits. Ecclesiastes also dwells on the crisis of faith caused by seeing the righteous suffer and the wicked prosper, and demonstrates how the ultimate wisdom consists of living a moral life in keeping with G-d's will.

Eitz Chaim Kabbalistic work by Rabbi Chaim Vital (1543–1620), recording the teachings of his teacher, Ari.

Elazar, Rabbi Rabbi Elazar ben Pedath, a prominent Talmudic sage who was active in both Babylonia and the Holy Land in the third century CE.

Elazar HaKalir, Rabbi One of the earliest and most prolific *payetanim* (composers of Jewish religious poetry). Some opinions place him in the Mishnaic era, while others place him in the 6th or 7th centuries. Many of his compositions, which are laced with much Midrashic material, are recited as part of the prayer services.

Eliezer Biblical figure; the servant of Abraham.

Eliezer, Rabbi Rabbi Eliezer ben Hyrcanus, 1st century, Lod, Israel. A Mishnaic sage, also known as Rabbi Eliezer ha-Gadol ("the great"). Rabbi Eliezer was an illiterate farm worker in his father's fields when he ran away from home to study in the academy of Rabbi Jochanan ben Zakai, where he developed into a leading Torah scholar; Rabbi Jochanan said of him that he could outweigh all of the other sages in his breadth of knowledge. His disciples included Rabbi Akiva.

Elijah the Prophet The leading prophet of his era in the 8th century BCE, Israel. The biblical book of Kings relates that Elijah ascended bodily to heaven on a chariot of fire, and Jewish tradition records his reappearances on earth through the generations to teach great sages, and to assist people in distress. The prophet Malachi foretells of Elijah's future appearance as the herald of Moshiach.

Elokim Stand-in for the divine name *Elohim*, which due to its sacredness, is pronounced only when reading from the Torah or in prayer.

Ethics of the Fathers Tractate of the Talmud, mostly containing ethical and religious maxims by sages of successive generations, from those of the "Great Assembly" (4th century BCE) to Rabban Gamliel III, son of Rabbi Judah HaNassi (early 3rd century CE).

Etrog Citron fruit. One of the Four Kinds taken on the festival of Sukkot.

Exile, The See *Galut*.

Exodus, The The miraculous liberation of the people of Israel from Egyptian slavery under the leadership of Moses, and their exodus from that land for the purpose of receiving the Torah at Mount Sinai and settling the Holy Land in fulfillment of their destiny as G-d's chosen people.

GLOSSARY

Exodus (book of) The second of the biblical Five Books of Moses.
Ezekiel Biblical prophet. The biblical book of Ezekiel contains vivid descriptions of the divine "chariot" (*merkavah*) and its angelic bearers, which are a primary source of the mystical teachings of kabbalah. The book also includes detailed descriptions of the future third Holy Temple of the messianic era.

F

First Tablets *See* Tablets of the Testament.
Five Books of Moses The core text of Judaism, which Moses received from G-d and taught to the people of Israel during their forty years in the Sinai Desert. Moses completed his transcription of these texts on the last day of his life, in the biblical year 2488 (1273 BCE). The five books are: Genesis, Exodus, Leviticus, Numbers, and Deuteronomy (in the Hebrew: *Bereishith, Shemot, Vayikra, Bamidbar,* and *Devarim*). The Five Books of Moses are also referred to as the Chumash (short for *chamishah chumshei Torah*, Hebrew for "the five fifths of the Torah"), the Pentateuch (Greek for "five books"), as well as simply the Torah ("teaching"). The five books constitute the first of the three sections (Torah, Prophets, and Scriptures) of the Jewish Bible.
Flood, The The great deluge that covered the earth during Noah's days, as related in the book of Genesis, chapters 6–8.
Four Kinds As instructed in Leviticus 23:40, four plant species are taken in hand on the festival of Sukkot: the citron fruit (*etrog*), palm frond (*lulav*), myrtle twigs (*hadasim*), and willow twigs (*aravot*).

G

Galut Lit., "exile." The state of physical and spiritual displacement experienced by the Jewish people for much of their history—in Egypt prior to the Exodus, in Babylonia and Persia following the destruction of the first Holy Temple, under the hegemony of Greece during the Second Temple Era, and following the destruction of the second Temple by the Romans.
Gaon of Rogatchov Rabbi Yosef Rozin, 1858–1936.
Gaon of Vilna *See* Gra.
Garden of Eden Where Adam and Eve were placed by G-d upon their creation, and from which they were expelled after partaking of the "Tree of Knowledge of Good and Evil" (as related in Genesis, chapter 3). "The Garden of Eden" also refers to the spiritual reward that souls enjoy in the afterlife.

Gematria Hebrew numerology. The Hebrew letters also serve as numbers, so that it is possible to speak of the *gematria* of an individual letter, a word, or an entire phrase. *Gematria* is frequently used in Torah commentaries of various genres.

Genesis First of the biblical Five Books of Moses.

Gershom, Rabbeinu 960–1028, leader of the Jewish communities in Germany and France.

Gevurah "Might." The fifth *sefirah* (divine attribute), associated with the holding back of divine revelation and the restriction of the flow of divine energy to lower levels of existence, or the corresponding human attributes of discipline and withdrawal.

Gevurot Hashem A work by Maharal (c. 1520–1609).

Giving of the Torah The revelation at Mount Sinai on the sixth of *Sivan* of the biblical year 2448 (1313 BCE), where G-d spoke the Ten Commandments to the assembled people of Israel and summoned Moses to the top of the mountain to receive the Torah, as related in the book of Exodus, chapters 19–20 and 24.

G-dly soul In chassidic teaching, one of the two souls that comprise the human psyche. The G-dly soul is described as "veritably a part of G-d," and the core essence of the human being, and the source of the person's striving for unity with G-d.

Golden Calf The idol made and worshipped by the people of Israel, thus violating their newly-made covenant with G-d only forty days after the revelation at Mount Sinai (as related in the 32nd chapter of the biblical book of Exodus).

Gra Rabbi Elijah, the "Gaon of Vilna," 1720–1797. Recognized as one of the greatest scholars in Jewish history.

Guide for the Perplexed Classic work of Jewish philosophy by Maimonides (Rabbi Moses ben Maimon, c. 1135–1204).

H

Haggadah Literally, "telling." The text used for telling and expounding on the story of the Exodus in the course of the Passover *seder* feast, including the instructions for each step of the procedure.

Halachah; halachic Torah law; the rulings pertaining to the details of the biblical commandments (*mitzvot*) and the rabbinical ordinances. In particular, those works of Torah literature devoted to weighing the different arguments and opinions appearing in the Talmud and the Talmudic commentaries to arrive at a final ruling. Central halachic works include the Mishnah (the core text of the Talmud); the codes authored by Maimonides and *Tur* along with their commentaries; the *Shulchan Aruch* and its commentaries; and the vast body of halachic responsa.

Havayah Stand-in for the most sacred name of G-d, which is consists of the four

Hebrew letters *yud-hei-vav-hei* but is not pronounced due to its holiness. It is therefore a common practice to transpose its four letters as *Havayah* when referring to it in writing and conversation.

Hillel First century BCE, Babylonia and Israel. A descendant of King David, Hillel served as president of the *sanhedrin* (highest court of Torah law) during the Second Temple Era, a position filled thereafter almost exclusively by his descendants. Famous for his legendary devotion to Torah study under conditions of extreme poverty in his first years as a student of Torah. Hillel was also famed for his approachability and patience, and is the author of the maxim: "What is hateful to you, do not do to your fellow. This is the entire Torah; the rest is commentary, now go and study it!" In his rulings on Torah law, Hillel tended toward the lenient position, in contrast with the more stringent approach of his colleague Shammai. Each of them gathered a following of like-minded disciples, which developed into two schools of Torah thought and law—the "House of Hillel" and the "House of Shammai."

Holy of Holies Heb. *kodesh hakodashim*. The innermost and most sacred room of the Tabernacle and later the Holy Temple, which housed the ark containing the Two Tablets inscribed with the Ten Commandments.

Holy Temple Heb. *beit hamikdash* (lit., "house of holiness"). The seat of G-d's manifest presence in the physical world, and the location where korbanot (animal and meal offerings) were to be offered exclusively; located on Mount Moriah (the "Temple Mount") in Jerusalem. The first Holy Temple was built by King Solomon and stood for 410 years (833–423 BCE) until its destruction by the Babylonians. The second Temple was built by the Jews returning from exile under the leadership of the "Great Assembly" and stood for 420 years (353 BCE to 69 CE) until its destruction by the Romans. The third Temple, whose details are described in the biblical book of Ezekiel, is to be built by Moshiach.

Holy, The Name given to the outer chamber in the Tabernacle (and the Holy Temple).

Hosea Biblical prophet of the late 7th to early 6th centuries BCE, Israel. His prophesies are collected in the biblical book that carries his name.

Hoshaanot Lit., "salvations." A bundle of five willow twigs used in the service of the seventh day of the festival of Sukkot. Also refers to the special prayers said on that occasion.

Hur Biblical figure. Son of Miriam (and the nephew of Moses and Aaron), and the grandfather of Bezalel, the chief architect of the Tabernacle. When Moses ascended Mount Sinai to receive the Torah, he placed Aaron and Hur in charge of governing the nation in his absence. According to Midrash Rabbah, Hur was killed while attempting to prevent the making of the Golden Calf.

I

Ibn Attar Rabbi Chaim ibn Attar, 1696–1743, Morocco and Jerusalem. Author of the *Ohr HaChaim* commentary on the Bible

Ibn Ezra Rabbi Abraham ibn Ezra, c. 1089–1164, Spain, Italy, and France. Author of one of the classic commentaries on the Bible.

Igrot Kodesh Literally, "holy letters." Name given to published collections of letters by saintly rabbis and leaders. In this book, it refers to the published letters of the Lubavitcher Rebbe (Rabbi Menachem Mendel Schneerson, 1902–1994).

Ikarim Work by Rabbi Yosef Albo (d. 1444, Spain) exploring the basics of Jewish belief.

Inner altar See entry for Altar.

Isaac 17th and 16th centuries BCE, the Holy Land. Son of Abraham and Sarah, and the second of the three patriarchs or founding fathers of the Jewish people.

Isaac Luria, Rabbi See entry for Ari

Isaiah Biblical prophet, active in the 7th and 6th centuries BCE. The biblical book of Isaiah contains his recorded prophesies, which include many references to the future coming of Moshiach (the messiah) and describe the universal peace, goodness, and perfection of the messianic era.

Ishmael, Rabbi Talmudic sage Rabbi Ishmael ben Elisha, d. c. 130 CE, Kefar Aziz, Israel. A colleague of Rabbi Akiva.

Israel Name given by G-d to Jacob, and to the Jewish people as a whole, who are referred to throughout the Bible as "the children of Israel," or simply "Israel." Israel can also refer to the Land of Israel—the land promised by G-d to the patriarchs as the eternal heritage of the Jewish people.

Isserlis, Rabbi Moses c. 1525–1572, Krakow, Poland. Known by the acronym "Rema." Author of glosses on *Shulchan Aruch*.

J

Jacob Also called "Israel." 16th and 15th centuries BCE; lived in the Holy Land, Charan, and Egypt. Son of Isaac and Rebecca, and the third of the three patriarchs or founding fathers of the Jewish people. His twelve sons became the progenitors of the twelve tribes of Israel.

Jeremiah Biblical prophet, 5th century BCE, Jerusalem. Also the name of the biblical book that records his prophesies.

Jerusalem Talmud During the talmudic era (see entry for Talmud), there were two major centers of Torah learning—in the Land of Israel and in Babylonia. Consequently there are two recensions of the Talmud: the "Jerusalem Talmud" and the "Babylonian Talmud." The Jerusalem Talmud records 150 years of teachings and discussions in the academies of the Land of Israel, approximately 200–350 CE. The term "Talmud," without further qualification, generally means the Babylonian version which, as the later and more comprehensive recension, is considered the more decisive conclusion in matters of Torah law.

Job One of the books of the Bible, which tells the story of Job, a prosperous, charitable, and G-d-fearing man who undergoes a litany of personal and family tragedies, leading to a series of debates between him and his three friends on the meaning of life and of suffering, and in particular, why bad things happen to righteous people. The Talmud cites an opinion attributing its authorship to Moses.

Jochanan ben Zakai, Rabbi c. 40 BCE to 80 CE, Israel. A Talmudic sage and disciple of both Hillel and Shammai, who served as vice-president of the *sanhedrin* (high court of Torah law) in the period before and after the destruction of the second Holy Temple and was instrumental in ensuring that Judaism would continue to flourish despite the loss of the Temple.

Joshua 1355–1245 BCE. Joshua was the principal disciple of Moses, whom he succeeded as leader of the people of Israel. Joshua brought the Israelites into the Promised Land, led them in the battles for the Land's conquest, and oversaw its apportionment amongst the twelve tribes of Israel. The biblical book of Joshua, which he authored, describes the events during his time of leadership.

Judah Fourth son of Jacob. Also refers to the Israelite tribe descendant from him. The tribe of Judah was assigned the role of the leadership of Israel: the kings of the royal House of David, as well as the future redeemer Moshiach, are descendants of Judah. The name "Judah" (and its derivatives, "Judean" and "Jew") also refers to the whole of the Jewish people.

Judah, Rabbi Rabbi Judah bar Ila'i, 2nd century, Israel. A disciple of Rabbi Akiva, he is the sage most cited by name in the Mishnah. The Midrashic work *Torat Kohanim* is largely based on his teachings.

Judah HaNassi, Rabbi c. 120–190 CE; Tiberias, Bet Shearim, and Sepphoris, Israel. President (*nassi*) of the *sanhedrin* (high court of Torah law) and redactor of the Mishnah, the first official transcription of the laws of the Oral Torah. He is also known simply as "Rebbi" ("master" and "teacher" *par excellence*) in recognition of this accomplishment, and of the great number of prominent sages who were his disciples.

K

Kabbalah; kabbalistic; kabbalist The mystical dimension of the Torah, transmitted by tradition from master to disciple (hence the name *kabbalah*, meaning "that which is received"). The teachings of kabbalah explore the relationship between G-d and creation, the significance of the various names of G-d, the structure of the spiritual cosmos, the nature and purpose of evil, the function of the *mitzvot*, and the mission of the human soul which descends into the world to repair its breaches and unite creation with its Creator. Core texts of kabbalah include *Zohar*, *Sefer Yetzirah*, and the teachings of the Safed kabbalists Ramak (Rabbi Moses Cordovero, 1522–1570) and Ari (1534–1572) and their contemporaries and disciples.

Kaddish An ancient and sacred prayer extoling the greatness and sanctity of G-d, written in Aramaic and recited in the course of communal prayer. A version of this prayer, called "Mourner's Kaddish," is traditionally recited for the merit of the soul of the deceased.

Kaporet The cover of the ark in the Tabernacle and the Holy Temple.

Keruvim Two winged figures, hammered out of a block of solid gold, that were part of the cover of the ark in the Tabernacle and the Holy Temple.

Kesef Mishneh Commentary on Maimonides' *Mishneh Torah*, by Rabbi Joseph Caro (1488–1575).

Ketoret The incense offered twice daily in the Tabernacle and later in the Holy Temple, as well as by the high priest in the Holy of Holies on Yom Kippur.

Kings (book) Biblical book, authored by the prophet Jeremiah. It describes the reign of King Solomon, and his building of the first Holy Temple in Jerusalem; the division of Israel into two kingdoms after Solomon's death; the deeds of Elijah the Prophet and of his disciple Elisha; the conquest and exile of the northern kingdom of Israel by the Assyrians; and the conquest and exile of the southern kingdom of Judah and the destruction of the Temple by the Babylonians. In medieval times it was divided into two books, I Kings and II Kings.

Kislev Ninth month of the Jewish calendar, or the third month counting from Tishrei. Approximately November–December. The holiday of Chanukah begins on the 25th of this month.

Kiyor "Laver"; the washstand that stood in the courtyard of the Tabernacle (and later, in the Holy Temple), for the *kohanim* to wash their hands and feet before performing their service or entering into the Sanctuary.

Kohen gadol The "high priest" elected as leader of the Kohanim. The *kohen gadol* wore special priestly garments, and performed the Yom Kippur service in the Holy Temple.

Kolbo Halachic work, first published in Naples in 1490. There are various opinions regarding its authorship.

Korach A cousin of Moses who led a mutiny against Moses' leadership, as related in the book of Numbers, chapter 16.

Korban; korbanot (pl.) Literally, "a bringing near." An offering brought to G-d (as a rule, in the Holy Temple), generally an animal, a bird, or a measure of flour. The various *korbanot* and their laws are enumerated in the biblical books of Leviticus and Numbers, and discussed at length in the Talmud.

L

Laver See Kiyor.

Lekach Tov Midrashic anthology and commentary on the Five Books of Moses by Rabbi Toviah ben Eliezer, late 11th century, Kastoria, Greece.

Levi; Levites The third of twelve sons of Jacob. Also refers to the Israelite tribe descendant from him, who served as spiritual leaders, and as kohanim (priests) and "Levites" (priestly assistants) in the Holy Temple.

Leviticus Third of the biblical Five Books of Moses.

Likutei Sichot A 39-volume collection of essays adapted from the talks of the Lubavitcher Rebbe (Rabbi Menachem Mendel Schneerson, 1902–1994) and edited by him.

Likutei Torah A book of discourses of chassidic teaching by Rabbi Schneur Zalman of Liadi (1745–1812). Also the name of a collection of teachings by Ari.

Lubavitch The town in White Russia, Lyubavichi, that served as the seat of the rebbes of the Chabad-Lubavitch branch of chassidism for 102 years, from 1813 to 1915. The Chabad-Lubavitch movement is also known by the name "Lubavitch."

Lubavitcher Rebbe, The The seventh rebbe or leader of Chabad-Lubavitch, Rabbi Menachem Mendel Schneerson (1902–1994). Commonly referred to as "The Rebbe."

Luria, Rabbi Isaac See entry for Ari.

M

Maggid of Kozhnitz Chassidic master Rabbi Israel of Kozhnitz, Poland, 1737-1814.

Maharal Rabbi Judah Loew, c. 1520–1609, Poland and Bohemia. Rabbi in several communities, most notably Prague. A prolific author on many areas of Torah, whose works strongly influenced later Jewish thinkers and schools of thought.

Maimonides Rabbi Moses ben Maimon, c. 1135–1204, Spain, Morocco, and Egypt. Also known by the acronym "Rambam." One of the foremost authorities in Torah law and in Jewish philosophy.

Malachi One of the last biblical prophets, who was active in the Land of Israel in the 4th century BCE. Also the name of the biblical book that contains his prophesies.

Malchut Lit., "kingship" and "sovereignty." The tenth and last of the sefirot (divine attributes) described in kabbalah.

Maror The "bitter herbs" eaten at the Passover seder to remember the bitterness of the Egyptian exile and enslavement.

Matzah; matzot (pl.) Unleavened bread, eaten during the holiday of Passover. Matzah is made and baked quickly before the dough can leaven and rise, and hence commemorates the haste with which the Children of Israel left Egypt during the Exodus.

Mechilta Midrash on the book of Exodus from the school of Rabbi Ishmael, first century, Israel.

Mechilta d'Rashbi Midrash on the book of Exodus from the school of Rabbi Akiva, first and second century, Israel. The acronym "Rashbi" is a reference to Rabbi Shimon bar Yochai, the first sage quoted in the work.

Megaleh Amukot Kabbalistic work by Rabbi Nathan Nata Spira, 1585–1633, Krakow, Poland.

Meir, Rabbi Mishnaic sage of the mid-2nd century, Israel. A prominent disciple of Rabbi Akiva. Rabbi Meir's formulation of the Mishnah served as the basis for the final text redacted by Rabbi Judah HaNasi a generation later.

Me'iri. Rabbi Menachem HaMeiri, c. 1249–1315, Perpignan, France.

Menachot The meal offerings brought in the Tabernacle and the Holy Temple. These offerings of flour, oil, and frankincense, baked in a variety of ways, were brought as an accompaniment to the animal offerings, or as offerings in their own right.

Menorah Candelabrum. In the Tabernacle and later in the Holy Temple, the *menorah* was made of gold and had seven branches. It was kindled every afternoon and burned through the night, representing the divine light which radiated to the entire world from the "dwelling place" of the divine presence. Also refers to the candelabrum (regardless of its shape) which holds eight lights, used on Chanukah to commemorate the miracle that occurred when the Temple's *menorah* remained lit for eight days on one day's supply of oil.

Messiah; messianic See Moshiach.

Midrash; *Midrashim* (pl.); **midrashic** General name given to explanations and expositions of biblical verses cited by the sages of the Talmudic era. These include the halachic *Midrashim*—expositions of Torah law using traditional exegetical methods (as in the midrashic works Mechilta, Torat Kohanim, and Sifri); or non-legal teachings, called aggadah, including ethics, homilies, narratives, etc. (as in Pirkei d'R. Eliezer, Midrash Rabbah, and Midrash Tanchuma). In a looser sense, the term "midrash" also includes post-Talmudic narratives and teachings.

Midrash Rabbah General name given to ten different collections of *Midrashim* on the Five Books of Moses and five other biblical books (referred to as the "five scrolls"), based mostly on the teachings of Talmudic sages from the Land of Israel from the 3rd and 4th centuries. The ten works are: *Bereishith Rabbah* on the book of Genesis; *Shemot Rabbah* on Exodus; *Vayikra Rabbah* on Leviticus; *Bamidbar Rabbah* on Numbers; *Devarim Rabbah* on Deuteronomy; *Esther Rabbah* on the book of Esther; *Shir HaShirim Rabbah* on Song of Songs; *Ruth Rabbah* on the book of Ruth; *Eichah Rabati* on Lamentations; and *Kohelet Rabbah* on

Ecclesiastes. The collections vary widely in date of compilation (between approximately the 3rd and 12th centuries) and their treatment of the source material, some parts being a running commentary on the biblical narrative while others consist of lengthy discourses on particular verses.

Midrash Tanchuma A Midrash on the Five Books of Moses, collected from the sermons of Rabbi Tanchuma bar Aba (though quoting numerous other Talmudic sages as well). Composed early to mid-4th century; Israel.

Midrash Tehilim An early Midrash on the book of Psalms, also known as *Shocher Tov*, from its opening words.

Migdal Oz Commentary on Maimonides' Mishneh Torah by Rabbi Shem-Tov ibn Gaon, 1287–1330, Spain.

Mikvah Lit., "pool." A ritual bathing pool used for the immersion of people, utensils, and other objects, as part of their transition to ritual purity.

Minchat Chinuch Halachic work by Rabbi Yosef Babad, 1800–1874, Ternopil, Ukraine. Written in the form of a commentary on the classic Torah work, *Sefer HaChinuch*.

Miriam Elder sister of Moses. A prophetess and leader during the Egyptian exile and in the period following the Exodus.

Mishkan See Tabernacle.

Mishnah; mishnaic The Mishnah is the basic summary text of the laws of the Torah, as redacted toward the end of the 2nd century by Rabbi Judah HaNassi. It is the first officially written text of any part of the "Oral Torah" which had hitherto been passed down orally from teacher to disciple. The Talmud is structured as commentaries on the Mishnah.

Mishneh Torah A fourteen-volume codification of halachah, covering all areas of Torah law, composed by Maimonides (Rabbi Moses ben Maimon, c. 1135–1204, Spain, Morocco, and Egypt).

Mitzvah; mitzvot (pl.) Literally, "commandment." A good deed or religious precept; more specifically, one of the Torah's 613 divine commandments, or of the seven ordinances enacted by the rabbis. In chassidic literature the word *mitzvah* is also seen as related to the Aramaic word *tzavta*, "attachment," indicating that a *mitzvah* creates a bond between G-d, who commands it, and the person who performs it.

Mizrachi Rabbi Eliyahu Mizrachi, c. 1440–1525, Constantinople (Istanbul), Turkey. Served as chief rabbi of the Ottoman Empire. Authored one of the most well-known supercommentaries on Rashi's commentary on the Torah.

Moses 1393–1273 BCE. First leader of the Jewish nation and the greatest prophet in Jewish tradition. Moses took the Israelites out of Egypt, performed numerous miracles for them, received the Torah from G-d and taught it to the people, and led the Children of Israel for forty years as they journeyed through the wilderness.

Moshiach Literally, "anointed one." The messiah. One of the fundamental principles of the Jewish faith is that G-d will send a leader and redeemer to return the dispersed people of Israel to their homeland, rebuild the Holy Temple, and usher in a messianic era of universal peace, wisdom, and perfection, as foretold in the Five Books of Moses (e.g., Numbers 24 and Deuteronomy 30) and extensively prophesied by Isaiah, Ezekiel, Zechariah, and virtually all the prophets of Israel. In the words of Maimonides, "In that time there will be no hunger or war, no jealousy or rivalry. For the good will be plentiful, and all delicacies available as dust. The entire occupation of the world will be only to know G-d... as it is written (Isaiah 11:9): 'For the earth shall be filled with the knowledge of G-d, as the waters cover the sea.'"

Mount Sinai See entry for Sinai.

Musaf Literally, "addition." Additional offerings brought on in the Holy Temple on special days (Shabbat, Rosh Chodesh, and the festivals). Also refers to an additional prayer service recited nowadays on those occasions.

N

Nachmanides Rabbi Moses ben Nachman, c. 1195–1270, Spain and Israel. Recognized as a leading authority in all areas of Torah, Nachmanides is the author of influential works of Talmudic analysis, Torah law, Jewish philosophy, and kabbalah, as well as an in-depth commentary on the Five Books of Moses.

Nassi; nessi'im (pl.) Literally, "exalted one." In biblical times, the title was used to refer to the head of any one of the twelve tribes of Israel, and sometimes also as a monarchical title. In later eras, the civil and/or spiritual head of the Jewish community at large; in particular, it was the title of the president of the high court of Torah law (*sanhedrin*).

Negative commandment The 613 *mitzvot* (divine commandments) of the Torah are generally divided into two categories: 1) prohibitions, or "negative commandments," such as the prohibitions against nonkosher foods or forbidden relations; 2) actionable *mitzvot*, or "positive commandments," such as the obligation to study Torah or to eat matzah on Passover.

Nimukei Shmuel Commentary on Rashi by 17th-century sage Rabbi Shmuel Zarfati of Fez, Morocco.

Nissan First month of the Jewish calendar, approximately March–April. Also the seventh month, counting from Tishrei. The Torah, in Exodus 12, declares *Nissan*—the month of the Exodus and of Israel's birth as a people—the "first of the months of the year." The holiday Passover, marking the liberation of the Jewish people from Egyptian slavery, begins on the 15th of *Nissan*.

Numbers (book) See Five Books of Moses.

O

Ohr HaChaim Commentary on the Bible by Rabbi Chaim ibn Attar, 1696–1743.

Ohr HaTorah A multivolume series of discourses of chassidic teaching by Tzemach Tzedek (Rabbi Menachem Mendel of Lubavitch, 1789–1866).

Onkelos Early Aramaic translation of the Five Books of Moses, regarded by commentaries of all generations as one of the most authoritative translations/explanations of the Torah. Composed by a Roman convert to Judaism in the first century CE.

Orach Chaim Lit., "Way of life." The first of the four sections of Shulchan Aruch (Code of Jewish Law). The *Orach Chaim* section includes the laws of prayer, of frequently performed mitzvot such as tzitzit and tefilin, and of Shabbat and the Jewish festivals.

Oral Torah Collective name for the entire body of interpretation, exposition, and commentary that is part of the Torah's "chain of transmission" from Moses onward, in contrast to the Written Torah canonized by Moses and the later prophets. Originally the Oral Torah was in fact oral, handed down from teacher to disciple without being officially put in writing. That changed when Rabbi Judah HaNassi —foreseeing the expansion of the Jewish Diaspora and the end of a single, centralized authority on Torah law—redacted the Mishnah in approximately 189 CE. The process was repeated some 300 years later when Rav Ashi and Ravina redacted the Talmud in the 5th century. In the centuries since, the Torah sages of each generation wrote and published their commentaries, responsa, and codifications of Torah law as their contributions to the constantly evolving Oral Torah.

P

Parashah; parashiot (pl.) Lit., "passage" or "chapter." A portion of the Bible as divided according to the annual Torah reading cycle. Can also refer to a biblical section discussing a single topic, marked off in the Torah scroll by an empty space before and after it.

Passover Heb., *Pesach*. A seven-day festival (eight days outside the Holy Land) beginning on the 15th day of the Jewish month of Nissan, commemorating the Exodus from Egypt.

Patriarchs, The Heb., *avot*. The three ancestors of the people of Israel, Abraham, Isaac, and Jacob.

Perez The first of the two twins born from the union of Judah and Tamar; the ancestor of King David and of Moshiach.

Pirkei d'Rabbi Eliezer A Midrashic work attributed to the Talmudic sage Rabbi Eliezer ben Hyrcanus (first century CE, Lod, Israel).

Positive commandment See entry for Negative commandment.

Priestly garments Specially designed garment that the *kohanim* and the *kohen gadol* are mandated to wear while performing the service in the Tabernacle and the Holy Temple, described in the 28th chapter of the biblical book of Exodus.

Promised Land The Holy Land, also called the "Land of Israel," promised by G-d to Abraham, Isaac, and Jacob as the eternal heritage of the Jewish people.

Proverbs Biblical book containing the teachings of King Solomon. Proverbs consists largely of aphorisms and parables on the importance of acquiring wisdom, the virtues of a moral life, and other themes.

Psalms Biblical book of religious poetry arranged by King David.

R

Rabbi Literally, "my master" or "my great one." Traditional honorific for Torah teachers and leaders, particularly those upon whom the authority to decide matters of Torah law has been conferred.

Ralbag Rabbi Levi ben Gershon, 1288–1344, France. Also known as "Gersonides." A prominent Bible commentator, philosopher, mathematician, and astronomer.

Ran Rabbi Nissim ben Reuben Gerondi, d. 1376, Barcelona, Spain. A leading authority on Torah law and an important voice of Jewish philosophy.

Rashba Rabbi Solomon ben Aderet, 1235–1310, Barcelona, Spain. Author of a collection of some three thousand responsa covering all areas of Jewish life; an analytical commentary on much of the Talmud; *Torat HaBayit*, an important work on Jewish law; and other works.

Rashi Rabbi Solomon Yitzchaki, 1040–1105, Troyes, France. Foremost of the biblical elucidators, Rashi's commentary on Torah is a first point of reference for schoolchild and scholar alike.

Rebbe A variant of the title "Rabbi." Generally used to refer to chassidic leaders. "The Rebbe" without qualification commonly refers to the Lubavitcher Rebbe, Rabbi Menachem Mendel Schneerson (1902–1994).

Rebbe, The See entry for Lubavitcher Rebbe.

Rebecca Second of the four matriarchs of the Jewish people. Wife of Isaac, and mother of Jacob.

Redemption, the See entry for Moshiach.

Reishith Chochmah A classic work on Jewish ethics and morals in a kabbalistic vein, authored by 16th-century sage Rabbi Eliyahu de Vidas, of Safed and Hebron, Israel

Reshimot Notebooks containing the teachings of the Lubavitcher Rebbe, in the form of handwritten notes, drafts of letters and talks, and diary entries, discovered in the Rebbe's desk after his passing in 1994.

Ritva Rabbi Yom-Tov ben Abraham Ashvili, 1250-1330, Seville, Spain. Authored many important works of Talmudic commentary and halachic responsa.

Ruth One of the books of the Bible, which tells the story of Ruth, a Moabite princess who converted to Judaism and loyally followed her impoverished mother-in-law Naomi to the Land of Israel after the death of her husband. Ruth's controversial marriage to the Judean leader Boaz produced a child, Obed, who was the grandfather of King David.

S

Sanctuary An alternate term for the Tabernacle and Holy Temple. More specifically, it refers to the roofed edifice at the center of the Tabernacle or Temple (as opposed to the unroofed courtyards).

Sarah The first of the four matriarchs of the Jewish people. Wife of Abraham.

Schneersohn, Rabbi Yosef Yitzchak 1880–1950, Russia and the U.S. Sixth "rebbe" or leader of the Chabad-Lubavitch branch of chassidism.

Schneerson, Rabbi Menachem Mendel See entries for Tzemach Tzedek and for Lubavitcher Rebbe.

Schneerson, Rebbetzin Chaya Mushkah 1901–1988, Russia and the U.S. Daughter of Rabbi Yosef Yitzchak Schneersohn, and wife of the Lubavitcher Rebbe.

Schneur Zalman of Liadi, Rabbi 1745–1812. Founder of the Chabad branch of chassidism.

Scripture A term for the Written Torah.

Second Tablets See Tablets of the Testament.

Second Temple See Holy Temple.

Seder Lit., "order." The step-by-step procedure for the meal on the first night of Passover. It includes the recital of the Passover Haggadah and the eating of matzah and bitter herbs. Outside of the Holy Land, the *seder* is held a second time on the second night of Passover.

Seder hishtalshelut Lit., "order of evolution." The chain of *sefirot* and "worlds" (i.e., realms of reality) by which G-d generates and relates to creation, as described at length in the works of kabbalah.

Sefer HaMitzvot Work by Maimonides enumerating and describing the 613 mitzvot of the Torah.

Sefer HaSichot A ten-volume collection of essays adapted from the talks of the Lubavitcher Rebbe (Rabbi Menachem Mendel Schneerson, 1902–1994) and edited by him during the years 1987 to 1992. Each volume is followed by a number representing the Jewish year in which the talks were delivered (e.g., *Sefer HaSichot 5748* includes talks from September of 1987 to September of 1988).

Sefer Ho'arochim Chabad A multivolume, comprehensive treatment, in encyclopedia form, of terms and concepts in teachings of Chabad Chassidism, authored by Rabbi Yoel Kahan.

Sefer Yetzirah An early work of kabbalah attributed to the patriarch Abraham.

Sefirah; sefirot (pl.) In kabbalistic literature, the term for the divine attributes or emanations which G-d manifested to create the world and relate to His creations.

Sforno Commentary on the Bible, by Rabbi Obadiah Sforno, c. 1475–1550, Rome and Bologna, Italy.

Shaar HaGilgulim Kabbalistic work by Rabbi Chaim Vital on the subject of reincarnation.

Shabbat Literally, "cessation" and "rest." The weekly day of rest observed on the seventh day of the week (i.e., Saturday) in remembrance that "six days G-d created the heavens and the earth... and He rested on the seventh day" (Exodus 20:11). Also the name of the tractate of the Talmud dealing with the laws of Shabbat.

Shach Commentary on the Shulchan Aruch by Rabbi Shabetai HaKohen, 1622–1663, Lithuania and Bohemia.

Shaloh Rabbi Isaiah Horowitz, c. 1560–1630, Poland, Austria, Germany, and Israel. Served as rabbi of numerous leading communities in Europe (including Dubna, Frankfurt am Mein, and Prague), and later in Jerusalem, Safed, and Tiberias. Author of *Shenei Luchot HaBerit*, an encyclopedic work blending Talmudic discourse, Torah law, kabbalah, biblical commentary, and ethics. Both the work and the author are commonly referred to as "Shaloh," an acronym for the work's title.

Shalom DovBer of Lubavitch, Rabbi 1860–1920. The fifth rebbe or leader of Chabad-Lubavitch. Also known by the acronym "Rashab."

Shammai First century BCE, Jerusalem, Israel. A Mishnaic sage who served as vice-president of the *sanhedrin* (high court of Torah law). In questions of Torah law Shammai tended toward the stricter view, as did his disciples (known as the "House of Shammai"), in contrast to the opinions of his colleague Hillel and his disciples.

Shavuot Lit., "weeks." A one-day festival (two days outside of Israel) commemorating the Giving of the Torah on Mount Sinai. Shavuot occurs on the 6th (and 7th) of the Jewish month of Sivan, but strictly speaking is defined as the day after the completion of the seven-week "counting of the omer" beginning on the second night of Passover.

Shechinah Lit., "indwelling." The divine presence in this world; equated in kabbalistic and chassidic literature with the feminine aspect of the divine.

Shekel Lit., "weight." A silver coin, equivalent to approximately 10–12 grams of silver, that served as the standard monetary unit in biblical and Talmudic times.

Shema Lit., "hear." The Jewish creed of belief in the unity of G-d, also including fundamental precepts as love of G-d, awe for G-d, Torah study, tefilin, mezuzah, tzitzit, and remembering the Exodus from Egypt. It consists of three passages from the Torah (Deuteronomy 6:4–9 and 11:13–21, and Numbers 15:37–41), opening with the declaration, "Hear O Israel, G-d is our G-d, G-d is one." The *Shema* is recited in the morning and evening prayers, and before retiring for the night. Its first two passages are inscribed on the parchment scrolls placed inside *tefilin* and *mezuzot*.

Shiloh A town in northern Israel where the Tabernacle (forerunner of the Holy Temple) was erected, and which served as the spiritual center for the people of Israel for 369 years, from the days of Joshua until its destruction by the Philistines in 890 BCE.

Shofar The horn of a ram or other animal, sounded on the festival of Rosh Hashanah and at the close of Yom Kippur, and by custom also throughout the month of Elul.

Showbread Twelve uniquely shaped loaves of unleavened bread that were baked each Friday in the Tabernacle and the Holy Temple. On Shabbat, these were placed on a specially designed Table in the Sanctuary, were they were displayed for one week, following which they were distributed to the *kohanim* serving in the Temple.

Shulchan Aruch Lit., "set table." The code of Torah law composed by Rabbi Joseph Caro (1488–1575) as a digest of his encyclopedic work *Beit Yosef*, with glosses added by Rema (Rabbi Moses Isserlis, 1525–1572). The *Shulchan Aruch* and its commentaries form the basis for virtually all subsequent deliberations of Torah law.

Siddur The Jewish prayer book. Its basic framework was developed by the sages of the early Second Temple Era. It includes selections from the Bible (particularly the book of Psalms), praise of G-d, requests for personal and national needs, and much else, and has been the subject of hundreds of commentaries spanning all genres of Jewish thought.

Sifri Midrash on the biblical books of Numbers and Deuteronomy, from the school of Rabbi Shimon bar Yochai (2nd century; Israel).

Siftei Chachamim Anthology of commentaries on Rashi, compiled by R. Shabetai Bass, 1641–1718, who lived in Bohemia, the Netherlands, and Poland.

Sinai; Sinaic Pertaining to the Giving of the Torah on Mount Sinai, as related in Exodus 19–20 and 24.

Sinai Desert Place of the Children of Israel's 40-year journey from Egypt to the Promised Land, 1313 to 1273 BCE.

Sivan Third month of the Jewish calendar, or the ninth month counting from Tishrei. Approximately May–June. The festival of Shavuot is on the 6th of this month.

Solomon, King 849–797 BCE; Jerusalem, Israel. Son and successor of King David, and builder of the first Holy Temple in Jerusalem. Regarded as "the wisest of all men," the wisdom of Solomon is contained in the biblical books of Proverbs, Song of Songs, and Ecclesiastes. Under Solomon's reign the people of Israel flourished as never before, both materially and spiritually.

Song of Songs Biblical book composed by King Solomon (849–797 BCE). Its form is a poetic dialogue between a shepherdess and her beloved, describing their mutual love and desire for each other through all the vicissitudes of their relationship. Classical Jewish tradition sees this as an extended allegory on the various phases of the relationship between G-d and the people of Israel throughout history.

Splitting of the Sea The miraculous splitting of the Sea of Reeds (commonly associated with the Red Sea) on the seventh day following the Exodus, allowing the Children of Israel to escape the Egyptians' attempt to force them back into slavery, and drowning the Egyptians (as recounted in the biblical book of Exodus, chapters 13 to 15).

Sukkot A seven-day festival, beginning on the 15th of the Jewish month of Tishrei. The festival takes its name from the temporary dwelling, called a *sukkah* ("shed"), in which the Torah (Leviticus 23:39–43) instructs to dwell during this period, commemorating the divine protection of the Children of Israel during their forty-year trek in the desert on their way to the Promised Land.

T

Tabernacle The portable sanctuary—also called *Mishkan* and "Tent of Meeting"—built by the Children of Israel to accompany them in their journeys in the desert, which served as the "dwelling" for the divine presence in the Israelite camp. The Tabernacle was the forerunner of the Holy Temple in Jerusalem.

Table, the One of the vessels of the Tabernacle; used to display the showbread.

Tablets of the Testament The two stone tablets on which G-d inscribed the Ten Commandments and which Moses brought down from Mount Sinai. The tablets were kept in a specially built ark in the innermost chamber of the Holy Temple (the "Holy of Holies"). There were actually two sets of tablets, as the first were broken by Moses when he witnessed the people of Israel worshipping the Golden Calf; when G-d forgave Israel's sin, He instructed Moses to carve a second set of tablets (see account in Exodus 32–34).

Tachash An animal whose skins were used in the making of the uppermost roof covering of the Tabernacle. There are various opinions among the sages as to its identity, as well as an opinion that it existed only for the purpose of the making of the Tabernacle.

Talmud; Talmudic The most important work of Judaism after the Bible, the Talmud is a multivolume compilation of teachings and deliberations by hundreds of sages over a period of close to 300 years, from the 3rd through 5th centuries CE. The term "Talmudic" is also used to refer to other works by the sages of that period (also called *Midrashim*), and to later works that explain or expound on the Talmud.

Tammuz Fourth month of the Jewish calendar, or the tenth month counting from Tishrei. Approximately June–July. The "Three Weeks" of mourning for the destruction of the Holy Temple begin with a fast day on the 17th of this month, also commemorating Moses' shattering of the Tablets of the Testament, the Roman penetration of Jerusalem, and various other calamities.

Tana d'Vei Eliyahu A Midrash which expands on the biblical narratives and stresses the importance of moral behavior. According to one tradition, it was taught by Elijah the Prophet to the sage Rabbi Anan.

Tanchuma See entry for *Midrash Tanchuma*.

Tanya A work by Rabbi Schneur Zalman of Liadi (1745–1812) in which he presents the fundamental doctrines of the Chabad branch of chassidism.

Tarfon, Rabbi Talmudic sage. Contemporary of Rabbi Akiva.

Targum Onkelos See Onkelos.

Taz Rabbi David Segal, 1586–1667, Poland. Known as "Taz," after the halachic commentary he authored on the *Shulchan Aruch*.

Tefilin Literally, "prayer accessories." Small leather cubes, dyed black and containing parchment scrolls inscribed with the *Shema* and other biblical passages, worn on the arm and head of adult men during weekday morning prayers. (See Exodus 13:9 and 13:16, and Deuteronomy 6:8 and 11:18.)

Ten Commandments Ten fundamental divine commandments which G-d spoke before the assembled people of Israel at the Giving of the Torah at Mount Sinai. The Ten Commandments are: belief in G-d; the prohibition to worship idols; the prohibition to take G-d's name in vain; observing the Shabbat; honoring one's parents; and the prohibitions of murder, adultery, theft, testifying falsely, and coveting another's property.

Ten Plagues Ten miraculous plagues brought upon the Egyptians to force them to release the Children of Israel from slavery, as described in chapters 7 to 12 of the biblical book of Exodus.

Tent of Meeting Another name for the Tabernacle.

Teshuvah Lit., "return." Repentance, seen in Jewish teaching as a return to G-d and to one's true essence.

Tiferet "Beauty" or "splendor." The sixth of the ten *sefirot* (divine attributes) and their corresponding attributes in the human psyche, *tiferet* fuses the qualities of *chesed* and *gevurah* into something that transcends both of them. It is also identified with the quality of compassion.

Tikkunei Zohar Addenda to the kabbalistic work *Zohar*.

Tishrei Month of the Jewish calendar, approximately September–October. Counting from Nissan (which the Torah designates as the "first of the months of the year") it is the seventh month, and is referred to in the Torah as such. However, it is also regarded as the beginning of the year, as the 1st of *Tishrei* is the anniversary of the creation of the first man and woman, Adam and Eve. *Tishrei* is a month replete with festivals: Its first two days are celebrated as Rosh Hashanah, followed later in the month by the solemn day of Yom Kippur and the joyous festivals of Sukkot and Simchat Torah.

Torah Lit., "teaching" and "instruction." In the narrow sense, the term refers to the Five Books of Moses. In its broader sense, the term refers to the entire body of Jewish teaching deriving from the divine communication received by Moses at Mount Sinai and handed down and expounded upon through the generations.

Torah reading cycle See entry for Annual Torah reading cycle.

Torah scroll A parchment scroll on which the Torah (i.e., the Five Books of Moses) is handwritten by a specially trained religious scribe. The Torah scroll is the holiest object in Judaism (other than the human being).

Torah Ohr A book of discourses of chassidic teaching, by Rabbi Schneur Zalman of Liadi (1745–1812).

Torat Kohanim A Midrash on the biblical book of Leviticus, compiled in 2nd-century Israel.

Torat Menachem Hitvaaduyot Transcripts of the talks delivered by the Lubavitcher Rebbe in the years 1950–1992, of which more than 100 volumes have been published to date. The volumes in the series are named in accordance with the year on the Jewish calendar in which they were delivered (e.g., *Torat Menachem Hitvaaduyot 5740* contains transcripts of the talks delivered during the Jewish year 5740—equivalent to 1979–1980 on the secular calendar).

Tosafot Collective name given to commentaries on the Talmud by dozens of sages who lived in Western Europe in the 12th and 13th centuries.

Tzaddik; tzaddikim (pl.) Perfectly righteous person.

Tzafnat Paaneach Collective name for the works of the "Gaon of Rogatchov," Rabbi Yosef Rozin (1858–1936).

Tzemach Tzedek Rabbi Menachem Mendel of Lubavitch, 1789–1866, the third rebbe of the Chabad-Lubavitch branch of chassidism. Known as "Tzemach Tzedek," after the collection of his responsa on Torah law and Talmudic commentary published under that title.

GLOSSARY

Tzimtzum Lit., "contraction." In the kabbalistic teachings of Ari and his successors, the *tzimtzum* is the process of G-d contracting and delimiting His "light" (i.e., the divine self-expression and self-revelation) in order to make possible the concept of a limited, worldly existence.

Tzitzit Lit., "fringes." An arrangement of knotted strings, mandated by the Torah (Numbers 15:37–41) to be attached to garments of four or more corners as a reminder to fulfill the 613 commandments (*mitzvot*) of the Torah.

V

Vessels (of the Tabernacle) The various furnishings that facilitated the divine service in the Tabernacle (and later, in the Holy Temple). This included: The ark, that contained the Tablets of the Testament; the *menorah* (candelabra), whose seven lamps were lit each afternoon and burned through the night; the table, on which the showbread was placed; the inner altar, on which the *ketoret* (incense) was burned); the outer altar, on which the *korbanot* (animal and meal offerings) were brought; and the *kiyor* (laver), from which the priests washed their hands and feet before performing the service.

Vital, Rabbi Chaim Safed kabbalist, 1543–1620. A disciple of Ari, and the one entrusted by him with recording his teachings.

W

World to Come Heb., *olam habah*. Can refer to the afterlife in which each individual soul receives its reward, or to the collective resurrection of the dead that will take place in the era of Moshiach.

Written Torah The twenty-four books of the Jewish Bible. Also called *Tanach*, which is an acronym for its three components: 1) *Torah*—the Five Books of Moses; 2) *Neviim* or "Prophets;" and 3) *Ketuvim*—"Scriptures." These are referred to as the "Written Torah," in contrast to the Oral Torah—the explanations and expositions of the Written Torah which were handed down through the generations and not officially committed to writing until the Mishnaic era. The final format of the Written Torah was set by the prophets and sages of the "Great Assembly" under the leadership of Ezra in the 4th century BCE. In some contexts, the term "Written Torah" refers more narrowly to the Five Books of Moses only.

Y

Yalkut Reuveni Anthology of kabbalistic teachings compiled by Rabbi Abraham Reuben ha-Kohen Sofer (d. 1673; Prague).

Yalkut Shimoni Comprehensive anthology of early Midrashim on the Bible, compiled in the 12th or 13th century by Rabbi Shimon HaDarshan of Frankfurt am Mein, Germany.

Yeshivah; yeshivot (pl.) Literally, "sitting" or "settling." A school for advanced Torah learning and study.

Yom Kippur Literally, "day of atonement." The holiest day on the Jewish calendar, occurring on the 10th of *Tishrei*. A solemn day of fasting and prayer, devoted to repentance and return to G-d.

Yom Tov Shel Rosh Hashanah 5666 A series of dozens of discourses of chassidic teaching authored by Rabbi Shalom DovBer of Lubavitch, and delivered by him in the course of the years 1905 to 1908 (5666 to 5668 on the Jewish calendar).

Yoreh De'ah "Instructor of knowledge." The second of the four sections of Shulchan Aruch (code of Jewish law). *Yoreh De'ah* codifies ritual laws requiring the expertise of a rabbi, such as the kosher dietary laws.

Z

Zechariah One of the biblical prophets, whose prophecies are collected in the biblical book which carries his name.

Zohar; Zoharic The fundamental work of kabbalah. Contains the esoteric teachings of 2nd-century sage Rabbi Shimon bar Yochai and his disciples, in the form of a series of discourses on the Five Books of Moses.

Zohar Chadash Portions of the kabbalistic work *Zohar* that came to light after the work's initial publication in the late 13th century.

INDEX

A

Aaron 34; 56–57; 58; 137; 191; 252; 254; 275
Abarbanel 19
Abolitionist Movement 42
Abraham 28–29; 31; 36; 37; 95
    also see: Patriarchs, The
Action 82–83; 107; 123; 173; 195; 199–202; 205; 216–220; 257–259; 263; 298; 309–310; 327–328
Adar 7 295
Administration 150–151
Afikoman 101
Aggadah 157; 301; 308
Akiva, Rabbi 81–84; 131; 132; 160–168; 173; 308
Alacrity see: Haste
Alexander I, Czar 51; 52
Altar 209; 210; 213; 222; 223; 228–229; 243; 264–266; 275–277
Altruism 187; 196–198
Amalek 140–145
Ambition 100–106
American Revolution 42; 49–50
Analogy 46–47
Angels 43; 200; 202; 224; 235
Animal Kingdom 219–220; 221
Animal Soul 211–212; 258
Annual Torah Reading Cycle 70; 295; 329
    also see: Name of the *Parashah*
Apathy 60
Apollo 8 (space mission) 173–174
Apple 256–258
Apron see: Ephod
Ari 21; 97; 270; 311

Ark 204; 209; 210; 212–214; 223; 229; 232–237; 238–239; 246; 248; 289
Aroma see: Smell
Ashes 321–324
Assyria 99
Astronaut 173–174
Atonement see: Forgiveness and Teshuvah
Authority 44–52
Authority, Delegation of 151
Avot d'Rabbi Nathan 85
Awareness; Consciousness 126
Azariah 61

B

Baal HaTurim 237; 295–296; 297
Baal Shem Tov, Rabbi Israel 14; 188; 237; 254; 261; 323
Baal Teshuvah 285–287; 289
Baalei HaTosafot see: Tosafot
Babel, Tower of see: Tower of Babel
Babylonian Exile 105
Bartenura 246
Beauty 255–259
Bechayei 241
Bechor see: Firstborn Offering
Behavior see: Action
Bells 252; 255–256; 257; 259
Betrothal see: Marriage
Betzalel 314
Binding of Isaac 28
Bittul 46; 74; 180–181; 220; 228; 249; 250; 258; 309
    also see: Nullification (halachic)
Blood 58–60; 211
Blood, Plague of 58–60

Bo, Parashah of 70–75
Body 174; 186; 246; 253–254
  also see: Materialism; Material world
Bonaparte see: Napoleon Bonaparte
Borrower see: Guardians, The Four
Bread 138; 276
Bread from Heaven see: Manna
Breaking of the Tablets 281; 282; 300–302
Bricks 5–7; 182
Burning see: Fire
Burning Bush 14–15; 16; 22; 95

C

Calendar, The Jewish 225–226; 295
Career; Earning a Living 8–9; 277–278; 317
Carrying Poles (of the Ark) 238–239
Cedar 206
Census (of the Israelites in the desert) 132; 151
Challenge 37; 98; 118–123; 169–170; 321
Challenging G-d 34–40
Chametz see: Leaven
Chanukah 282
Character 179–180; 311
Chariot, The Divine 235
Charity 268; 328
Chassidism 174–175; 254; 311–312; 322
Chatzitzah 125
Cherubs see: Keruvim
Chidush (innovation in Torah) 156
Child; Children; Childhood 112; 114–115; 217; 235; 236–237
  also see: Parent-Child Relationship
Children of Israel see: Jewish People
Chiya, Rabbi 283

Chizkuni 93; 207
Chochmah 103
Choice see: Free choice
Choshen 262–263
Chronicles, Book of 228
Chronology (in Torah) 149; 282–284
Chumash see: Written Torah
Chutzpah 144
Civil Law 172–182
Cohen see: Kohen; Kohanim
Coldness 60; 62; 141
Commitment 216–220; 272–274
  also see: Kabbalat Ol
Community 329–333
Comprehension see: Intellect; Reason
Conflict 176–177
Consciousness see: Awareness
Converts (to Judaism) 84; 97; 155
Copper 266; 328
Copper Altar see: Altar
Counting 2–4; 330
Counting of the *Omer* 42; 90–91; 92
Courtyard (of the Tabernacle) 222–223; 228–229
Covenant Between the Parts 95
Creation 24; 27–28; 71; 86–88; 97; 214; 223–224; 269; 286; 291; 320
  also see: Something from Nothing and *Seder Hishtalshelut*
Creativity 87
Crowns 199–202
Custom 53–54

D

Damages see: Torts
Daniel, Book of 61
Darkness, Plague of 96
Daughters of Zelophehad 150
David, King 21; 40

INDEX

Death 323–324
Debate (in Torah) 244; 249–250; 288–289
Deed see: Action
Derech Mitzvotecha see: Tzemach Tzedek
Digestion 138; 225
Dira Betachtonim see: Dwelling for G-d in the Physical World
Divine Attributes see: *Sefirot*
Divine Chariot see: Chariot, The Divine
Divine Presence 209; 210; 212–215; 242; 276; 312; 317
Divine Providence 52–53; 204; 261; 295; 329
Divine Revelation 306
Divrei Dovid see: Taz
Donkey 27–32
Doubt 140–145; 170
Dov Ber of Mezheritch, Rabbi 287
Dovid Horodoker 46
Duality 165–168
Dwelling for G-d in the Physical World 6–7; 29–32; 136; 213; 217–218; 221–222; 230–231; 265; 279–289; 308–310; 311–316; 320; 326–327

E

Earth 221–222
East 244
Eating see: Food
Ecclesiastes 199; 304
Echad 23–26
Ego see: Selfhood and Ego
Egypt 58–59; 78; 92; 95; 99; 115; 142; 208; 283
Eh-he-yeh (divine name) 16–20

Eitz Chaim see: Ari and Vital, Rabbi Chaim
Elazar, Rabbi 243; 246; 249
Eliezer 271
Eliezer, Rabbi 81–83; 131; 132–133
Elijah Mizrachi, Rabbi see: Mizrachi
Elijah of Vilna, Rabbi see: Gra
Elijah the Prophet 253–254; 258
Elokim (divine name) 17; 18
Emotions 37–40; 83; 200; 220; 246; 248–250; 263
Employee 181
Ephod 260–261; 262–263
Ephraim 127
Erev Pesach 76; 101
Essence 73; 79–84; 237; 290–299
Ethics of the Fathers 42; 57; 269; 276
Evil 37; 53; 70–75; 78; 173; 193–194; 287
Evil Inclination 179–180; 287
Exile see: *Galut*
Exodus, The 22; 41–42; 44; 45; 58; 70–71; 76; 83; 90–93; 108; 110; 118–119; 130; 140; 142–143
Ezekiel 41; 71; 73; 235; 236

F

Face 277–278
Faith 38–40; 83; 135–136; 163; 299
Farming 277
Fat 211
Fate 189
Fear of G-d see: G-d, Fear of
Feeling see: Emotions
Feet 109; 263; 277–278
Fire 14–15; 80–81; 82; 100–106; 253; 319–324
First Temple 105
   also see: Holy Temple
Firstborn, Plague of 103

Firstborn Offering 101–102
Fish 124–128
Five Books of Moses
    see: Written Torah
Food 78; 138; 225; 228; 252–253; 275–276
Foolishness 180
Forgiveness 281; 282; 283; 293–294
Form and Substance 78–82
Foundation 220; 272–274; 286
Foundation Sockets (of the Tabernacle) 219; 272–274
Four Elements 81–83
Four Expressions of Redemption 110
Four Guardians
    see Guardians, The Four
France 54–55
Franklin, Benjamin 42
Free Choice 37; 43; 188
Freedom 41–55; 58–60; 71; 85–93; 112
Freedom of Religion 49–50
French Revolution 49
Frogs 61–62
Frogs, Plague of 61–62

G

Galoshes 278
Galut 3; 94–99; 105–106; 111; 206–208
Gaon of Rogachov 11; 89; 234
Gaon of Vilna see: Gra
Garden of Eden 187
Gematria 22–23
Generation Gap 114–115
Gershon, Rabbeinu 244
Gevurah 105
Gibeon 222
Gilgal 222

Giving of the Torah
    see: Torah, Giving of
G-d 38; 42; 43; 60; 74–75; 87; 111; 135–136; 163; 188; 200; 201–202; 209; 214; 237; 246; 271; 279–280; 311; 312
    also see: Challenging G-d; Chariot, The Divine; Divine Presence; Divine Providence; Divine Revelation; *Shechinah*; *Sefirot*; and the next six entries below
G-d, Fear of 37; 298
G-d, Love for 14–15; 37
G-d, Names of 16–20; 190; 297
G-d, Service of 44–45; 59–60; 91; 97–98; 181; 197; 211–215; 216; 227; 254; 268; 275; 313
G-d, Unity of 23–26
G-d, Yearning for 14–15; 68; 104; 322
Gold 266; 281; 284; 328
Golden Altar see: Altar
Golden Calf 39; 279–289; 290; 300–301
Good; Goodness 311
    also see: Good and Evil
Good and Evil 173
Good Deed see: Action and Mitzvah
Gra 156; 205
Guardians, The Four 177; 183–189; 193

H

Haggadah 41; 76; 81; 83; 92; 103; 112; 142
Hail, Plague of 63–68
HaKalir, Rabbi Elazar 111
Halachah 174–175; 186; 210–212; 244–245; 248; 265; 275; 301; 308
Half-Shekel 268–271; 272
Hammer 157

Hananiah 61
Hands 214; 277–279
Haste 108
Havayah (divine name) 17; 18
Hearing 160–165
Heart see: Emotions
Heat see: Warmth
Heaven 30
Hem 259
Heresy 60
High Priest see: *Kohen Gadol*
Hillel 172–173
Hips 109
History 52; 178–182
Holiness; Holy Object 7; 18–19; 87; 240–241; 276; 281; 304–306; 313
also see: Spirituality; and Sparks of Holiness
Holy Land see: Israel, Land of
Holy of Holies 204; 214; 222–223; 230; 241–242; 246; 289`
Holy Temple 101; 105; 209–215; 216–220; 221–231; 239; 240–241; 245–246; 268; 275–276; 279
also see: Tabernacle; Vessels (of the Temple); Priestly Garments
Holy, The (outer chamber of the Tabernacle) 222–223; 229–230
Hope 207–208
Hosea 237
Human Being 43; 45–46; 90; 124; 186; 212; 220; 221–222; 224; 230–231; 246; 265–266; 273; 300–303; 312
Human Character see: Character
Humility 27; 126
Hur 191

I

Ibn Attar, Rabbi Chaim
see: *Ohr HaChaim*

Ibn Ezra 93; 207
Idolatry 8–9; 11; 58–59; 74; 103; 281
Ikarim 19
Incense see: *Ketoret*
Individuality; Personal Initiative 3–4; 134; 136; 153; 173; 174; 273; 329–333
Indoor Altar see: Altar
Infinity 17; 71; 90–93; 135; 213–214; 309
Inheritance 150
Innerness 278
Intellect; Reason 37–39; 83; 135–136; 141; 199–202; 220; 225; 230; 246–250; 277–278; 300–303; 311
Isaac 36; 37; 271
also see: Patriarchs, The
Isaiah 2; 5; 21; 25; 40; 99; 111; 128; 214; 306; 312
Ishmael, Rabbi 160–168
Isolationism 120–121
Israel see: Jacob; Israel, Land of; and Jewish people
Israel of Kozhnitz, Rabbi 50; 51–52
Israel, Land of 206–207
Isserlis, Rabbi Moshe see: Rema

J

Jacob 36; 37; 43; 98; 127; 206; 208
also see: Patriarchs, The
Jeremiah 41; 66; 157; 317
Jerusalem 101; 222; 240; 242; 264; 279
Jerusalem Talmud 94; 156; 157; 173; 308
Jethro 148–156
Jewish People 23; 41; 103; 108; 130; 132; 144; 204–205; 227–228; 235–237; 254; 256–259; 266; 270; 280; 289; 290; 291–294; 298–299
Job, Book of 126; 169; 193; 258; 271

Jochanan ben Zakai, Rabbi 196–197
Jochanan HaSandlar, Rabbi 277
Joshua, Book of 302
Joshua ben Levi, Rabbi 42; 277
Josiah, King 239
Judah, Rabbi 80; 82; 184–186
Judah, Tribe of 21
Judah HaNassi, Rabbi 243; 246; 250
Jurisprudence 150–151; 162
Justice 103

K

Kabbalah 48; 53; 103; 212; 233; 235
Kabbalat Ol (submission to divine authority) 44–45; 173–174; 199–202; 216–220; 272–274
Kaddish 324
Kaporet 232–237
Keruvim 223; 232–237
Kesef Mishneh 18
Ketoret 222; 227; 229
King; Kingship 44; 46–48; 258; 317
Kings, Book of 252; 254; 279
Kiyor 223; 229; 275–278
Kohen; Kohanim 103; 227
Kohen Gadol 223; 228; 230; 238; 254; 255
  also see: Priestly Garments
Kolbo 81
Korach 53
Korban; Korbanot 210; 211–212; 223; 227; 228; 268–271; 275
Korban Bechor
  see: Firstborn Offering
Korban Maaser see: Tithe Offering
Korban Pesach see: Passover Offering

L

Land 124–128
Laver see: *Kiyor*
Leadership 13; 45; 53; 129–134; 153; 208; 298–299
Learning 218
  also see: Torah Exegesis
Leaven 76–84
Lekach Tov 21
Length 245; 249
Levi, Tribe of see: Levites
Levi Yitzchak of Berditchev, Rabbi 50
Levites 21; 227
Light 242
Likutei Torah see: Ari and Schneur Zalman of Liadi, Rabbi
Logic 38
Lost Object 177; 180–181; 193
Love 249
Love for G-d see: G-d, Love for
Love Your Fellow see: Self and Fellow
Luria, Rabbi Isaac see: Ari

M

Maaser see: Tithe Offering
Machloket see: Debate (in Torah)
Maggid of Kozhnitz
  see: Israel of Kozhnitz, Rabbi
Maggid of Mezheritch
  see: Dov Ber of Mezheritch, Rabbi
Maharal 19; 41; 43; 45; 90; 158
Maimonides 15; 249
  Guide for the Perplexed 19; 43; 223–224
  Mishneh Torah 11; 18; 21; 24; 37; 43; 81; 85; 89; 103; 107; 122; 173; 197; 210; 211; 219; 226; 228; 239; 249; 268; 275; 276
  Thirteen Principles 24; 65; 298

Sefer HaMitzvot 90
Commentary on Mishnah 243
Majority 245
Malachi 149; 290
Malchut 103; 249
Manasseh 127
Manna 137–139
Manual Labor 277–278
  also see: Work
Maror 101; 112
Marriage 32; 202; 270–271
Marseillaise, The 55
Martyrdom 144
  also see: Self-Sacrifice
Mashal see: Analogy
Mashpiah 46–47
Mask 304–306
Materialism; Material World 7;
  29–32; 94–99; 103; 138; 161;
  211–212; 213; 215–215; 221–231;
  240; 252–254; 263; 275–278; 306;
  309–310; 312–313; 322; 327
  also see: Body and Dwelling for
  G-d in the Physical World
Matzah 101; 108; 112
Me'il 252–259
Me'iri 244
Meat 211
Mechilta 41; 81; 119–120; 129; 132; 137;
  149; 160–168; 290
Mechilta d'Rashbi 226; 317; 320
Megaleh Amukot 208
Meir, Rabbi 184–186
Memory 145; 330
Menachem Mendel of Lubavitch,
  Rabbi see: Tzemach Tzedek
Menachem Mendel of Riminow,
  Rabbi 50
Menorah 121; 223; 227; 229; 240–250;
  256; 258; 296
Mesirat nefesh see: Self-sacrifice

Messiah, The see: Moshiach and the
  Future Redemption
Midot, The Seven 248
Midnight 105
Midrash 301; 308
Midrash Mechilta see: Mechilta
Midrash Rabbah
  Bereishith Rabbah 22; 27; 37; 86;
    166; 291
  Shemot Rabbah 11; 12; 13; 17; 20; 21;
    39–40; 53; 56; 89; 96; 148; 153; 202;
    204; 282; 301
  Vayikra Rabbah 201
  Bamidbar Rabbah 5; 111; 235; 273
  Shir HaShirim Rabbah 256
Midrash Tanchuma see: Tanchuma
Midrash Tehillim 41; 55; 87
Migdal Oz 90
Mikvah 125; 264
Minchat Chinuch 90
Mind see: Intellect and Mind Rules
  the Heart
Mind Rules the Heart 141; 142–143
Mineral Kingdom 210–220; 221
Miracles 64; 161
Miriam 10
Mishael 61
Mishkan see: Tabernacle
Mishnah 157; 247–248; 308; 324
Mishpatim, Parashah of 175
Mitzvah; *Mitzvot* 32; 44; 123;
  165 168; 197; 199 202; 218; 226;
  244; 257; 259; 269; 313; 317; 320;
  326–327
  also see: Prohibitions (of the
  Torah)
Mizrachi 256; 288
Modeh Bemiktzat 190–198
Monarchy see: Kings; Kingship
Money 278
Monotheism 8

Moses 10–12; 13; 15; 16; 21–26; 27; 28–29; 31–32; 34–40; 42; 53; 56; 58; 70; 95; 100; 110; 118; 126–127; 129; 132; 137; 149; 152–156; 191; 209; 217; 232; 280–281; 290–299; 300; 304; 308; 314; 317; 319
Moshe Maizlish of Vilna 51
Moshiach and the Future Redemption 21–26; 27–32; 42–43; 50; 53; 99; 128; 179; 306
Mount Sinai 309
also see: Torah, Giving of
Mussar 311

N

Nachmanides 93; 210; 211; 212–213; 233–236; 244; 255–256; 258; 283; 287–288; 289; 297
Name 2–4; 16–20; 71; 295–300; 329
Name of the *Parashah* 70–72; 148–149; 329–333
Names of G-d see: G-d, Names of
Napoleon Bonaparte 49–52
Nassi; Nessi'im 210
Nature 62; 64–66; 90; 93; 103; 161
Nebuchadnezzar 61
Nechemiah, Rabbi 132; 133–134
Neck 142–143
Negative Commandments
see: Prohibitions (of the Torah)
Ner HaMaaravi see: Western Lamp
Nicholas II, Czar 46
Night 105–106
Nile River 8–9; 11–12; 58–60; 72
Nimukei Shmuel 158; 256
Nisayon 169–170
Nissan 282
Nissim Gerondi, Rabbi 65; 161; 244
Nob 222
Noise 252–259

Nullification (halachic) 77; 265
Numbers see: Counting; Duality; and Gematria

O

Oath (legal) 190–198
Obedience see: Kabbalat Ol
Oceans; Seas 124–128
Offerings see: Korbanot
Ohr HaChaim 130
Ohr HaTorah see: Tzemach Tzedek
Oil 253; 258
Olive Oil 258
Oneness 23–26
Onkelos 11
Oral Torah 154–156; 247–248; 301–302; 308
Outer Altar see: Altar
Outreach 13; 112; 115; 238–239; 259; 315–316

P

Paid Guardian
see: Guardians, The Four
Parashah see: Annual Torah Reading Cycle and Name of the *Parashah*
Parent-Child Relationship 32; 38; 39; 205; 237
Partial Conceder
see: *Modeh Bemiktzat*
Partnership 178; 181–182; 212; 268–271
Passion 211
Passover 85; 89–90; 92; 103; 130
also see: Seder; Matzah; and Second Passover
Passover Offering 100–106; 107; 108; 149
Past, The 67–68
Patriarchs, The 35–39; 277

INDEX

Patriotism 45
Pekudei, Parashah of 329–333
Penitent see: *Baal Teshuvah*
Perfection 257–258; 268–269
Persecution 50–51
Personal Initiative
   see: Individuality; Personal Initiative
Pharaoh 8; 34; 42; 57; 63; 66–68; 70–75
Philosophy 163
Physical Space see: Space
Physicality 29–32
   also see: Materialism
Pilgrimage Festivals 264
Pirkei d'Rabbi Eliezer 28; 214
Plagues, The see: Ten Plagues
Plants 219
Pomegranates 255–258
Positive Commandments 165–168
Poverty 252–253; 266
Prayer 122–123; 214; 242; 254; 275–276; 323
Priestly Garments 252–259; 260–261; 262–263; 309
   also see: *Ephod*; *Choshen*; and *Me'il*
Priests see: *Kohen; Kohanim*
Prohibitions (of the Torah) 65–66; 77–81; 165–168
Proof 163
Prophecy 105; 126
Proverbs 57; 122; 138; 246; 276; 286
Psalms 30; 40; 111; 169; 188; 277; 285
Punishment 56–57; 58; 63–68; 94–95
Purpose 220; 227; 260–261; 278; 311–316; 321–324

R

Raavad 244
Rain 59
Ralbag 19
Ran see: Nissim Gerondi, Rabbi
Rashba 244
Rashbatz 82
Rashi 2; 14; 20; 57; 63; 64; 86; 98; 102; 112; 114; 132; 138; 152; 157–158; 175; 205; 206–207; 233–235; 236–237; 242; 244; 255–256; 260–261; 262; 280–281; 282; 283; 285; 287; 288; 291; 292; 297; 320
Ratzo v'Shuv 322–324
Reality; Existence 19–20; 160–168; 254; 306; 308–310
Reason see: Intellect; Reason
Rebbe, The 134; 173–174
Rebecca 271
Reciprocity 188
Redemption 99
   also see: Moshiach and the Future Redemption; Four Expressions of Redemption
Regret 193
Reishith Chochmah 265
Religion 45–46; 49–50; 112; 173
Rema 241
Renter see: Guardians, The Four
Repentance see: *Teshuvah*
Rephidim 140
Responsibility 183–189
Rest 85–89
Revelation 25–26
   also see: Divine Revelation
Revelation at Mount Sinai
   see: Torah, Giving of
Reward 181
Ritual Impurity 149; 264–266; 289
Ritva 82
Roasting 100–106
Rosh Hashanah 51
Russian Revolution 46

S

Salt 276
Sanctuary see: Tabernacle, The and Holy Temple
Sapphire 300
Sarah 36
Satan 280–281
Schneerson, Rabbi Yosef Yitzchak 134
Schneerson, Rebbetzin Chayah Mushka 324
Schneur Zalman of Liadi, Rabbi 25; 48; 51–52; 87; 97; 111; 144; 167; 257; 266; 280; 287; 289; 297; 298–299; 327
Sea see: Oceans
Second Passover 149
Second Temple 105
   also see: Holy Temple
Seder (Passover) 101; 108; 110–113
Seder Hishtalshelut 103; 104; 240; 245
Seeds 257
Sefer Torah see: Torah Scroll
Sefer Yetzirah 269
Sefirot (divine attributes) 37; 103; 248
Segal, Rabbi David see: Taz
Self and Fellow 172–182
Self-Abnegation see: *Bittul*
Self-Improvement 216–217
Self-Sacrifice 61–2; 83; 144; 170; 258; 266
Selfhood and Ego 73–75; 76–77; 127; 180–181; 187–188; 197; 218; 309; 312; 317
Selflessness see: Altruism; *Bittul*; and Selfhood and Ego
Service of G-d see: G-d, Service of
Sforno 43
Sha-dai (divine name) 17

Shabbat 55; 86–90; 226; 239; 317–318; 319–321
Shabetai Hakohen, Rabbi see: Shach
Shach 191–192; 193
Shaloh 65–66; 172; 230–231; 241; 265; 295
Shalom DovBer of Lubavitch, Rabbi 60; 278; 311–312
Shammai 277
Shavuot 42; 91; 281
Shechinah 202; 210
   also see: Divine Presence
Shekel 328
   also see: Half-Shekel
Shema 23; 41; 44
Shepherding; Shepherds 12; 13; 277; 298–299
Shevat 10 134
Shiloh 23; 219; 222
Shittim **Wood** 206
Shlomo of Karlin, Rabbi 50
Shoes 109
Shofar 51–52
Showbread 223; 227; 229–230
Shulchan Aruch 18; 205
Siddur 22; 23; 93; 111; 220
Sifri 111; 159
Siftei Chachamim 288
Sight 38; 160–165; 225; 229
Silver 272
Simplicity 14–15; 236–237
Sin; Sinner 193–194; 198; 279–289; 291; 293
Sinai see: Torah, Giving of
Sixties, The 54
Skepticism see: Doubt
Smell 225; 227; 229
Solomon, King 198; 202; 219; 222; 239; 279
Something from Nothing 68
Son-in-Law 204–205

INDEX 373

Song at the Sea 128; 129–134; 136;
Song of Songs 201–202; 256–257
Soul, The 3–4; 43; 97; 98; 111; 126; 174–175; 186; 193–194; 195; 211; 224–225; 246; 266; 269; 270; 271; 322; 324
Space (physical) 214; 240–241; 309
Space Travel 173–174
Sparks of Holiness 97–98
Speech 87; 225; 230
Spiritual; Spirituality 46–47; 87; 98; 103; 122–123; 138; 174–175; 179–182; 186; 193; 211; 212; 221–231; 240–241; 245; 263; 280; 286; 309; 327
  also see Sparks of Holiness
Splitting of the Sea 118–123; 124–128; 140
Staff 109
Stars 224
Stone 7; 182; 219–220
Struggle 169–170; 252–258; 286; 301; 302–303; 310
Submissiveness 45–46
Substance and Form
  see: Form and Substance
Suffering 17–20; 34–40; 51; 169

T

Tabernacle 204–205; 206; 209–215; 216–220; 221–231; 238; 265; 272–274; 279–289; 305; 308–310; 311–316; 319–321; 326; 329–331
  also see: Vessels (of the Temple); Priestly Garments
Table, The (in the Temple) 210; 222–223; 227; 246
  also see: Food

Tablets, The Two 172; 204; 210; 223; 232; 234; 238; 248; 271; 281; 289; 300–303
Talmud 157; 308
  Berachot 16; 32; 44; 96; 135; 195; 257; 269; 275; 286; 298
  Shabbat 6; 26; 43; 88; 157; 161; 173; 199–200; 244; 256; 276; 280–281; 284; 320
  Eruvin 32; 194; 244; 288
  Pesachim 41; 61; 76; 83; 92; 97; 149; 244; 283
  Rosh Hashanah 88; 162; 219
  Yoma 37; 112; 214; 239; 241; 294
  Sukkah 238
  Taanit 14; 281
  Megillah 188
  Chagigah 180; 268; 275; 317
  Nedarim 193; 302
  Sotah 11; 131–132; 134; 193
  Gittin 122
  Kidushin 112; 187; 197; 216; 311; 318
  Nezikin 176–182
  Bava Kama 176–177; 179–180; 190; 191
  Bava Metzia 53; 176; 177; 180–181; 183; 186; 191
  Bava Batra 150; 176; 178; 181–182; 289
  Sanhedrin 36; 111; 112; 128; 157; 174; 235; 242; 285; 292
  Makot 295
  Shevuot 18
  Zevachim 101; 149; 229
  Menachot 89; 243; 244; 308
  Chulin 98; 124
  Nega'im 273
  Nidah 195
  also see: Ethics of the Fathers
  and Jerusalem Talmud
Tammuz 17 281

Tanchuma 6; 29; 30; 124; 128; 141; 206–207; 220; 221; 280; 281; 283; 287; 310; 312; 326
Tanna D'vei Eliyahu 237; 291
Tanya 6; 12; 23; 24; 26; 29; 43; 71; 81; 111; 126; 132; 136; 141; 144–145; 153; 169; 172; 193; 194; 211; 217; 221; 266; 271; 280; 285; 286; 298–299; 310; 312; 326; 327
Taste 225
Taz 158; 207
Technology 109
Temptation 169
Ten 269–271
Ten Commandments 42; 71; 88; 148; 152; 165–168; 172; 204; 210; 232; 238; 248; 269; 271; 301
Ten Plagues 58; 61; 63; 81–82; 96; 103; 140
Ten Utterances 87; 269
Terumah, Parashah of 209; 222
Teshuvah 66–68; 84; 197; 285–289; 294; 303
    also see: Baal Teshuvah
Teshuvah **movement** 54
Test see: Nisayon
Tetzaveh, Parashah of 295–297
Theft 135; 177
Thornbush 14–15
Thought 87
Time 53; 67–68; 225–226; 309
Tithe Offering 101–102
Tools 109
Torah, The 22; 36; 59; 91; 102; 111; 137–139; 148; 157–159; 174–175; 186; 212; 213; 233; 235–236; 237; 239; 244; 247–248; 265; 289; 290–299; 300–303; 305
    also see: Chronology (in Torah); Debate (in Torah); Halachah; Oral Torah; Torah, Giving of;
Torah Exegesis; Torah Scroll; and Written Torah
Torah Exegesis 156; 157–159; 300–303; 308; 319
    also see: Debate (in Torah)
Torah Law see: Halachah
Torah Scroll 111; 190; 204; 233
Torah, Giving of 22; 25–26; 29–31; 42; 45; 59; 71; 91; 92–3; 119; 148–156; 160–168; 169; 175; 199–202; 204; 280; 282; 284
Torat HaOlah see: Rema
Torat Kohanim 144; 234; 243
Torts 176–177
Tosafot 102; 149; 158; 207
Tower of Babel 6
Tradition 136
Transgression see: Sin; Sinner
Tree of Knowledge, Sin of 53
Trees 14
Truth 135; 137–139; 141; 247
Tumah see: Ritual Impurity
Two Tablets, The
    see: Tablets, The Two
Tzaddik; Tzaddikim 126; 208; 258; 284; 285–287; 289; 291; 295
Tzafnat Paaneach
    see: Gaon of Rogachov
Tzemach Tzedek 195; 257; 266
Tzeva'ot (divine name) 17
Tzimtzum 87

U

Unity 129–134
Unity of G-d see: G-d, Unity of
Unpaid Guardian
    see: Guardians, The Four

V

Vayak'hel, Parashah of 329–333
Vegetable Kingdom 219–220; 221
Veil see: Mask
Vessels (of the Temple) 209–210;
 233–234; 238; 264; 309; 330
Vital, Rabbi Chaim 211; 296

W

Waist 262–263
Walls 182
Warmth 60
Washstand see: *Kiyor*
Waste 138; 229; 300–303
Water 104; 124–128
Wealth 94–99; 170; 252–253; 266;
 273; 302–303
Weight 328
West 241–242; 245
Western Lamp 242–244; 248; 249
Width 245; 247–248
Wisdom 302
 also see: Intellect; Reason
Wood 219–220; 253; 264
Wood Gatherer, The 150
Work 86; 87; 226; 277–278; 317–318;
 319–321
Written Torah 247–248; 301–302;
 308
 also see: Torah, The

Y

Yabbok River 98
Yachid 23–26
Yahrzeit 324
Yalkut Reuveni 103
Yalkut Shimoni 27; 41; 205
Yearning for G-d
 see: G-d, Yearning for
Yesod 249
Yetzer HaRa see: Evil Inclination
Yitro, Parashah of 148–149; 175
Yitzchaki, Rabbi Shlomo
 see: Rashi
Yom Kippur 223; 226; 230; 238; 282;
 283; 285
Yom Tov Shel Rosh Hashanah 5666
 see: Shalom DovBer of Lubavitch,
 Rabbi
Youth 217; 236–237

Z

Zechariah 23; 27
Zelophehad
 see: Daughters of Zelophehad
Zohar 18; 70; 72–73; 76; 87; 103; 111;
 126; 141; 172; 186; 214; 235; 237;
 256; 270; 283–284; 286–288; 311;
 312
 Zohar Chadash 11; 103